# AN OUTLINE OF
# ESOTERIC SCIENCE

## CLASSICS IN ANTHROPOSOPHY

# AN OUTLINE OF ESOTERIC SCIENCE

RUDOLF STEINER

*Translated by* CATHERINE E. CREEGER

ANTHROPOSOPHIC PRESS

The previous English edition of this work was published by Anthroposophic Press with the title *An Outline of Occult Science*. It was translated by Henry B. Monges and revised for later editions by Lisa D. Monges. This edition was translated by Catherine E. Creeger from the German edition *Die Geheimwissenschaft Im Umriss,* which is volume 13 in the Bibliographic Survey, published by Rudolf Steiner Verlag, Dornach, Switzerland.

This edition Copyright © 1997 by Anthroposophic Press
Introduction Copyright © 1997 by Clopper Almon

Published by SteinerBooks / Anthroposophic Press
www.steinerbooks.org

Library of Congress Cataloging-in-Publication Data

Steiner, Rudolf, 1861–1925.
  [Geheimwissenschaft im Umriss. English]
  An outline of esoteric science / Rudolf Steiner ; translated by
Catherine E. Creeger.
      p. cm. — (Classics in anthroposophy)
  Includes bibliographical references.
    ISBN 978-0-88010-409-8 (paper)
    1. Anthroposophy. I. Creeger, Catherine E. II. Title. III. Series.
BP595. S894G44613   1997
299'.935—dc21                                           97-37188
                                                         CIP

Cover design: Barbara Richey

10 9 8 7 6

Printed in the United States of America by McNaughton & Gunn, Inc.

# CONTENTS

# INTRODUCTION

*by* CLOPPER ALMON

We and the world around us evolve. This evolution is nowhere more marked than in our own consciousness. When
we try to enter into the religious texts of the ancient Egyptians, we have to admit that they are total enigmas to us.
Our science would almost certainly be equally incomprehensible to them. They were, for example, obvious masters
of what, in physics today, we call *force*; however, they used
it in a completely intuitive way, without any *concept* of it.
They may well have had visions of force, but no concept.

Concepts appear first with the Greeks, and even then they
seem to have reached only into things of the intellect, logic,
geometry, and philosophy. Only with the arrival of the scientific revolution did a new power seem to unfold in us.
Suddenly we could comprehend that the same force that
makes the apple fall also holds the moon in orbit. The excite-
ment of discovering that new inner capacity swept all before
it. What could be understood with this new capacity was *Science* with a capital *S*; what could not was considered faith,
religion, or superstition, according to one's point of view.

Initially, Science consisted of physics and astronomy.
Gradually, new domains were conquered; chemistry, geology, biology, economics, and psychology led to a
whole new way of viewing the world. Darwin's theory of
evolution opened even the question of human origins to

the march of Science. One field, however, remained beyond the scope of Science—the inner, nonmaterial, spiritual being within each human individual, as well as all spiritual beings not incarnated in human bodies.

Religion and myth had long spoken of such beings, but to most students of Science they were invisible and hidden. Some enthusiasts of Science felt that if they themselves could not perceive such beings, then they simply do not exist. Talk of such beings in myths was considered merely human behavior explained on the basis of material processes. Other, wiser heads recognized that their own inability to perceive something did not prove its nonexistence; it did mean, however, that they themselves were in no position to develop a science concerning it. Thus, they lived in a divided world—one of Science and one of Religion.

Rudolf Steiner undertook the enormous work of extending Science into this ultimate domain. As the son of a railway stationmaster, he had studied the natural sciences in high school and what we now call the Technological University of Vienna—then, as now, the leading technological institute in Austria. He was at home in the natural sciences with their logical, conceptual structure. He admired their care and objectivity. But for him, they left out the essential. To him, the spiritual beings of which myth and religion spoke are *not* imperceptible but present realities. He had developed a remarkable, controlled clairvoyance, which he used as an instrument of scientific investigation. Although there had been clairvoyants before, what set Steiner apart was his *conceptual* presentation of clairvoyantly perceived facts, which made them accessible to the understanding of those who do not have such direct perception. As one studies his work, the gap between Science and Religion fades. The inner capacity for comprehending the material world begins to comprehend the world of spirit. Our divided world begins to knit together.

There remains, of course, the problem of the perception of spiritual beings. Can we take an interest in a science of things we cannot perceive? Now in the first place, most modern research in the natural sciences rests on observations that I am in no position to verify for myself. I have to take the word of a scientist's report. I have to trust that, had I spent the many years that a scientist has spent preparing, and if I had built similar instruments, then I might have been capable of having similar experiences. Mostly, however, the natural scientist asks that we follow along in thought. Steiner makes very similar demands. He asks primarily that we follow him in thought and ask ourselves if such thinking makes sense. He is also at pains to explain a path of development that leads slowly but safely to an ability to perceive the spiritual for oneself. This differs from the natural sciences only in that the instruments we must build are our own organs of perception. The process is longer, probably stretching over a number of lifetimes. The first step on that path, however, is a diligent, open-minded study of the results of spiritual research expressed in conceptual form. And this brings us directly to the present book.

*An Outline of Esoteric Science* is Steiner's most complete and orderly presentation of the results of his work. Written in 1909 when he was 48, it represents his mature thinking; nevertheless, it has the careful structure and development characteristic of a young author's work. The original title *Die Geheimwissenschaft in Umriss* indicates that the subject of the book is just those realities and beings that are—at least initially—hidden from most of us. At the same time, however, it makes clear that it is no collection of "tales of the supernatural," but a clear, conceptual, thoroughly scientific account of these matters. Because the terrain is unfamiliar, a substantial portion of the book necessarily consists of what might be called "conceptual description." The final word of the title, *Umriss* ("Outline"), must also be taken seriously. Nearly every subject discussed here is treated in greater detail in other books or lectures. This book is terse, concise, and demands the utmost attention from the reader, as well as the energy to visualize inwardly the pictures presented. It is not a book to be skimmed. Nor is it to be sampled here and there—although one man who tried hit a passage that changed his life.

There is no proper English translation of "*Geheim*" in the German title. The "*heim*" is cognate with our "home" and so connotes something intimate, held close, hidden, inner. Hence the "esoteric" in the title of the present translation, for *esoteric* means fundamentally "inner." Earlier translations used the title *Occult Science*. In Latin, *occult* simply means "hidden." *Occult*, however, has a fallen meaning in English that *Geheim* does not have in German. The book is about the majestic, full spiritual being present in each of us, and about the lofty beings above us. *Occult* is clearly inappropriate. Other possibilities might be *Spiritual Science* or *Science of Inner Realities* or, to use Goethe's expression developed in the early pages of the book, *Science of Manifest Secrets*.

This is probably not the best book by Steiner to read first. It might be better to begin with *How to Know Higher Worlds* for a "hands-on," practical introduction to Steiner's approach to self-development. *Theosophy* is more conceptual but still introductory, and is concerned with the structure of the human individual as a being of body, soul, and spirit. It also deals with reincarnation and karma. After reading one or both of these, *Cosmic Memory* may be appropriate; it deals with earthly and human evolution through metamorphosis and reincarnation. One may then want to read some of the lecture cycles, which are available to us only as stenographic notes, unrevised by Steiner himself. I would suggest starting with those given before 1910. Reading a few of these will soon awaken a desire to see all the ideas put together and laid out in an orderly fashion. One is then prepared for *An Outline of Esoteric Science*.

If you want to get quickly to the heart of the matter, you can safely skip the prefaces (most of which have been moved to the back of the present edition) and go straight to chapter 1 and read through to chapter 7. Afterward, look at the prefaces, including those in the appendix, which should now be more meaningful.

Chapter 1 makes a careful statement of the nature of this science. In chapter 2, Steiner deals with our own inner nature as beings of body, soul, and spirit. It will recall parts of *Theosophy* but at a deeper level. Chapter 3, on sleep, death, and reincarnation, similarly extends ideas from the earlier book.

Chapter 4 on evolution, however, is the great advance over anything Steiner had previously written. Just as we cannot understand ourselves or any human being without recognizing the reality of reincarnation, so it is with the whole world, with the Earth itself. In order that we may understand what stands before us as outer nature and as our inner nature, Steiner takes us back through three prior incarnations of the whole Earth and universe. Evolution is the great theme of this book and, indeed, of Steiner's life work. It is, however, an evolution that goes far beyond anything dreamed of today in biology or geology.

Chapter 5 then explains the path of individual spiritual development. Here one senses an advance over the previous expositions in *How to Know Higher Worlds* and *Theosophy*. I suspect that such an advance is largely the result of several years of work with individual students. The final chapter looks into the future evolution of the Earth.

Why should one bother with all this science of the unseen? If what is seen makes perfect sense to you as you see it, then this book is not for you. But if life is full of unanswered questions, such as: Where did we come from? How can we grow inwardly? Why is there suffering? Why joy? Why birth? Why death?—then this book will have meaning for you, just as it has meaning for me.

---

*Clopper Almon was a co-founder of the Rudolf Steiner Institute and has taught courses there on this book and other subjects. He is professor of economics at the University of Maryland, where his professional work is in building quantitative models of economics.*

Now that fifteen years have elapsed since this book first appeared in print, I may well be permitted to say something in public about the state of mind that gave rise to it.

My original plan was to make the essential content of this book into the final chapter of *Theosophy*,[1] another book of mine which was published much earlier. This did not work. When *Theosophy* was going to press, the subject matter of this current book had not achieved closure in me as was the case with that of *Theosophy*. In my imaginations, the spiritual being of the individual stood before my soul and I was able to describe it, but this was not yet true of the cosmic relationships that were to be presented in *Esoteric Science*. Individual details were there, but not the total picture. So I decided to have *Theosophy* published in its present form, containing what I had seen as the essential spiritual being in the life of the human individual, and to complete *Esoteric Science* in the near future at my own pace.

In keeping with my mental attitude at that time, the content of this book had to be presented in the form of

---

1. *Theosophy: An Introduction to the Spiritual Processes in Human Life and in the Cosmos*, Anthroposophic Press, Hudson, NY, 1994.

thoughts that were further elaborations of thoughts applied in the natural sciences, adapted for presenting what is spiritual. You will note in the introduction to the first edition, reprinted here, that I felt a strong responsibility toward the natural sciences in everything I wrote about spiritual cognition at that time.

However, the spiritual world as it reveals itself to spiritual sight cannot be presented exclusively in thoughts of this sort, since this revelation does not conform to a mere thought content. Anyone who has directly experienced the nature of such revelations knows that the thoughts of our ordinary consciousness are suitable only for expressing sensory perceptions, but not for spiritual perceptions. The content of spiritual perception can only be conveyed in images (imaginations) through which inspirations speak, while these inspirations in turn stem from a spiritual entity perceived intuitively. (Necessary information on the nature of imagination, inspiration, and intuition can be found here in *Esoteric Science* and also in my book *How to Know Higher Worlds.*)[2]

At present, however, those who describe imaginations from the spiritual world cannot present only these imaginations. Doing so would be to present the contents of a completely different consciousness, something that would stand alongside contemporary knowledge without relating to it at all. People who have such imaginations must fill our present-day consciousness with what can be

---

2. *How to Know Higher Worlds: A Modern Path of Initiation*, Anthroposophic Press, Hudson, NY, 1994.

seen by a different consciousness that looks into the world of the spirit. The content of what they present will be the spiritual world, but in order to become fully comprehensible to our ordinary consciousness, which thinks in modern terms and does not yet see into the world of the spirit, this spiritual world must flow into our thoughts and appear in thought form. It will remain incomprehensible only if we ourselves place obstacles in its path; that is, if we subscribe to contemporary prejudices about "the limits of knowledge" that result from an incorrectly conceived view of nature.

In spiritual cognition everything is immersed in subtle soul experience—not only spiritual perception itself, but also the type of understanding that ordinary unseeing consciousness brings to it. If people of superficial knowledge claim that others who believe they understand are merely talking themselves into it, this demonstrates that they themselves do not have the faintest idea of this subtle experience. But the fact of the matter is that the merely conceptual expression of truth or error in our understanding of the physical world becomes an actual experience for us when we face the spiritual world.

If we allow our opinion to be even ever so slightly influenced by the assertion that the limitations of an ordinary consciousness that does not yet perceive prevent this consciousness from understanding spiritual perceptions, then this judgment, this feeling, blankets our comprehension like a dark cloud, and we really cannot understand. But to an unperceiving but unbiased consciousness, spiritual perceptions are fully comprehensible if seers cast them in the form of thoughts. They are comprehensible in the same way that a painter's finished picture is comprehensible to a non-painter. However, understanding the spiritual world is not an artistic, feeling process like understanding a work of art, but a thinking process like that of science. But in order to make this understanding really possible, those who present spiritual perceptions must be able to cast them in the form of thoughts without having them lose their imaginative character.

All this stood before my soul as I drew up my *Esoteric Science*.

In 1909 I then felt that the prerequisites were in place for me to be able to produce a book that 1) cast the content of my spiritual vision in the form of thoughts to a certain provisionally adequate extent, and 2) could be understood by any thinking people who placed no obstacles in the way of their own understanding. I say this today and state at the same time that in 1909 I thought I was taking a risk in publishing this book. I knew that professional scientists were incapable of mustering the necessary impartiality, as were numerous others who depended on science for their judgment. But the fact that stood before my soul most clearly was that in an age when humanity's consciousness was furthest removed from the spiritual world, there was an urgent need for communications from this world. I counted on the fact that there were also people who experienced being distanced from all spirituality as such an impediment to life that they were grasping at communications from the spiritual world with inner longing.

The years that followed confirmed this completely. *Theosophy* and *Esoteric Science,* books that require the goodwill of the reader in dealing with a difficult style of writing, have both enjoyed wide circulation. I tried very consciously not to supply a "popular" exposition of these themes, but one that requires the reader to exert a good deal of thought in approaching the content. Because of the character I imprinted on my books, merely reading them is already the beginning of spiritual training. Exerting one's thinking in the calm and collected way that this reading requires strengthens the reader's soul forces and makes these forces capable of approaching the spiritual world.

Calling the book *Esoteric Science* caused immediate misunderstandings. I was informed from all different directions that something that intends to be a "science" must not be esoteric or secret.[3] How thoughtless such objections were! As if anyone who actually publishes a content wants to be secretive with it! The whole book shows that nothing was meant to be labeled "secret"; it was meant to be cast in a form that made it as understandable as any "science." When we use the term "natural sciences," don't we mean to indicate that we are dealing with

---

3. For instance, the early review by Wincenty Lutoslawski, *"Rudolf Steiners sogen. 'Geheimwissenschaft'"* ("Rudolf Steiner's So-called 'Esoteric Science'") in the magazine *Hochland,* vol. 1910/11, no. 1, Munich, October 1910, pp. 45–58. Its opening paragraph immediately presents this objection: "The expression *esoteric science* contains a contradiction just like *dry wetness* or *light darkness.* Science and esotericism, science and petty secrecy, are as far apart as day and night."

the knowledge of "nature?" "Esoteric science" is the science of what takes place "esoterically" in the sense that it is perceived, not outside in nature, but where one's soul turns when it directs its inner being toward the spirit. "Esoteric science" is the opposite and the counterpart of "natural science."

My perceptions of the spiritual world repeatedly met with the objection that they were reproductions and transformations of concepts about the spiritual world that came to the fore in ancient times. It was said that I had read many of these things, absorbed them into my subconscious, and then presented them in the belief that they sprang from my own perceptions. I was said to have derived my reports from Gnostic teachings, the poetic wisdom of the Orient, and so on.

The thought that went into these claims is very superficial. I am fully conscious of the fact that my knowledge of spiritual things is the result of my own perception. Whether with regard to details or in the broader surveys, I subjected myself to strict tests to make sure that each step in the progress of my perception was made in full and deliberate consciousness. I told myself that just as a mathematician proceeds from one thought to another without autosuggestion or the unconscious playing any role in the process, spiritual perception must proceed from one objective imagination to another, without anything being active in the soul except the spiritual content of clear and collected consciousness.

Knowing an imagination to be not merely a subjective image but a reproduction in image form of an objective spiritual content is an achievement of healthy inner experience. It is achieved on the level of the soul and spirit in the same way that a healthy person distinguishes between fantasy and objective perception in the realm of sensory observation.

So there I stood with the results of my perception before me. To begin with, they were perceptions without names. Later, I needed words in order to describe and communicate them, so I then went looking in older accounts of spiritual matters for ways to express these still nameless things in words. I made free use of the terms I found, so my usage almost never coincides with the ancient meaning. However, in every case, I went looking for such possibilities of expression only after the content had become apparent in my own perception. I was able to eliminate what I had previously read from my own perception and research by means of the state of consciousness that I have just described.

It was also claimed that the terms I used were reminiscent of ancient ideas. People fixed their attention on the expressions themselves without going into the content. If I spoke of "lotus flowers" in the human astral body, that was proof that I was repeating ancient Indian teachings in which that term is found. If I used the terms "angeloi," "archangeloi," and so on, then I was simply reviving concepts of Gnostic Christianity. I was constantly confronted with the objections of entirely superficial thinking of this sort. I wanted to point to this fact too, now that a new edition of *Esoteric Science* is being published. This book, since it contains the outline of anthroposophy as a whole, is especially susceptible to all the misunderstandings anthroposophy is exposed to.

Since the time when the imaginations presented in this book first merged into a complete picture in my soul, I have constantly been developing my ability to perceive the human being, the historical development of humanity, and the cosmos. But the outline I offered in *Esoteric Science* fifteen years ago remains unshaken as far as I am concerned. Everything I have been able to say since then, if inserted into this book in the right place, seems only to elaborate on that outline.[4]

RUDOLF STEINER
*The Goetheanum*
*January 10, 1925*

---

4. This preface was written for the sixteenth through twentieth editions of *An Outline of Esoteric Science.*

## Publisher's Note

*As an aid to readers wishing to follow the text in German, the numbers that appear in the margins indicate Rudolf Steiner's original paragraphing in the German edition.*

*An index has not been included because it proved to be unfeasible for the text. As a resource for further study, it has been decided to subsequently publish a separate "study guide."*

# CHAPTER 1

# THE CHARACTER
# OF ESOTERIC SCIENCE

The ancient term *esoteric science* is used to describe the [1] contents of this book. This term immediately rouses the most contradictory feelings among contemporary people. For many it is somewhat repellent or calls forth derision, pitying smiles, and perhaps even contempt. They imagine that a way of thinking that describes itself in this way can only be based on idle, fantastic dreaming, that this alleged science can only conceal an impulse to reinstate all kinds of superstitions that those familiar with the "true scientific approach" and "real striving for knowledge" are quite right in avoiding. To others, what is meant by this term seems to provide them with something they cannot acquire in any other way; depending on their personal predispositions, they are drawn to it either out of a deep inner longing for knowledge or out of the curiosity of a refined soul. Between these sharply divergent opinions there are all kinds of possible intermediate stages of conditional rejection or acceptance of what different individuals may think of on hearing the words *esoteric science*.

For many people the term *esoteric science* has a magical ring to it because it seems to appease their fateful obsession with knowing of something unknown, mysterious, or even obscure, with a knowledge that cannot be acquired naturally. Many people do not want to satisfy their souls' deepest longings with something that can be clearly known. They tend to believe that in addition to what is recognizable and knowable in the world, there must also be something that eludes cognition. Regarding their deepest longing for knowledge, and with a peculiar illogicality they do not notice, they reject everything known and choose to accept only something that cannot be said to be knowable through any natural form of research. Anyone who speaks of "esoteric science" would do well to keep in mind the need to confront misunderstandings caused by some of its advocates who are striving not for knowledge but for its opposite.

*[2]*   This account is aimed at readers who will not allow their impartiality to be shaken by the fact that a term calls forth prejudices under certain circumstances. There can be no talk here of a knowledge that is "secret" in the sense of being accessible only to certain people because of some especially favorable destiny. We will do justice to the term *esoteric science* as it is used here if we think of what Goethe had in mind when he spoke of the "revealed mysteries" in the phenomena of the universe.[1]

---

1. "There are so many revealed mysteries because the feeling for them becomes conscious in so few people, and these few, fearing to harm themselves and others, do not give voice to their inner explanations." Goethe in a letter to C.L.F. Schultz, November 28, 1821, in *Goethes Werke* (*Goethe's Works*), Weimar ed., sec. 4, vol. 35, 1906, p. 192.

His view sees what remains secret, "esoteric," or unrevealed in the phenomena we grasp only with our senses and our sense-bound intellect as the content of a supersensible way of knowing.[2] Of course, to those who restrict science to what is revealed through the senses and the intellect that serves them, what is meant here by *esoteric science* does not constitute a science. If such people wish to understand themselves, however, they must admit that they reject esoteric science not on the basis of well-founded insight, but simply on the authority of their purely personal feelings.

In order to realize this, all we need to do is to consider how sciences come about and what significance they have in human life. The definitive factor in the birth of a science is not the object that is studied but the type of human soul-activity that takes place during the scientific quest. The activity and attitude of the soul involved in the study of science is what we need to look at. If we acquire the

---

2. Some people have rejected the term *esoteric science*, as used by the author in earlier editions of this book, on the grounds that a science cannot be something that is secret or "esoteric" to anyone. This objection would have been correct if that had been the intent in using this term, but that is not the case. The natural sciences, the sciences of nature, cannot be called "natural" in the sense that they belong to everyone "by nature." Similarly, the author understands *esoteric science* to be not a "secret" science but a science "of the esoteric," a science that deals with what is "secret" and unrevealed in the phenomena of the universe as far our ordinary means of cognition are concerned. This science, however, should not remain a secret for anyone who searches for its knowledge in appropriate ways [note by Rudolf Steiner; see also note, page 29.]

habit of exercising activity of this sort only when dealing with what the senses disclose, we may easily succumb to the opinion that the sense perception is the essential factor. In that case, we fail to look at the fact that specific activities and attitudes of the human soul have been applied, but only to what is sense-perceptible. However, it is possible to transcend this arbitrary, self-imposed limitation and look at the character of scientific activity itself without regard to its specific application.

This is our basis for speaking of knowledge of the non-sensory content of the world as "scientific." The human power of cognition tries to become involved with this content in the same way that it would otherwise become involved with the world's natural scientific content. It is the intent of spiritual science to free the methods and attitudes of scientific research from their particular application to the relationships and processes of sensory facts while preserving their way of thinking and other attributes. Spiritual science attempts to speak about non-sensory things in the same way that the natural sciences speak about sense-perceptible things. While natural-scientific methods of research and ways of thinking stop short at the sensory world, esoteric science views the soul's work in the natural world as a means of self-education and attempts to apply the faculties that develop in this way to non-sensory domains. Instead of attempting to speak about sensory phenomena as such, esoteric science speaks about the non-sensory contents of the world in the same way that scientists speak about its sense-perceptible contents. In this process, it retains the inner attitude of the scientific method, which is what makes the study of nature a science in the first place. This permits esoteric science to call itself a science.

When we begin to consider it, we will find that the significance of the natural sciences in human life is not exhausted in acquiring knowledge about nature, since this knowledge can never lead to anything except experiences of what the human soul itself is *not*. The soul principle does not live in what we know about nature; it lives in the process of knowing. The soul experiences itself during its active involvement with nature, and the result of this living involvement is something other than knowledge about nature itself, namely the self-development experienced in acquiring this knowledge. Esoteric science attempts to apply the result of this self-development to areas that transcend mere nature. It is not the intent of esoteric scientists to underestimate the value of the natural sciences. On the contrary, they try to acknowledge it even more than the natural scientists do. They know that it is impossible to establish any science without the exacting way of thinking that is the rule in the natural sciences, but they also know that after this exactitude has been acquired by genuinely entering into the spirit of natural scientific thought, the soul's strength can hold it fast and apply it to other fields. [3]

Something appears at this point, however, that may cause misgivings. While observing nature, the soul is guided by the object under observation to a much greater extent than it is while observing the world's non-sensory contents, when it has to be able to hold fast to the essence [4] of the scientific way of thinking out of purely inner impulses to a much greater extent. Since many people believe—although not consciously—that only the guidance of natural phenomena allows us to retain this essence, they tend to decide dogmatically that as soon as this guidance is abandoned, the soul with its scientific method is left groping in the dark. These people have not become aware of the distinctive character of this method; for the most part, they base their judgment on errors that necessarily arise when someone whose scientific attitude has not been sufficiently reinforced by observing natural phenomena nonetheless proceeds to observe non-sensory domains. Such cases naturally give rise to a lot of unscientific talk about the world's non-sensory content. However, this is not because such talk is essentially incapable of being scientific, but only because in this particular instance the scientific self-education that comes from observing nature was neglected.

[5]     With regard to what has just been said, however, anyone wanting to speak about esoteric science must keep a sharp eye out for all the distractions and illusions that can arise from conjecturing about the revealed mysteries of the world without approaching them scientifically. And yet it would be counterproductive, right at the beginning of an account of esoteric science, to speak about all the possible aberrations that discredit its research in the minds of biased people, because these people conclude from the very existence of the aberrations—and it is true that they are very numerous—that the entire undertaking is unjustified. In most instances, however, scientists or

scientifically minded critics reject esoteric science dogmatically, as was described earlier, and their reference to
the aberrations is merely a pretext that is often unconscious. Discussion with such opponents will prove futile.
Indeed, nothing prevents them from raising the very justified objection that there is no way of determining from
the outset whether the person who believes others are in
error actually possesses the firm foundation described
above. Therefore, all that can be done by people who are
striving in the direction of esoteric science is to present
what they believe is permissible for them to say. Whether
this belief is justified can only be decided by others, and
in fact only by those who avoid dogmatic statements of
any sort and are able to enter into how these esoteric
researchers communicate the revealed mysteries of cosmic events. Of course the researchers will be obliged to
show how what they present relates to other achievements
of knowledge and of life. They will also need to show
what opposition is possible and to what extent life's
immediate outer, sense-perceptible reality confirms their
observations. However, they should never attempt to
present things in a way that depends on the art of persua-
sion rather than on content for its effect.

Esoteric scientific accounts often meet with the objec-   *[6]*
tion that they do not prove what they present, that they
merely make some assertion or other and say that esoteric science has determined this to be true. Do not misunderstand the account that follows by thinking that any
part of it is being presented in this manner. An effort is
being made here to allow the capability that unfolds in

the soul through studying nature to continue to develop according to its own essence. In the course of this development the soul encounters supersensible facts. It is assumed that every reader who is able to really go into what has been presented will necessarily run up against these facts. The moment we enter the domain of spiritual science, however, we encounter a difference between it and purely natural scientific observation. In the natural sciences, facts are present in the field of the sensory world; scientists who present these facts regard the activity of the soul as something that recedes into the background in the face of sense-perceptible relationships and processes. Those who present spiritual scientific facts must place this soul activity in the forefront, because their readers only arrive at the facts by making this activity their own in the right way. Unlike the facts of natural science, which—although not understood— are still available for human perception even without any soul activity, spiritual scientific facts enter into our perception only through activity on the part of the soul. Thus those presenting spiritual science presume that the readers are accompanying them on the search for these facts. Their presentation consists of recounting the discovery of these facts and is governed not by personal whim, but by a scientific attitude trained by natural science. Therefore, they must also speak about the means they use to become able to observe non-sensory, supersensible things.

By attempting to present an esoteric scientific subject, we will soon see that this leads us to acquire concepts and ideas that we did not possess before. The new thoughts we acquire about the nature of proof are also different from our previous conceptions of it. We learn to recognize that when natural science is explained, "proof" is something brought toward it from the outside, so to speak. In spiritual scientific thinking, however, the activity applied to proving something in natural scientific thinking is already present in the search for the facts. We cannot find these facts if the path that leads to them does not constitute a proving process in itself. Anyone who really follows this path already experiences the element of proof, and nothing more can be accomplished by means of a proof applied from outside. Failure to recognize this characteristic of esoteric science has led to many misunderstandings.

The whole of esoteric science must spring from two   [7] thoughts that can take root in each human being. For the esoteric scientist, as the term is used in this book, these two thoughts express facts that can be experienced if we apply the right means. For many other people, these thoughts constitute extremely debatable claims that can provoke a great deal of argument and may even be "proved" to be impossible. The first of these thoughts is   [8] that behind the visible world there is an invisible one, a world that is temporarily concealed, at least as far as our senses and sense-bound thinking are concerned. The second is that by developing human capacities that lie dormant in us, it is possible to enter this hidden world.

Some people may say that there is no such hidden   [9] world, that the world we perceive with our senses is the only one, that it contains everything necessary to solve its riddles, and that even if we are far from being able to answer all our existential questions at present, a time will come when sensory experiences and the science based on them will be able to provide the answers.

[10]    Others say that we cannot state definitively that there is no hidden world behind the visible one, but our human powers of cognition cannot penetrate this world because they have limits that they cannot overstep. Although those who need "faith" may take refuge in a world of that sort, a true science based on the guarantee of fact cannot be concerned with such a world.

[11]    A third group sees it as rather presumptuous to want to penetrate into a domain where we must renounce "knowledge" and be content with "faith." Those who adhere to this position find it wrong for the feeble human being to want to penetrate into a world that is supposed to be the exclusive province of religious life.

[12]    Still others raise the objection that it is possible for everyone to share a common knowledge of the facts of the sense-perceptible world, but since knowledge of supersensible things is only a matter of personal, individual opinion, we should not speak of universal certainty in such things.

[13]    And there are others who make many other assertions.

[14]    It becomes clear that observing the visible world presents us with riddles that can never be solved on the basis of the facts of this world alone. They will never be solved in this way, regardless of how far the science of these facts may advance, because the very inner nature of the

visible facts points clearly to a hidden world. If we do not realize this, we are shutting ourselves off to the riddles that spring up everywhere out of the facts of the sensory world. We *choose* not to see certain questions and riddles, and so we believe that all questions can be answered by means of sense-perceptible facts. The questions we choose to ask may indeed all be answered by the facts we expect will be discovered in the future. There is no reason not to concede that this is the case. But why should we wait for answers to certain things if we ask no questions about them? Those who aspire to an esoteric science are only saying that the questions they ask are a matter of course for them and should be acknowledged as fully legitimate expressions of the human soul. After all, science cannot be forced into narrow confines by forbidding people to ask unbiased questions.

In response to the opinion that there are limits to human cognition which we cannot overstep and which force us to come to a halt in front of any invisible world that may be there, it must be said that there can be no doubt in anyone's mind that it is *not* possible to push one's way into an invisible world with that particular kind of cognition. For anyone who believes that form of cognition to be the one and only form, it is impossible to arrive at any other view of the matter than that human beings are denied access to any higher world that may exist. But it can also be said that if it is possible to develop another form of cognition, this could lead into the supersensible world. If we consider this form of cognition impossible, we reach a viewpoint that makes any talk of a supersensible world seem like pure

*[15]*

nonsense. To an impartial judge, however, the only possible reason for this viewpoint is that its champions are unfamiliar with any other form of cognition. Yet how can people pass judgment on something while insisting that they know nothing about it? Unbiased thinking must concur with the statement that we should speak only about things we know and not make statements about things we do not know. This kind of thinking can only speak of people's right to communicate what they have experienced, but not of any right on their part to declare something impossible if they know (or choose to know) nothing about it. No one can ever deny others the right to ignore the supersensible, but there is never any legitimate reason for people to declare themselves authorities, not only on what they themselves are capable of knowing, but also on what they suppose cannot be known by any human being.

[16]    In the case of those who declare it presumptuous to enter the domain of the supersensible, an esoteric scientific view must call their attention to the fact that it is possible to enter this domain and that we sin against the faculties we have been given if we allow them to stagnate instead of developing them and putting them to use.

[17]    However, anyone who believes that views concerning the supersensible world are strictly a matter of personal opinions and feelings denies what is common to all human beings. It is certainly true that individuals must find insight into such things on their own, but it is also a fact that all people who go far enough come to the same insight about these things rather than to different insights. Differences exist only when people try to approach the

highest truths through an arbitrary personal whim rather than by a scientifically guaranteed path. It must be admitted without reservation, however, that only those who are willing to immerse themselves in the unique character of the esoteric scientific path are capable of acknowledging that it is correct.

If we acknowledge—or even merely assume or surmise [18] from the manifest world—the existence of a hidden world, and if our awareness that our powers of cognition are capable of development compels us to feel that this hidden world can reveal itself to us, then each one of us will be able to find the way to esoteric science at the individually appropriate time. When individuals have been led to esoteric science by these soul experiences, several prospects open up before them. One is the prospect of finding the answer to certain questions posed by their craving for knowledge; another is the quite different prospect of victory over everything that impedes and weakens life.

In a certain higher sense, it signifies a weakening of life or even a soul death when a person is forced to deny or turn away from the supersensible world. Under certain circumstances it even leads to despair when someone loses hope that the hidden will be revealed. At the same time, the various forms of this death and despair oppose esoteric scientific efforts on the inner level of the soul. They set in when our inner strength dwindles. If we are then to have any strength for life at all, it must come from outside. Then we perceive the things, beings, and processes that appear to our senses, and we analyze them with our intellect. They cause us joy and sorrow; they drive us to whatever actions we are capable of. We can carry on like this for a while, but eventually we reach the point of dying inwardly, because we have exhausted what can be drawn from the world in this way for a human being's sake. This is not a statement stemming from the personal experience of one individual; it results from an unbiased consideration of all human life. What shields us from exhausting this source is the hidden element that rests within the depths of things. Ultimately, if the strength to descend into these depths to draw up new strength for life dies away in a human being, the outer aspect of things also proves to be no longer conducive to life.

[19]    This is by no means a matter of concern only to the individual human being with his or her personal well-being and misfortune. Precisely through true esoteric scientific observations, we arrive at the certainty that from a higher standpoint, an individual's well-being and misfortune are intimately related to the well-being or misfortune of the whole world. We come to the insight that we are causing damage to the whole world and all the beings in it when we do not develop our own forces in the right way. If we ravage our life by losing our connection to the supersensible world, not only do we destroy something within us, something that can ultimately drive us to despair as it dies off, but our weakness also creates a hindrance to the evolution of the entire world in which we live.

[20]    Now, it is possible for human beings to deceive themselves. We can succumb to the belief that there is no hidden element, that what appears to our senses and our intellect includes everything that can possibly exist. This

deception, however, is only possible on the surface of consciousness, not in its depths. Our feeling and desire do not submit to this deceptive belief. In one way or another, they will always long for something hidden. If this is withheld from us, it forces us into doubt, into uncertainty in life, or even into despair. Cognition that reveals what is hidden is suited to overcoming all this hopelessness, uncertainty, and despair—in short, everything that weakens a life and makes it incapable of performing the services required of it within the world as a whole.

This is the beautiful fruit of spiritual scientific knowledge—rather than merely gratifying our passion for knowledge, it gives our life strength and steadfastness. It draws strength for work and confidence in life from an inexhaustible source. No one who has ever truly approached this source and returns repeatedly to take refuge there will ever go away unstrengthened. *[21]*

There are people who do not want to know anything about such knowledge because they see something unhealthy in what has just been said. As far as the outer, superficial aspect of life is concerned, these people are right. They do not want what life offers in its so-called reality to be diminished in any way. They see it as a weakness when people turn away from reality and seek salvation in a hidden world that seems fantastic and dreamed-up. If we do not want to fall into a state of pathological dreaminess and weakness in our spiritual scientific search, we must acknowledge that such objections are partially justified. They rest on healthy judgment that leads to a half-truth rather than to a whole one *[22]* only because it does not thrust its way into the depths of things but remains on the surface. If striving for supersensible knowledge were likely to weaken life and turn people away from true reality, then such objections would certainly be strong enough to pull the foundation out from under this spiritual trend.

[23]    However, it is not appropriate for esoteric scientific efforts to respond to such opinions by "defending" themselves in the usual sense of the word. In this case, too, they can speak only out of their own merit, which is apparent to any unbiased person, and make it evident that they supplement the life forces and strength for life of anyone who immerses him or herself in them in the right way. Such efforts cannot turn a person into a dreamer or someone who is alienated from the world; the strength they provide comes from the sources of life that are the origin of the soul and spiritual parts of us.

[24]    Still other obstacles may confront many people when they first approach an esoteric scientific search. It is a fundamental truth that readers of esoteric scientific accounts find descriptions of soul experiences which they can follow in order to approach the world's supersensible contents. But while this is the ideal, it still has to be realized in actual practice.

Readers must first absorb a fairly large number of supersensible experiences recounted by others without experiencing them personally. This cannot be otherwise, and will also be true of this book. The author will describe what he believes he knows about the nature of human beings and what happens to them at birth, at death, and in the body-free state in the spiritual world. He will also describe the evolution of the Earth and of humanity. It could seem that a certain amount of alleged knowledge is being presented like dogma, as if belief based on authority were called for. However, this is not the case. In fact, what can be known about the world's supersensible content is present in the author as a living soul content, and immersing yourself in this content kindles impulses in your own soul which then lead to the corresponding supersensible facts. In reading about spiritual scientific knowledge, you are active in a different way than you are in reading accounts of sense-perceptible facts. If you read accounts of the sense-perceptible world, you read *about* them, but if you read accounts of supersensible facts in the right way, you immerse yourself in the stream of spiritual existence. By taking in the results of spiritual research, we also set out on our own inner path toward discovering these results for ourselves.

It is true that to begin with, what is meant here is often not noticed at all by those who read it. People imagine entering the spiritual world to be much too similar to a sensory experience, and so they find their experiences in reading about this world much too thought-like. But if we are *truly* absorbing these things as thoughts, we are already in the midst of the spiritual world and must only realize that we are already experiencing (although we do not notice it) what we believed we were merely receiving in the form of thoughts communicated to us.

The real nature of what we have experienced will become completely clear to us if we actually practice what is described in the second and last part of this book as the path to supersensible knowledge. It would be easy to believe the opposite—that the path would have to be described first. But that is not the case. To anyone who simply does exercises in order to enter the supersensible world without paying any soul-attention to specific facts about it, this world will remain an indistinct and confused chaos. We learn to find our way into that world naively, so to speak, in the process of learning about some of its specific facts; only after that do we abandon our unsuspecting naïveté and realize that we are fully consciously acquiring for ourselves the experiences that have been communicated to us.

If you go into esoteric scientific accounts in depth, you will be convinced that this is the only sure path to supersensible knowledge. You will also realize that the opinion that supersensible knowledge might initially affect us like dogma—through the power of suggestion, as it were—is unfounded, because we acquire the content of this knowledge by means of a soul activity that strips it of any merely suggestive power and only allows it to speak to us in the same way as any truth that addresses our level-headed judgment. Our initial failure to notice that we are living in the spiritual world is not due to lack of thought on our part or to being influenced by suggestion in taking in what we have read, but only to the subtlety and unfamiliarity of what we have experienced while reading. When we first take in communications such as those in the first part of this book, we begin to participate, with help, in knowledge of the supersensible world; through practical application of the soul exercises given in the second part, we begin to know this world independently.

No real scientists will be able to find any essential contradiction between their science, which is based on the facts of the sense world, and how the supersensible world is investigated. These scientists use certain tools and methods. They produce these tools by transforming what "nature" gives them. Supersensible cognition also makes use of a tool—the human being—that must also first be made suitable for higher research. The human abilities and forces that nature provides without any involvement on the part of the individual must be transformed into higher ones. This is how we can transform ourselves into instruments for investigating the supersensible world.

*[25]*

CHAPTER 2

# THE MAKEUP OF
# THE HUMAN BEING

[1] When we observe the human being from the viewpoint of a supersensible mode of cognition, the general principles of this cognitive mode take effect immediately. This way of looking at the human being is based on recognizing the "revealed mystery" in our human makeup. Of all the elements supersensible knowledge includes in this, the *physical body* is the only one that is accessible to our senses and our sense-based intellect. To clarify this concept of the physical body, we must turn our attention first to a great riddle that envelops all of our observations of life: the phenomenon of death and, connected with it, so-called inorganic nature, the mineral kingdom, in which death is always inherent. This points to facts that can only be fully explained through supersensible knowledge, and a significant portion of this book will have to be devoted to them. At this point, however, the intent is simply to offer a few ideas for the sake of orientation.

[2] Within the manifest world, the physical human body is the part of the human being that is the same as the mineral

world. In contrast, everything that differentiates us from minerals cannot be considered part of the physical body. To an unbiased view, the most important fact is that death exposes the aspect of our human makeup that is of the same nature as the mineral kingdom. We can refer to the corpse as the aspect that, after death, is subject to processes that are found in that kingdom. It can be emphasized that in this element of our human makeup—the corpse—the same substances and forces are at work as in the mineral kingdom. However, it is necessary to emphasize equally strongly that this physical body begins to break down when death sets in. Yet we are also justified in saying that while the same substances and forces are at work in the physical human body as in minerals, as long as we are alive they work in the service of something higher. Only after death do they work in the physical human body as they do in the mineral kingdom. They then appear in the form that is true to their own nature: that is, as disintegrators of the physical body's form.

Thus, in the human being we must distinguish clearly [3] between what is manifest and what is hidden. During life, a hidden something has to wage a constant battle against the mineral substances and forces in the physical body. If this battle ceases, their mineral effects come to the fore. At this point, supersensible science must get involved. Its job is to look for what wages the battle, for something hidden from sensory observation and accessible only to supersensible observation. A later chapter in this book will discuss how to reach the point where this hidden something becomes as evident to us as sensory phenomena are to our ordinary eyes. For the moment, however, what is revealed to supersensible observation will simply be described.

*[4]*    It has already been stated that information on how to approach higher vision can only be of value to people if they first become familiar with accounts of what supersensible research reveals. In this field it is indeed possible to comprehend things that we cannot yet observe. In fact, understanding is the first step toward achieving vision in the right way.

*[5]*    Although the hidden something that fights off the disintegration of the physical body is only visible to higher sight, its *effects* are clearly evident to a faculty of judgment restricted to manifest phenomena. These effects express themselves in the shape or form that the physical body's mineral substances and forces share during life. Once death sets in, this form gradually disappears and the physical body becomes part of the rest of the mineral kingdom. However, what prevents the physical substances and forces from going their own way during life, which would cause the physical body to disintegrate, can be observed by supersensible perception as an independent part of our human makeup. This independent element will be called the "ether body" or "life body."

In order to prevent misunderstandings from creeping in right at the outset, there are two things that must be considered with regard to the terms applied to this second element of our human makeup: First, the use of the word *ether* is different here than it is in modern physics, which describes the medium of light as "ether." Here, however, the meaning of the word will be restricted to the one given above. It will be applied to this entity that is accessible to higher vision but recognizable to sensory perception only because of its effects—that is, because it is capable of giving a particular shape or form to the mineral substances and forces present in the physical body. Second, the word *body* should also not be misunderstood. After all, we have to use words taken from ordinary language, words that express only sense-perceptible things, to designate the higher things of existence. In sensory terms, of course, the ether "body" is nothing bodily at all, no matter how fine or delicate a body we might imagine. (As the author has discussed in his book *Theosophy*, his intention in using the terms *ether body* and *life body* is *not* simply to revive the old scientifically outdated idea of "life force," or "vital force.")

Having arrived at the point of mentioning the "ether body" or "life body" in describing supersensible things, we have also reached a point where this description necessarily contradicts some modern-day views. The evolution of the human spirit has led to a situation where talking about such an element of our human makeup is necessarily seen as unscientific nowadays. The materialistic view has reached the point of seeing nothing more in the living human body than an assemblage of physical substances and forces such as are also found in minerals, in so-called inanimate objects. The only difference is supposed to be that the way they are put together is more complicated in living things than in lifeless matter.

Not too long ago even ordinary science had different views on this subject. If you track down the writings of

*[6]*

serious scientists from the first half of the nineteenth century, you will find that, at that time, even some "real" scientists were also aware of something in living bodies that is different from what is present in lifeless minerals. Back then, people spoke of a "vital force" or "life force." Admittedly, they did not imagine this life force as the life body described above, but their concept was based nonetheless on an inkling that something of this sort does exist. They imagined this "life force" as supplementing the physical substances and forces of the living body, just as the force of magnetism supplements the plain iron in a magnet.

Then came a time when this "life force" was removed from the stock of scientific concepts, and people tried to explain everything in terms of mere physical and chemical causes. More recently, however, a reaction against this has again set in among some scientific thinkers. In some quarters, it is admitted that assuming the existence of something like a "life force" is not total nonsense after all. However, even scientists who deign to admit this possibility will not want to make common cause with the view of the "life body" that has been presented here. As a general rule, engaging these people in dialogue from the viewpoint of supersensible knowledge will lead nowhere. Instead, supersensible knowledge should make a point of recognizing that the materialistic view is a necessary concomitant of our era's great progress in natural science, which is based on a tremendous refining of our methods of sensory observation. In the course of evolution, it is simply part of human nature to raise some specific individual capabilities to a certain degree of perfection at the expense of others from time to time. Human faculties that lead to "hidden worlds" had to be forced into the background by the exact sensory observation that the natural sciences developed to such a significant extent. But now a time has again come when we need to cultivate these faculties. We will win acknowledgment of what is hidden, not by combating judgments that are the logical consequence of denying the existence of hidden elements, but by showing these elements themselves in the right light so that they can then be acknowledged by those for whom the time is right.

This needed to be said here to keep people from assuming that the author is ignorant of the views of natural science when he talks about an "ether body"—something that is necessarily seen in many quarters as a figment of the imagination.  *[7]*

This ether body, then, is a second part of our human makeup. Supersensible knowledge attributes a higher degree of reality to it than to the physical body. A description of this body as supersensible knowledge sees it can only be given in later chapters of this book, once the sense in which such descriptions are meant to be taken has become evident. For the moment, let it suffice to say that the ether body permeates the physical body in all its parts and is to be seen as its architect, so to speak. The shape and form of all our organs are maintained by the ether body's currents and movements.[1] Our physical heart is  *[8]*

---

1. See also Rudolf Steiner's lecture cycle *Occult Physiology*, Prague, March 20–28, 1911 (GA 128), particularly the fifth lecture.

based on an "ether heart," our physical brain, on an "ether brain," and so on. The ether body is differentiated just like the physical body, but it is more complicated. In the ether body, everything is in a living, flowing state of interpenetration, whereas in the physical body, distinctly separate parts are present.

[9]     Having an ether body is common to plants and human beings in the same way that having a physical body is common to humans and minerals. Every living thing has its own ether body.

[10]     From the ether body, we move on to a further component of our human makeup. To help us visualize this next part, supersensible observation points to the phenomenon of sleep, just as it pointed to death in the case of the ether body. As far as everything manifest is concerned, all our productive actions are based on activity in the waking state. Waking activity, however, is only possible if we repeatedly draw new strength for our exhausted forces from sleep. Doing and thinking disappear during sleep; all suffering and pleasure are submerged as far as our conscious life is concerned. When we awaken, conscious forces rise up out of sleep's unconsciousness like water out of hidden and mysterious springs. The consciousness that sinks down into the dark depths when we fall asleep is the same as the one that rises up when we awaken. According to supersensible cognition, what awakens life again and again from the unconscious state is the third part of our human makeup. We can call it the "astral body."

Just as the physical body cannot maintain its form by means of the mineral substances and forces it contains, but only by being permeated by the ether body, the forces of the ether body are incapable of illumining themselves with the light of consciousness. Left to its own devices, the ether body would have to remain in an ongoing state of sleep. We might also say that it would only be able to support a plant-like existence within the physical body. A waking ether body is illumined by an astral body. As far as sensory perception is concerned, the effects of the astral body disappear when a person falls asleep. To supersensible observation, however, the astral body is still present but appears to have separated from the ether body or lifted out of it. Sensory perception does not deal with the astral body itself but only with its effects on manifest elements. These effects are not directly present while we sleep.

In the same sense that having a physical body is something we share with minerals and the ether body something we share with plants, with respect to our astral body we are of the same nature as animals. Plants exist in a continuous state of sleep. If we do not judge these things accurately, it is easy to fall into the error of crediting plants with a consciousness similar to what animals and humans have in the waking state. This error is only possible if we form an inexact concept of consciousness. When an external stimulus is applied to a plant, it makes certain movements just as an animal would do; we can say that plants whose leaves curl up under certain external stimuli are "sensitive" to these stimuli. The deciding factor in consciousness, however, is not the fact that a being responds to stimuli, but the fact that it inwardly experiences something new in addition to the mere response. Otherwise, we would also be able to speak of consciousness when a piece of iron expands under the influence of heat. Consciousness is only present when the being in question has an inner experience—of pain, for example—as a result of the heat's effect.

[11]    The fourth element that supersensible cognition ascribes to our human makeup has nothing in common with the manifest world that surrounds us. It is what distinguishes us from our fellow creatures and makes us the crown of creation, of the created world that belongs to us at least temporarily. Supersensible cognition forms a concept of this next part of our human makeup by pointing out essential differences among our waking experiences. These differences immediately become apparent when we turn our attention to the fact that in the waking state we are constantly in the midst of experiences that are necessarily transient, while, on the other hand, we also have experiences of which this is not true. This difference becomes especially clear when we compare our human experiences to those of animals. Animals experience the influences of the outer world with great regularity; under the influence of the warmth and the cold, of pain and pleasure, and certain regularly recurrent processes in their bodies, they become aware of hunger and thirst. Such experiences do not constitute the entire scope of our human life; we can develop desires and wishes that transcend all this. It would always be possible, if we were able to go far enough, to demonstrate where the cause of an animal's action or sensation lies, whether within its

body or outside of it. This is by no means the case with human beings. We can produce wishes and desires that are not adequately accounted for by causes either within or outside of our bodies. We must acknowledge that everything falling into this domain has a special source. In spiritual scientific terms, this source can be seen in the human "I," which can therefore be called the fourth part of our human makeup.

If the astral body were left to its own devices, pleasure and pain and sensations of hunger and thirst would take place in it, but there would be no sense of anything permanent in all of this. What we are calling the "I" is not the permanent factor itself, but what experiences permanency. In this field, we must formulate our concepts very clearly so that no misunderstandings arise. When we become aware of something lasting or permanent within the changing flow of our inner experiences, the feeling of I begins to dawn on us. The fact that a being feels hunger, for instance, cannot give it a feeling of I. Hunger sets in when its recurrent causes make themselves felt in the being in question, which then attacks its food with gusto simply because these recurrent causes are present. The feeling of I does not appear when recurrent causes of hunger drive us to seek food; it appears when, in addition to this, we retain an awareness of our pleasure on a previous occasion when our hunger was satisfied, so that our desire for food is driven by past experience, as well as by our current experience of hunger.

The physical body would fall apart if the ether body did not hold it together. The ether body would sink into unconsciousness if the astral body did not illumine it. Likewise, the astral body would repeatedly forget the past if the I did not rescue this past and carry it over into the present. What *death* is to the physical body and *sleep* to the ether body, *forgetting* is to the astral body. We can also say that life belongs to the ether body, consciousness to the astral body, and memory to the I.

*[12]*     Falling into the error of ascribing memory to animals is even easier than ascribing consciousness to plants. It is natural to think of memory when a dog recognizes its owners after perhaps not having seen them for a long time. In reality, however, this recognition is not based on memory but on something totally different. The dog feels a certain attraction for its owners, which proceeds from their very being. This gives the dog pleasure when its owners are present. Each time they are again present after an absence, the dog's pleasure recurs. Memory, however, is only present when a being not only feels its experiences in the present but also retains those of the past. Even if we acknowledge this, we might still fall into the error of thinking that the dog remembers. We could say, for instance, that since the dog grieves when its owners leave, it retains a memory of them. This, too, is an incorrect assessment of the situation. Through sharing life with its owners, the dog comes to need their presence and thus feels their absence in the same way that it feels hunger. If we do not make such distinctions, life's true circumstances will not become clear to us.

*[13]*     Certain biases might make us object to this presentation and say that we cannot know whether or not anything

similar to human memory is present in animals. This objection is based on untrained observation. If we are really capable of observing factually how an animal behaves in the context of its experiences, we will notice the difference between its behavior and that of a human being and will realize that the animal's behavior is in keeping with the absence of memory.

This fact is immediately clear to supersensible observation. But in addition, the effects of what enters human consciousness directly during supersensible observation enable our thought-permeated sensory perception to recognize it. If we say that we become aware of our own memory by inwardly observing our own souls, while we cannot do the same with the soul of an animal, this statement is based on a fateful error. What we can say about our own capacity for memory does not come from inwardly observing our souls, but only from what we experience with regard to ourselves in relationship to the objects and processes of the outer world. We experience this with regard to ourselves, with regard to other human beings, and also with regard to animals in exactly the same way. We are blinded by illusion when we believe that we assess the presence of memory only on the basis of inner observation. Although we may say that the power that underlies memory is an inner power, our assessment of it, even with regard to ourselves, is acquired from the outer world by looking at the context of life. We are able to assess this context with regard to an animal in the same way that we can assess it with regard to ourselves. Contemporary psychology suffers a great deal in this respect from its totally untrained and inexact ideas, which are highly deceptive due to errors in observation.

[*]     It would be very easy to misunderstand this book's explanations of the faculty of memory.[2] It will not be immediately apparent to people who consider only outer processes that there is a difference between what happens in memory-like occurrences in animals or even in plants and what is described here as real memory in human beings. It is true that when an animal does something for the third or fourth time, to all outer appearances it may well seem that memory and the learning associated with it are actually present. Like some natural scientists and their followers, we might even extend the concept of memory to include what happens when a chick creeps out of its shell and begins pecking at grain—it even knows the precise movements it needs to make with its head and body in order to do this. We might say that since it cannot have learned this while still in the shell, it must have learned it from the thousands and thousands of creatures who were its ancestors. This is what Hering says, for example.[3] It is quite possible to describe this phenomenon as something that looks like memory. But if we do not consider the unique process that takes place in human beings—which is a process of really *perceiving* earlier experiences at later points in time rather than merely a

---

2. Paragraphs indicated by [*] in the margins were included at the end of previous editions as "Special Remarks."
3. Ewald Hering (1834–1918), *Über das Gedächtnis als eine allgemeine Funktion der organisierten Materie* ["Memory as a General Function of Organized Matter"], Vienna, 1870.

process by which earlier conditions influence later ones—
we will never be able to really grasp the essence of human
nature.

In this book, the *perception* of the past—and not merely     [*]
its reappearance, even in a changed form, at a later time—
is what will be called *memory*. If we chose to use this
word for the corresponding processes in the plant and animal kingdoms, we would need to have another one to
apply to human beings. The word itself is not what is
important in the discussion above; what is important is
that with regard to understanding the essential nature of
the human being, *we must recognize the difference*. It is
equally impossible to relate the apparently highly intelligent accomplishments of animals to what is being called
"memory" here.

For the I, remembering and forgetting signify some-     [14]
thing very similar to what waking and sleeping signify for
the astral body. Just as sleep allows the cares and troubles
of the day to disappear into nothingness, forgetting
spreads a veil over life's bad experiences, blotting out
part of the past. And just as we need sleep to strengthen
our exhausted life forces again, we also need to eradicate
certain parts of our past from our memory in order to
approach new experiences freely and without bias. Forgetting is precisely what develops our strength to perceive
something new. Think about things like learning how to
write, for instance. All the detailed steps that children
have to go through in learning how to write are forgotten,
and what remains is the ability to write. How could we
possibly write if all our past experiences of learning how

to do it arose again in our souls as memories each time we put pen to paper?

[15]    Now, memory appears in various stages. Its simplest form is when we perceive an object and can then turn away from it and reawaken a *mental image* of it. This mental image was formed while we were perceiving the object, in a process that took place between our astral body and our I. The astral body made the outer impression of the object become conscious, but we would have been aware of the object only for as long as it was actually present if the I had not absorbed this knowledge and taken possession of it.

This is the point where supersensible observation separates our bodily nature from our soul nature. We speak of the astral *body* as long as we have in mind the birth of knowledge about an object that is present. What gives permanence to this knowledge, however, we then call the *soul*. But from what has just been said, we can immediately see how closely the human astral body is linked to the part of the soul that gives permanence to knowledge. These two things are united into a single element of our human makeup, so to speak, and, therefore, this union can also be called the astral body. If we want exact terms, we can also call the human astral body the *soul body* and the soul, to the extent that it is united with this soul body, the *sentient soul*.

[16]    The I rises to a higher level of its essential nature when it directs its activity toward the aspects of this object-knowledge that it has made its own. Through this activity, the I detaches itself more and more from perceived

objects in order to work within what it has made its own. The part of the soul where this happens can be called the *intellectual soul* or *mind soul*. It is characteristic of both the sentient and mind souls that they work with what they receive through impressions of objects perceived by the senses and then retained in memory. Here the soul is totally given over to something external to it. Even what it takes possession of through memory has been received from outside.

However, the soul can transcend all this. It consists of more than just the sentient and mind souls. It is easiest for the supersensible view to provide some idea of this by pointing to a single simple fact whose comprehensive significance needs to be appreciated: Within the entire scope of our language, there is only one name whose essential character distinguishes it from all others. That name is *I*. Any other name can be applied to the thing or being to whom it belongs by any human being, but as a designation for a being, *I* has meaning only when that being applies it to itself. The name *I* can never be heard coming from outside as the name of the listener; one can only apply it to oneself. I am an "I" only to myself; I am a "you" to anyone else and anyone else is a "you" to me.

This state of affairs is the outward expression of a deeply significant truth. The actual essential nature of the I is independent of anything external; *therefore,* nothing outside of it can call it by its name. Religious denominations that have consciously maintained their connection to the supersensible view call the term *I* the "ineffable name of God." This points to what has just been indicated. Nothing external has access to the part of the human soul we are looking at now. This is the soul's "hidden shrine," and only a being that is of the same nature as the soul can gain entrance there. The God who dwells within the human being begins to speak when the soul recognizes itself as an I. Just as the sentient and mind souls dwell in the outer world, a third soul element immerses itself in the divine when the soul achieves perception of its own being.

[17]    It is easy to misunderstand this view as a declaration that the I and God are one and the same. However, it does not state that the I is God, but only that it is of the same character and essence as the divine. If we took a drop of water out of the sea, would we be claiming that it *is* the sea if we said that the drop is of the same essence or substance as the sea? If we absolutely want to use a comparison, we can say that the drop is to the sea as the I is to the divine. We can find a divine element in ourselves because our own primal being is taken from the divine. Thus, through this third part of the human soul, we acquire inner knowledge of ourselves, just as we acquire knowledge of the outer world through the astral body. This is why esoteric science can call this third soul element the *consciousness soul*. In an esoteric scientific sense, the soul consists of three parts: the sentient soul, the mind soul, and the consciousness soul, just as the body consists of three parts: the physical body, the ether body, and the astral body.

[18]    Psychological errors in observation, similar to those already mentioned regarding the erroneous assessment

of the capacity for memory, make it difficult to acquire the right kind of insight into the essential nature of the I. Many things we believe we understand can seem to refute what is presented above, while in reality they confirm it. This is the case, for example, with Eduard von Hartmann's comments on the I in his *Outline of Psychology*:

> In the first place, self-awareness is older than the word *I*. Personal pronouns are a rather late product of the evolution of languages; they are of value to language only as abbreviations. The word *I* is a shorter substitute for the speaker's own name, but a substitute that each speaker, as such, uses for him or herself, regardless of what proper name others may apply to him or her. Self-awareness can develop to a very great extent in animals and in untaught people with severe speech and hearing impairments, even without reference to a proper name. Awareness of one's own name can fully replace the absence of the use of the word *I*. This insight eliminates the magical aura that envelops the little word *I* in the minds of many people. This word cannot contribute in the least to the concept of self-awareness; rather, it receives its entire content from that concept.[4]

---

4. Eduard von Hartmann (1842-1906), *System der Philosophie im Grundriss* (*An Outline of a System of Philosophy*), vol. 3 *Grundriss der Psychologie* (*An Outline of Psychology*).

We can agree completely with such views; we can also agree that no magical aura should be attached to the little word *I* to darken our thoughtful consideration of the matter. But the nature of a thing is not determined by how gradually the word designating it came about. The important point is that the essential being of the I in self-awareness is "older than the word *I*," and that we are compelled to use this particular little word, endowed with qualities belonging to it alone, for the element in our interrelationship with the outer world that is different from what an animal can experience. Nothing can be shown about the nature of a triangle by showing how the word "triangle" came about; similarly, nothing can be concluded about the nature of the I by knowing how the word developed out of a different verbal usage in the course of the evolution of language.

[19]     The true nature of the I first reveals itself in the consciousness soul. The soul loses itself to other things in feeling and intellect, but as the consciousness soul it takes hold of its own being. That's why the consciousness soul's perception of the I can take place only through a certain inner activity. Mental images of outer objects, formed as these objects come and go, work on in our intellect through a power of their own. However, if the I is to perceive itself, it cannot simply surrender itself. In order to be conscious of its own being, it must first use inner activity to lift its being up out of its own depths. When the I is perceived—that is, when self-reflection takes place—an inner activity of the I begins. Through this activity, perceiving the I in the consciousness soul

acquires a quite different meaning for the human being than perceiving everything that approaches us through our three bodily elements and the other two parts of the soul.

The force that makes the I manifest in the consciousness soul is actually the same force that makes itself known in all the rest of the world, but in the body and in the lower soul elements, it does not appear directly, but reveals itself in stages through its effects. Its lowest manifestation takes place through the physical body; it then rises step by step to what fills the mind soul. We might say that at each step in its ascent, another veil cloaking the hidden element falls away. In what fills the consciousness soul, this hidden element steps unveiled into the innermost temple of the soul where it appears as only a drop in the sea of all-pervading spirituality. Here, however, we must first take hold of this spirituality. We must recognize it in ourselves so that we are then also able to find it in its manifestations.

What makes its way like a drop into the consciousness [20] soul is called the *spirit* by esoteric science. In this way the consciousness soul is united with the spirit, which is the hidden element in everything manifest. When we want to grasp the spirit in all of the revealed world, we must do so in the same way that we grasp the I in the consciousness soul. The activity that led us to perceive this I must now be directed toward the manifest world. In doing this, we evolve to higher levels of our being and add something new to the body and soul elements of our human makeup. To begin with, we conquer what lies hidden in the lower parts of the soul. This takes place through work on the soul that proceeds from the I. How a person is involved in this work becomes evident when we compare a noble idealist to someone who is still totally given up to lower desires and so-called sensual pleasures. Such a person can become a "noble idealist" by withdrawing from certain base inclinations and turning toward higher ones; that is, by working out of the I to have an ennobling and spiritualizing effect on his or her own soul. The I becomes the master within that person's soul life. This can be taken to the point where no desire or craving can find a place in the soul unless the I allows it to enter. In this way, the entire soul becomes a revelation of the I, as was previously true only of the consciousness soul. Fundamentally, all of our cultural activity and spiritual endeavors consist of work that aims for this mastery by the I. All human beings who are alive at present are involved in this work, whether or not they choose to be and whether or not they are conscious of it.

[21]     But this work leads to higher levels of our essential human nature and develops new parts of our makeup that are hidden behind what is manifest to us. Not only can we master the soul by working on it out of the I so that it reveals what is hidden in the manifest, but we can also take this work further and extend it to the astral body. The I then takes possession of the astral body by uniting with its hidden nature. This astral body that is conquered and transformed by the I can be called the *spirit self*. (This is the same as what is called *manas* in the traditions of Eastern wisdom.) The spirit self constitutes a higher element of our human makeup, one that is present in it in

embryonic form, as it were, and emerges more and more in the course of working on ourselves.

Just as we conquer the astral body by making our way through to the hidden forces standing behind it, this also happens with the ether body in the course of our inner development. Working on the ether body, however, is more intensive than working on the astral body because what is concealed in the ether body is cloaked in two veils, while what is hidden in the astral is cloaked in only a single veil. [22]

We can get an idea of the differences in working on each of these two bodies by pointing to certain changes that can take place in us in the course of our development. First, let's think about how certain soul qualities develop when the I works on the soul, how passion and desire, joy and sorrow may change. All we need to do is to think back to our childhood. What gave us pleasure then? What caused us pain? What have we learned, what have we added to what we were able to do as children? All of this is only an expression of how the I gained mastery over the astral body, because the astral body is the vehicle of passion and sorrow, of joy and pain.

In contrast, there are certain other qualities of ours, such as our temperament and the deeper idiosyncracies of our character, that change relatively little over time. Someone who was hot-tempered as a child will often retain certain aspects of this violent temper in later life. This point is so striking that there are theorists who totally deny the possibility of any fundamental change in a person's character. They assume that this remains constant throughout a person's life, simply revealing itself in one direction or another. However, this conclusion is based on lack of observation. It is clear to anyone who has the capacity to observe such things that even a person's character and temperament change under the influence of the I, although this change is slow in relationship to the change in the qualities described above. To use a comparison, the relationship between the two kinds of change is like the movement of the hour hand of a clock in relationship to the minute hand.

Now, the forces that bring about changes in a person's character or temperament belong to the hidden domain of the ether body. They are of the same nature as the forces that govern the living kingdom—that is, the forces that serve the processes of growth, nutrition, and reproduction. Explanations that will be presented later on in this book will shed the right light on these things.

[*]    It is not possible to draw a fixed boundary between the changes that take place as a result of the activity of the I in the astral body and those that take place in the ether body, since they blend into each other. If something we learn enhances our faculty of judgment, a change has taken place in the astral body, but if this judgment changes our state of mind so that we become accustomed to *feeling* differently about a subject after having learned about it, then a change has taken place in the ether body. Everything we take possession of in such a way that we can recall it again and again is based on a change in the ether body. Anything that gradually becomes an entrenched part of the wealth of our memory rests on the

fact that the work performed on the astral body has been transferred to the ether body.

The I is not working on the astral body when we simply give ourselves up to pleasure and suffering, joy and pain, but only when the idiosyncracies of these soul qualities begin to change. Likewise, this work extends to the ether body when our I applies its activity to changing our traits of character, our temperament, and so on. Every individual is working on this change, too, whether consciously or not. In ordinary life, the strongest impulses working on behalf of this change are religious ones. When our I allows impulses that flow from religion to work on it again and again, these impulses develop a strength within the I that works right through into the ether body and transforms it, just as lesser impulses in life cause a transformation of the astral body. These lesser impulses, which come to us through learning, thinking, ennobling our feelings, and so on, are subject to the many and various changes in our life, but religious feelings leave a uniform imprint on all our thinking, feeling, and willing. They shed a common, uniform light on our whole soul life, so to speak. We think and feel one way today, another way tomorrow, prompted by a great variety of causes. But if, because of religious feelings of whatever sort, we divine the presence of something that remains constant through all these changes, we will relate both today's and tomorrow's soul experiences to this fundamental feeling. Religious belief, therefore, has a far-reaching effect on our soul life that becomes stronger and stronger with time because it works through constant repetition. This is why it acquires the strength to work on our ether body.

True art has similar effects on us. If, through the outer form, color, or tone of a work of art we are able to penetrate to its spiritual foundation with our thought and feeling, then the impulses our I receives as a result actually work right through to the ether body. If we think this thought through to its conclusion, we can assess art's tremendous significance for all of human development and evolution.

We have referred here to only a few examples of things that provide the I with impulses to work on the ether body. There are many such influences in our lives that are not so readily apparent to the observing eye as the ones that have been mentioned here. From these, however, it is evident that there is an additional part of our human makeup hidden within us, and that the I is gradually developing it. We can call this second spiritual element the *life spirit*. (This is the same as what is called *buddhi* in the traditions of Eastern wisdom.) "Life spirit" is the appropriate term for this because the forces active within it are the same forces that are active in the life body. The only difference is that when they manifest as the life body, the human I is not active in them. However, when they manifest as the life spirit, they are imbued with the activity of the I.

[23]     Our intellectual development and the extent to which we purify and ennoble our displays of feeling and will are the measure of our transformation of the astral body into the spirit self, while religious and other related experiences leave an imprint on our ether body and turn it into

the life spirit. In the course of ordinary life, this happens more or less unconsciously. In contrast, in what is known as *initiation*, supersensible knowledge points out the means that allow us to take this work on the spirit self and life spirit quite consciously in hand. These means will be discussed in later sections of this book. For the moment, the most important thing is simply to show that in addition to the body and the soul, the spirit is also active within the human being. Later, we will also see how this spirit belongs to the human being's eternal aspect, in contrast to the transitory body.

The activity of the I, however, is not limited to working on the astral body and the ether body. It also extends to the physical body. A trace of the influence of the I can be seen, for instance, when a person blushes or turns pale under certain circumstances. In this case, the I actually triggers a process in the physical body. When changes take place in a person through the activity of the I, specifically with regard to its influence on the physical body, the I is actually united with the physical body's hidden forces, with the same forces that bring about physical processes in it. We can then say that the I is working on the physical body through this activity. This statement must not be misunderstood; we must not assume that this work is something crudely material. What appears in a crudely material way in the physical body is only the manifest aspect of this work. Its essential forces are spiritual in nature and lie hidden behind this manifestation. We are not speaking here of work on the physical body's manifest material aspect, but of spiritual work on the invisible

*[24]*

forces that bring the body into existence and later cause it to disintegrate again.

In ordinary life, the work of the I on the physical body enters our consciousness to only a very limited degree of clarity. We arrive at complete clarity only when we take this work consciously in hand under the influence of supersensible knowledge. At that point, however, it becomes apparent that there is a third spiritual part to the human being. This may be called the *spirit body*, in contrast to the physical human being. (In Eastern wisdom this spirit body is called the *atma*.)

[25]   It is also easy to be misled with regard to the spirit body because we view the physical body as the human being's lowest component and, therefore, have difficulty coming to terms with the fact that working on this physical body is supposed to result in the highest part of our human makeup. But the very fact that the physical body conceals the spirit active in it behind three veils is the reason why the highest form of inner work is needed to unite the I with the spirit hidden there.

[26]   Thus, the human being appears to esoteric science as a being made up of different elements. Those of a bodily nature are the physical body, the ether body, and the astral body. Those belonging to the soul are the sentient soul, the mind soul, and the consciousness soul. The light of the I shines forth within the soul. The spiritual elements are the spirit self, the life spirit, and the spirit body. It follows from the descriptions above that the sentient soul and the astral body are closely united and constitute a unity in a certain respect. Likewise, the consciousness soul and the

spirit self constitute a unity, because the consciousness soul is where the spirit flares up and radiates outward into the other parts of our human makeup. Taking this into consideration, we can speak of the following configuration of the human being: The astral body and the sentient soul can be combined into a single element, as can the consciousness soul and the spirit self. We can simply call the mind soul the I because it takes part in the nature of the I; in a certain respect, it already is the I that has not yet become aware of its spiritual nature. This results in seven components of the human being: 1) the physical body; 2) the ether body or life body; 3) the astral body; 4) the I; 5) the spirit self; 6) the life spirit; and 7) the spirit body.

This sevenfold configuration of the human being need not have anything "vaguely magical" about it—as people who are used to materialistic concepts so often claim—if these people would simply stick closely to the meaning of the descriptions above and not superimpose this element of magic from the very beginning. We ought to speak of these seven parts of the human being no differently from how we speak of the seven colors that make up light or the seven notes that constitute a scale (if we consider the octave to be a repetition of the tonic). The only difference is that we are speaking from the viewpoint of a higher method of observing the world. Just as light appears in seven colors and sound in a sevenfold scale, homogeneous human nature appears in the seven differentiations described above. Just as there is nothing inherently superstitious about the number seven in tone and color, this is also the case with regard to differentiation in the human being.

*[27]*

(During one oral presentation on this subject someone remarked that, in the case of colors, the number seven is not correct, because there are other colors, invisible to the eye, that lie beyond red and violet. Even taking this into account, however, the analogy to colors holds good, because our human makeup actually extends beyond the physical body on the one hand and the spirit body on the other. These extensions, however, are "spiritually invisible" to methods of supersensible observation, just as the colors beyond red and violet are invisible to the physical eye. It was necessary to respond to this remark, because it is so easy to think that supersensible observation is amateurish and imprecise in how it uses ideas from the natural sciences. However, anyone who pays strict attention to the intended meaning of what is said here will find that it actually never contradicts true natural science, neither when natural-scientific facts are used for purposes of illustration, nor when remarks made here point to a direct relationship to natural scientific research.)

# CHAPTER 3

# SLEEP AND DEATH

Just as we cannot solve the riddle of life without consider-    [1]
ing death, we also cannot break through to understanding
the essence of waking consciousness without considering
the state we pass through during sleep. Someone who has
no feeling for the significance of supersensible knowledge
may entertain doubts about this knowledge simply because
of its views on sleep and death. We can appreciate the reason for these doubts. There is nothing incomprehensible
about it if someone states that human beings are here in
order to lead an active and effective life, that purposeful
activity depends on being able to devote ourselves to this
life, and that delving into conditions like sleep and death
can result only from a penchant for idle dreaminess and
lead only to empty fantasies. It is easy for people to believe
that rejecting such "fantasies" is a sign of a healthy soul
and that devoting oneself to "idle dreaminess" is a pathological trait that is present only in people who lack both joy
in life and the strength to tackle it and who are incapable
of real "purposeful activity."

It would be doing this opinion an injustice to present it as totally false, because there is a certain kernel of truth in it. It is a quarter-truth that needs the other three-quarters for completeness. If we attack the one-quarter of it that is true, we will simply arouse the suspicions of those who see that quarter very clearly but have no inkling of the other three.

It must be acknowledged without reservation that investigating what is hidden behind the veils of sleep and death actually is pathological if it leads to weakness and estrangement from real life. Likewise, we must agree that much of what called itself esoteric science in the past, as well as much of what is practiced today under that name, bears the imprint of something unhealthy and hostile to life. But this unhealthy element does not spring from *true* supersensible knowledge. On the contrary, the real fact of the matter is this: Just as we cannot always be awake, when it comes to the real circumstances of life in the broadest sense, we also cannot get along without what the supersensible element can offer us. Life continues while we are asleep, and our forces for the working and creating we do while we are awake gain strength and refreshment from what sleep gives them; this is how things stand with what we can observe in the manifest world. But the world is broader in scope than that particular field of observation, and what we know in the visible world must be complemented and fructified by what can be known about the invisible worlds. If we did not repeatedly draw strength for our depleted forces from sleep, we would destroy our life. Similarly, a worldview not fructified by a knowledge of the hidden element inevitably leads to desolation.

Something similar is true of "death." Living things succumb to death so that new life can come about. Knowledge of the supersensible element is precisely what can shed light on Goethe's beautiful words, "Life is [Nature's] most beautiful invention, and death is a trick it plays in order to have abundant life."[1]

Just as there would be no life in the usual sense of the word if there were no death, there can be no real knowledge of the visible world without insight into the supersensible realm. All knowledge of the visible must immerse itself in the invisible again and again in order to be able to evolve. Thus it is evident that the science of the supersensible is what makes the existence of revealed knowledge altogether possible. When it appears in its true form, this science of the invisible never weakens life; it repeatedly strengthens it and makes it fresh and healthy when it has become weak and sick from having been left on its own.

When we fall asleep, the connection between the elements of our makeup changes. The part of a human being that lies sleeping on the bed contains the physical body and ether body, but not the astral body or ego. Life's processes continue during sleep because the ether body remains united with the physical body. If the physical [2]

---

1. An aphorism on "Nature" in Goethe's *Naturwissenschaftlichen Schriften* (*Works on Natural Science*), edited and with commentary by Rudolf Steiner in Kürschner's *Deutsche National-Literatur* (*National Literature of Germany*), 5 vols. (1884–1897), (GA 1a, e, vol.2, GA1b), p. 8.

body were left to itself, it would have to disintegrate. What is extinguished in sleep, however, are our mental images, our pain and pleasure, joy and sorrow, our ability to express our conscious intentions, and similar realities of our existence. The astral body is the vehicle of all these, however. If we are unbiased in our assessment of this situation, we will never be able to entertain the notion that the astral body is destroyed during sleep, along with all our pleasure and pain and the entire world of our ideas and will. It is simply present in a different state. For our I and astral body to have a conscious perception of our pain and suffering and all the other things just listed, rather than simply being filled with them, the astral body must be connected to the physical body and the ether body. And in fact it is connected when we are awake, but not when we are asleep. In sleep, the astral body withdraws. It takes on a different form of existence than the one it has when it is connected to the physical and ether bodies.

So the next task for supersensible knowledge is to consider the astral body's other form of existence. As far as observation in the external world is concerned, the astral body disappears during sleep. Now supersensible perception's job is to follow it until it takes possession of the physical and ether bodies once again when we wake up. As in all cases involving knowledge of the world's hidden things and processes, discovering the particulars of what is really going on in the state of sleep requires supersensible observation. Once what can be discovered by this means has been stated, however, it is immediately understandable to truly unbiased thinking, because processes in the hidden world have effects that are visible in the manifest world. Once we see how the contribution of supersensible observation makes sense-perceptible processes understandable, such corroboration by life itself constitutes the proof that can be required for such things. Those who choose not to use the methods of attaining supersensible perception that will be explained later will still be able to have the experience of accepting the statements of supersensible knowledge and applying them to manifest things in their own experience. By doing so, they will find that life becomes clear and understandable. The more precisely and thoroughly they consider ordinary life, the more they will come to this conviction.

Even though the astral body experiences no mental images during sleep, no pleasure or pain or anything similar, it does not remain inactive. On the contrary, it is obliged to maintain a lively activity in the sleeping state, an activity it must take up again and again in rhythmical succession after periods of being involved in the activity that it shares with the physical and ether bodies. Just as the pendulum of a clock that has swung to the left and then come back to the middle must then swing to the right because of the momentum gained by swinging to the left, the astral body and the I that rests in its bosom, having been active for a while in the physical and ether bodies, must then spend the next period of time being busy and active in the body-free state in an environment of soul and spirit. As far as our normal state of life is concerned, unconsciousness sets in when the astral body and the I are in this body-free state, because this represents the

*[3]*

counterbalance to the state of consciousness that develops in the waking state through union with the physical and ether bodies, just as the pendulum's swing to the right is the counterbalance to its swing to the left.

The soul-spiritual principle in the human being experiences needing to enter this state of unconsciousness as fatigue. However, this fatigue is the expression of the fact that during sleep the astral body and I are preparing themselves to re-form, during the next period of wakefulness, what has arisen in the physical and ether bodies through purely organic—and unconscious—formative activity while they were free of the spirit and soul principles. This unconscious formative activity is the polar opposite of what happens in the human being during consciousness and by means of consciousness; these states must alternate in rhythmical succession.

[*]     The usual views on the connection between sleep and fatigue are not in line with the facts. We think that sleep sets in as a consequence of fatigue. This is an oversimplified idea, as is shown by the fact that people often fall asleep during uninteresting lectures or on other similar occasions even if they aren't tired at all. Anyone who insists that such occasions make us tired is trying to explain this phenomenon by applying a method that lacks cognitive integrity.

[*]     Unbiased observation will certainly show us that waking and sleeping represent different relationships of the soul to the body. Like a pendulum swinging alternately to the right and to the left, these relationships alternate in rhythmic succession in the ordinary course of life. This

same unbiased observation reveals that the state of being filled with impressions of the outer world awakens within the soul a desire to follow this state with a different one in which the soul is absorbed in enjoying its own bodily nature. Two states of soul alternate—surrendering to outer impressions and surrendering to one's own bodily nature. During the first state, the desire for the second is produced unconsciously. The second state then runs its course in unconsciousness. Fatigue is the expression of wanting to enjoy our own bodily nature, so instead of saying that we want to sleep because we feel tired, we actually ought to say that we feel tired because we want to sleep. Since the human soul can, as a sort of adaptation, evoke at will states that normally appear as a matter of necessity, it is also possible for us to evoke the desire to enjoy our own bodily nature when we have numbed ourselves to a given outer impression. That is, we fall asleep even though our inner condition gives us no reason to do so.

The physical body can only be maintained in a shape and form suitable for a human being by means of a human ether body, which must in turn receive the appropriate forces from an astral body. The ether body is the sculptor or architect of the physical body. However, it can only shape the body in the right way if it receives the stimulus to do so from the astral body. The astral body contains the prototypes according to which the ether body gives the physical body its form. During the waking state, the astral body is not filled with these prototypes of the physical body, or only to a certain extent, because the soul puts images of its own in their place. When we direct our senses to our surroundings, we form mental images by means of perception, mental images that are likenesses of the world around us. Initially, these likenesses disturb the images that stimulate the ether body to maintain the physical body. If our own activity were to supply our astral body with images that would stimulate the ether body in the right way, this disturbance would not happen. In fact, however, this disturbance, which is expressed in the fact that the prototypes for the ether body are not fully effective during the waking state, plays an important role in human existence. In the waking state the astral body carries out its activity within the physical body, while in sleep it works upon it from outside.

*[4]*     Just as the physical body, which is of the same nature as the outer world, needs the outer world to supply it with nourishment, for example, something similar is also true of the astral body. Imagine a physical human body removed from the world that surrounds it. It would have to perish. This demonstrates that without its whole physical environment, it could not exist. In fact, the entire Earth must be just the way it is if physical human bodies are to exist on it. In reality, the entire human body is simply a part of the Earth, or, in a wider sense, part of the whole physical universe. In this connection, its relationship is similar to that of a finger on one hand to the entire human body. If we sever the finger from the hand, it can no longer remain a finger. It withers away. The same thing would happen to a human body if it were removed from the body it is part of, from the living conditions provided by the

Earth. If we were to raise it a sufficient number of miles above the Earth's surface, it would die just as a finger severed from the hand dies. If we pay less attention to this fact with regard to our own physical bodies than with regard to fingers, this is simply because fingers cannot stroll around freely on the body the way people can on the Earth, so the dependence of fingers is more obvious.

Just as the physical body is embedded in the physical    *[5]*
world to which it belongs, the astral body is also embedded in a world of its own. However, it is torn out of this world during our waking life. An analogy will illustrate what happens in this case. Imagine a container full of water. A single drop in this volume of water is not something separate and independent. But then suppose we take a little sponge and absorb one drop out of the whole amount. Something similar happens with the human astral body when we wake up. During sleep, it is in a world that is like itself; in a certain sense, it constitutes something belonging to that world. But when we wake up, the physical body and the ether body absorb it and fill themselves with it. They contain the organs through which it perceives the outer world, but in order to acquire this perception, it must separate itself from the other world to which it belongs. However, it can only receive the prototypes it needs for the ether body from this other world.

In the sleeping state, the astral body receives *images* from the world that surrounds it, just as the physical body receives nourishment from its surroundings, for example. The astral body actually lives out there in the universe, outside the physical and ether bodies, in the same universe that gave birth to the entire human being. This universe is the source of the images we use to maintain our form, and we are harmoniously incorporated into it during sleep. As we awaken, we lift ourselves up out of this all-encompassing harmony in order to acquire outer perception. During sleep our astral bodies return to the harmony of the universe again. When we awaken, we bring enough strength with us out of the cosmic harmony into our bodies so that we can go without being in that state for a while. The astral body returns home during sleep and brings renewed forces back into our life when we awaken. The outer expression of this is the refreshment that healthy sleep bestows on us. Further esoteric scientific descriptions will show that the astral body's home is more encompassing than the aspect of the physical environment that belongs to the physical body in the narrower sense. While we humans, as physical beings, are part of the Earth, our astral bodies are part of a world that embraces additional heavenly bodies. During sleep, therefore, we enter a world that encompasses other worlds in addition to our Earth. As mentioned before, this fact will only become clear from later descriptions.

[6]     It ought to be superfluous to point to a misunderstanding that can easily arise with regard to these facts, but this is not the case in an age when certain materialistic ways of thinking are present. Of course people who subscribe to these views can say that the only scientific thing to do is to investigate the physical conditions of something such as sleep. They can say that even though experts are not yet united on the subject of the physical cause of sleep, one thing is certain—we must assume that specific

physical processes are the basis of this phenomenon. If only people would admit that supersensible knowledge in no way contradicts this claim! It agrees with everything that is said from this point of view, just as we all agree that in the physical construction of a house, one brick must be placed on top of another, and that when the house is finished, its structure and the fact that it holds together can be explained in terms of purely mechanical laws. In order for the house to come about, however, the architect's idea is needed, and this idea is nowhere to be found when we investigate only the physical laws that apply.

Just as the thoughts of the person who created the house lie behind the physical laws that make it explainable, the statements of supersensible knowledge also lie behind what physical science quite correctly presents. It is true that this comparison, which may be considered trivial, is often used to justify the idea of a spiritual backdrop to the world. But in such matters the important thing is not that we are familiar with specific concepts, but that we attach the right value to them in arguing the point. The mere fact that opposing ideas exercise so much power over our capacity for judgment can prevent us from assessing this value correctly.

Dreaming is an intermediate state between waking and  [7] sleeping. To thoughtful consideration, dream experiences consist of a colorful intermingling of images in a world that conceals an element of regularity and lawfulness within it, although at first glance this world seems to reveal an often confusing ebb and flow. In dreaming, we are released from the laws of waking consciousness that fetter us to sensory perception and to the rules that govern our power of judgment. And yet, dreams obey certain mysterious laws that are fascinating and alluring to our faculty of surmising and are the deeper reason why we so readily compare "dreaming" to the beautiful play of imagination that supports artistic sensitivity. We will find this confirmed if we simply recall a few characteristic dreams: We dream, for example, about driving off a dog that is about to pounce on us. We wake up to catch ourselves in the unconscious act of throwing off the covers where they were weighing on an unaccustomed body part and starting to bother us.

What does dreaming do to a sense-perceptible process in this case? Our sleeping life allows what our senses would perceive in the waking state to remain fully unconscious for the moment, but it does hold fast to one essential thing—the fact that we are trying to get rid of something. It spins a pictorial process around this fact. The images as such are echoes of our daily waking life, but there is something arbitrary in the way they are borrowed from it. We have the feeling that although the same external provocation might also conjure up other pictures in our dream, these would still symbolically express the sensation of wanting to get rid of something. Dreams create symbols; they are symbolists. Inner processes can also be transformed into dream symbols. Suppose we dream that a fire is crackling nearby; we see the flames in our dream. We wake up and find that we have been too warmly covered and are getting hot. The feeling of too much warmth expresses itself in the dream image.

Very dramatic experiences can be enacted in dreams. We dream, for instance, that we are standing at the edge of a cliff. We see a child running toward the edge. The dream lets us experience all our tormenting thoughts: If only the child would pay attention and not fall over the cliff! We see the child fall and hear a dull thud as the body lands. We wake up and find that something hanging on the bedroom wall has fallen down with a dull thump. In the dream, this simple process is expressed in exciting images. At the moment, we need not wonder about how it is possible for the momentary dull thud of a falling object to trigger a whole series of events that seemed to take place over a certain span of time. We only need to consider how the dream makes an image out of what sense-perception would offer if we were awake.

We see that as soon as our sensory activity comes to a halt, something creative asserts itself in us. This is the same creativity that is also present in completely dreamless sleep, where it appears as the soul state that is the opposite of the waking state. In order for this dreamless sleep to set in, the astral body must have withdrawn from the ether body and the physical body. During dreams, it is separated from the physical body in that it is no longer connected to our sense organs, but it still maintains a certain connection to the ether body. That we can perceive the astral body's processes in image form is due to this connection. When it ceases, the images immediately sink down into the darkness of the unconscious, and we have dreamless sleep. *[8]*

That dream pictures are arbitrary and often absurd is due to the fact that the astral body is not able to relate its images to the right objects and processes in our external surroundings because it is separated from the physical body's sense organs. This state of affairs becomes much clearer when we consider a dream in which the I seems to split into two, for instance when someone dreams of sitting in a classroom and being unable to answer a certain question, which the teacher then answers immediately. In this case the dreamer cannot make use of the physical body's organs of perception and is therefore not in a position to relate these two occurrences to one and the same person, namely his or her self. In order for each of us to recognize the enduring I in ourselves, we must first be equipped with organs of outer perception. This enduring I would only be perceptible to us outside the physical body if we had acquired the ability to become aware of it in some way other than through these organs of perception. It is up to supersensible consciousness to acquire the faculties needed for this. We will talk about the means of acquiring these faculties later on in this book.

*[9]*     Death, too, occurs only because of a change in the relationship between the elements of our makeup. Here again, the effects of what supersensible perception describes can be seen in the manifest world, and—if our power of judgment is unbiased—we will be able to confirm the communications of supersensible knowledge by observing outer life. However, in this case the expression of the invisible in the visible is less apparent, and it is more difficult to fully recognize the significance of how the processes of outer life confirm what supersensible knowledge communicates. To those who refuse to understand how the sense-perceptible

contains a clear indication of the supersensible, claiming that these communications are mere figments of the imagination seems even more natural than saying the same of many things that have already been discussed in this book.

During the transition to sleep, the astral body is simply *[10]* released from its connection to the ether body and the physical body, which remain connected to each other. At death, however, the physical body also separates from the ether body. The physical body is given over to its own inherent forces; as a corpse, it must disintegrate. After death the ether body, however, finds itself in a condition that it never experienced between birth and death, except under certain exceptional conditions that will be spoken of later. It is now united with the astral body, but without the presence of the physical body, because the ether and astral bodies do not separate from each other immediately after death. It is easy to understand the need for the force that holds them together for a time. If that force were not present, the ether body would not be able to extricate itself from the physical body at all. In sleep, for example, they are held together and the astral body is incapable of tearing them apart. The requisite force takes effect at death, severing the ether body from the physical body so that the ether body is now connected with the astral body. Supersensible observation shows that this connection is different in different people, but lasts for a matter of days. (For the moment, this time period will be mentioned only as a point of information.)

Later, the astral body separates from its ether body and continues on its way without it. While these two bodies are still connected, we are in a state that allows us to perceive the experiences of our astral body. As long as the physical body is present, the work of restoring its worn-out organs must begin from outside as soon as the astral body is released from it, but once the physical body has been cast off, this work is no longer necessary. However, the force formerly used for this purpose during sleep persists after death and can now be used to make the astral body's own processes perceptible.

[11]     If our processes of observation cling to life's externalities, we may still say that these are all claims that may be clear to those gifted with supersensible sight, but for everyone else there is no possibility of arriving at the truth of the matter. This is not the case. After supersensible knowledge discovers something in this or any other domain that is removed from ordinary perception, it can be grasped by our ordinary power of judgment. We must simply give the right consideration to relationships in life in the manifest world. The relationships among thinking, feeling, and willing and their relationship to our experiences in the outer world remain inherently incomprehensible as long as the character of their revealed activity is not seen as the expression of an unrevealed activity. This revealed activity becomes transparent to judgment only when the activity and the course it runs in the physical life of a human being can be seen as resulting from what supersensible knowledge concludes about non-physical things. If we confront this activity without benefit of supersensible knowledge, it is as if we were in a dark room with no light. Just as we see the physical objects in

our surroundings only when light is present, what takes place in our soul life becomes explainable only in the presence of supersensible knowledge.

As long as we are connected to the physical body, the outer world enters our consciousness in the form of images or reproductions, but after we cast that body off, we begin to perceive what our astral body experiences when it is not connected to the outer world by physical sense organs. At first, the astral body has no new experiences; its connection to the ether body prevents it from experiencing anything new. However, it does possess a memory of the life that is just over. The still-present ether body allows this memory to appear as a comprehensive living picture, so our first experience after death is a perception of life between birth and death as a series of images spread out in front of us. During that life, memory was present only during the waking state, during union with our physical bodies, and only to the extent that these physical bodies permitted. But nothing that makes an impression on the soul during life is ever lost to it. If the physical body were the perfect instrument for this, it would be possible at any moment in life to make our entire life appear to the soul. At death, the physical body's hindrance disappears. As long as the ether body persists, a certain perfect memory is present, but this disappears to the extent that the ether body loses the form, similar to the physical body, that it had while dwelling in that body. This is also the reason why the astral body separates from the ether body after a while—it can only remain united with an ether body whose form still corresponds to the physical body.

*[12]*

During life between birth and death, the ether body separates from the physical body only in exceptional instances and only for brief periods. For example, a portion of the ether body can separate from the physical because of excessive pressure on one of our limbs. In this case, we say that the limb in question has "gone to sleep." That peculiar feeling comes from the separation of the ether body. (Of course this is another opportunity for a materialistic view of things to deny the presence of the invisible in the visible, saying that this all stems from the physical disturbance caused by the pressure.) In a case like this, supersensible observation can see how the corresponding part of the ether body slips out of the physical.

If a person experiences extreme fright or some similar unusual shock, the ether body may separate from the greater part of the physical body for a very short time. This happens if, for whatever reason, we suddenly find ourselves near death—on the verge of drowning, for example, or in danger of falling while rock climbing. The accounts of people who have experienced such things actually come very close to the truth and can be confirmed by supersensible observation. They state that in such moments their entire lives passed in front of their souls like a great picture in their memories.

Of the many examples that could be given here, only one will be referred to because it comes from a man whose personal philosophy would consider everything said about such things here to be sheer fantasy. For those who have made a few steps in the direction of supersensible observation, it's always very useful to become familiar with such accounts by people for whom supersensible science is mere fantasy, since it is not so easy to attribute these accounts to bias on the part of the observer. (It is to be hoped that spiritual scientists will learn a great deal from those who consider their efforts ridiculous, and it need not confuse them if their critics do not return their affection. Of course, supersensible observation itself does not aim to verify its own results through such things; it refers to them not in order to prove its findings, but only to clarify them.) In his memoirs, *Moritz Benedikt*, an eminent criminologist and well-known researcher in many other fields of natural science, relates a personal experience: Once he nearly drowned while swimming and saw his whole life flash before him in retrospect as if in a single picture.[2]

If the images seen by others on similar occasions are described differently and even seem to have little to do with the events of their past, this does not contradict what

---

2. Moritz Benedikt (1835–1920); in his autobiography *Aus meinem Leben. Erinnerungen und Erörterungen* (*Excerpts from My Life: Recollections and Commentary*) Vienna, 1906, p. 35, Benedikt describes this instance as follows: "I have had a great love for water ever since childhood, and this has prompted several experiences that stick in my memory. I went to great lengths to be able to swim out-doors, and once it happened that I went under while swimming in the Danube. Fortunately I was driven up against a post that served as a marker for swimmers. For scarcely more than half a minute, I was conscious of the fact that I was drowning and made the remarkable observation that in that brief time my memories of my entire life passed in front of me at top speed. Psychologists are familiar with this observation, but few people have experienced it personally. I was about twelve years old at the time...."

was said above. The images that arise in this unusual state of separation from the physical body are often not readily explainable in terms of their relationship to life. However, if they are considered in the right way, this relationship can always be recognized. If someone was once near drowning and did not have the experiences described here, this in no way detracts from the general description. We must keep in mind that these experiences can take place only when the ether body is really separated from the physical body but remains united with the astral body. When the shock also causes a loosening of the connection between the ether body and the astral body, these experiences do not take place because complete loss of consciousness occurs, as it does during dreamless sleep.

[13]     In the time immediately after death, our experiences of the past appear, combined into a single memory-picture. After that, the astral body separates from the ether body and continues its journey on its own. It is not difficult to see that everything the astral body acquired through its own activity during its stay in the physical body now remains in it. The I developed the spirit self, the life spirit, and the spirit body to a certain extent. To the extent that these have been developed, they do not owe their existence to the organs of the various bodies, but to the I, which needs no outer organs, either for self-perception or to remain in possession of what it has united with itself. In that case, we might wonder why we have no perception during sleep of the spirit self, life spirit, and spirit body that have developed. The reason for this is that the I is fettered to the physical body between birth and death. Even

when it is with the astral body outside the physical body during sleep, it is still closely connected to the physical body because the astral body's activity is directed toward the physical body at that point. In this state, the I and its perception are directed toward to the outer sensory world and prevented from receiving the revelations of the spirit directly. Death allows these revelations to reach the I for the first time, because death frees the I from its connection to the physical and ether bodies. The moment the soul withdraws from the physical world that lays claim to all of its activity during life, another world lights up for it.

Even during this time, not all of our connections to the outer sense-perceptible world have been terminated. Instead, they are maintained by certain desires that are still present. These desires are the ones we create through being conscious of the I as the fourth element of our makeup. Desires and wishes that spring from the nature of the three lower bodies can only be active in the external world, and they cease when these bodies are discarded. Hunger, for example, comes about through the external body and is silenced as soon as this body is no longer connected to the I. If the I had no desires other than those that originate in its own spiritual nature, it would be completely satisfied by the spiritual world into which it is transported at death. Life, however, has given it other desires. Life kindled a longing in it for pleasures that can only be satisfied by physical organs, although these pleasures are not inherent in the organs themselves. The three bodies are not the only elements that expect satisfaction from the physical world; the I also finds certain pleasures in this world, pleasures that the spiritual world has no means of providing. For the I, there are two types of desires in life: those that originate within the bodies and must also be satisfied there, coming to an end when the bodies disintegrate, and those that originate in its own spiritual nature. The latter are also satisfied by means of bodily organs as long as the I inhabits the bodies, since the hidden element of the spirit manifests in bodily organs. Along with everything the senses perceive, they also take in something spiritual. This spiritual element is also present after death, although in a different form. Everything of a spiritual nature that the I desires within the sense-perceptible world is also still there when the senses are no longer present.

If there were not a third type of desire in addition to these two, death would signify only a transition from desires that can be satisfied by the senses to those that find fulfillment in the revelation of the spiritual world. The third type of desire consists of the ones the I creates for itself during life in the sense-perceptible world because it also takes pleasure in aspects of this world in which the spirit does not manifest.

The lowest pleasures can be manifestations of the spirit. The satisfaction a hungry being gains from taking in food is a manifestation of the spirit, because if it did not take in nourishment, the spiritual element would not be able to evolve in a certain respect. However, the I can also move beyond the enjoyment offered by this necessary state of affairs. It can long for food that tastes good, regardless of how eating serves the spirit. The same thing happens with regard to other things in the sensory world. This creates desires that would never appear in the sense-perceptible world if the human I were not incorporated into it. Such desires, however, also do not originate in the spiritual nature of the I.

Even as a spiritual being, the I *must* have sensory pleasures as long as it lives in a body. The spirit manifests in sense-perceptible things, and the I is enjoying nothing other than the spirit when it gives itself up to sense-perceptible things through which the light of the spirit shines. The I will continue to enjoy this light even when sensuality is no longer the medium for the rays of the spirit.

In the spiritual world, however, no gratification exists for desires not already inhabited by the spirit in the sense-perceptible world. When death occurs, the possibility of satisfying these particular desires is cut off. The desire to enjoy good-tasting food can only be satisfied when the physical organs used in taking in food are present—the palate, the tongue, and so on. After shedding the physical body, we no longer have these, and if the I still needs to have these desires satisfied, this need must remain unmet. To the extent that this desire is in accord with the spirit, it is present only as long as the physical organs are there, but to the extent that the I has created it without serving the spirit, it persists after death as a desire that yearns in vain for satisfaction. We can only get an idea of what then takes place in the human being by imagining that someone is suffering from raging thirst in an area where there is no water far or near. That is how things stand with the I after death, to the extent that it still cherishes unextinguished desires for the pleasures of the outer world and no longer possesses organs that could satisfy them. Of course we must imagine the raging thirst that is an analogy for the state of the I after death as being intensified immeasurably and encompassing all other remaining desires that cannot possibly be satisfied.

After death, the I immediately finds itself in the situation of having to free itself from the shackles of this attraction to the outer world. In this respect, the I has to bring about purification and liberation within itself. It must eradicate all the desires that came about in it during life in the body, which therefore have no right to exist in the spiritual world. The world of these desires is dissolved and destroyed after death like an object that is seized and consumed by fire. This offers us a glimpse into the world that supersensible knowledge calls the "consuming fire of the spirit." Any desire that is sensual in nature in a sense that is *not* an expression of the spirit is seized upon by this "fire."

We might feel terrified and inconsolable when we confront the conceptions of these processes that spiritual science inevitably supplies. It might seem shocking that a hope that needs sense organs for its fulfillment must turn into hopelessness after death, and that a desire that can only be satisfied by the physical world must be transformed into searing deprivation. However, it is possible to maintain this view only as long as we fail to consider that all the desires seized upon by this "consuming fire" after our death are not beneficial ones in any higher sense but represent destructive forces in life.

Through such forces, the I binds itself more closely to the world of the senses than is necessary for taking in its beneficial aspects. This world is a revelation of the spiritual element concealed behind it. If the I chose not to make use of the senses to enjoy this spiritual element, it would never be able to enjoy the spirit in this form, in which it can reveal itself only through the bodily senses. However, to the extent that the I desires the aspects of the sense world in which the spirit does not speak, it deprives itself of the world's true spiritual reality. If sensory enjoyment as an expression of the spirit signifies an elevation and development of the I, then enjoyment that is not such an expression signifies impoverishment and desolation. If a desire of this latter sort is satisfied in the sense world, its devastating effect on the I, although present, does not become visible until after death. That is why enjoying such pleasures in life can create new, similar desires, although we are not at all aware that we are enveloping ourselves in a "consuming fire." What becomes visible after death is nothing other than what was already present around us during life, and when it becomes visible its healing, beneficial consequences also become evident.

For example, a person who loves someone else is not attracted only to the aspects of the other person that can be experienced through physical organs. However, these are the only aspects that can be said to become inaccessible to perception at death. After death, the aspect of the beloved person for which physical organs were only a means to an end becomes visible. In fact, the only thing that prevents this other, higher aspect from being completely visible is the presence of desires that can only be satisfied by means of physical organs. If this desire were not eradicated, conscious perception of the beloved person after death could not come about at all. Seen in this way, the terrifying, inconsolable conception we might have of post-death events as they are described by supersensible knowledge is transformed into a conception that is deeply satisfying and consoling.

[14]    The experiences we have immediately after death differ from life's experiences in still another respect. During purification, we live life in reverse, so to speak. We go through everything we experienced during life since birth, but in reverse order back to childhood, beginning with events immediately preceding our death. In this process, everything in our life that did not originate in the spiritual nature of the I appears spiritually before us, but we experience its inverse. For example, if a person dies at age sixty but injured someone else in body or soul at age forty, he or she will experience this event again on reaching this point in his or her fortieth year on the journey back through life. However, what is experienced this time will not be the satisfaction that came from attacking the other, but the pain the other person suffered as a result.

From what has just been described, we can immediately see that the only part of such an incident that can be perceived as painful after death is the part originating in a desire of the I that has its source purely in the outer physical world. In reality, the I not only harms the other person by satisfying such a desire, it also harms itself, but this damage remains invisible during life. After death, however, this whole damaging world of desire becomes visible to the I. The I then feels drawn to every being and thing that once kindled such desires in it so that these desires can be eradicated in the "consuming fire" in the same way that they were created.

On our journey back through life, all our desires of this sort will have gone through the fire of purification only when we reach the point of our birth again. From that point onward, nothing prevents us from dedicating ourselves completely to the spiritual world. We enter a new level of existence. Just as we discarded the physical body at death and the ether body soon after, the part of the astral body that can survive only in our consciousness of the outer world now disintegrates. For supersensible knowledge, therefore, there are three corpses—the physical, the etheric, and the astral. We discard the last of these at the end of the purification period, which is about one-third as long as the time that elapses between birth and death. The reason for this will become clear later on, when we consider the course of a human life on the basis of esoteric science. Just as physical corpses are physically perceptible in the world we live in, for supersensible observation astral corpses are constantly present in the surroundings, having been discarded by human beings who are moving from the state of purification into a higher level of existence.

As far as the I is concerned, a totally new state of consciousness sets in after purification. Before death, outer perceptions had to flow toward the I for the light of consciousness to shine on them, but now a world virtually flows outward from within and comes to consciousness. [15]

The I lived in this world between birth and death, too, but then it was veiled in sense-perceptible manifestations, only appearing in its real form when the I disregarded all sense perceptions and perceived itself in its own inner sanctuary. Just as pre-death self-perception on the part of the I took place within, in its inner being, the world of spirit in all its fullness is also revealed from within after death and purification.

Actually, this world is already revealed as soon as the ether body is discarded; it is simply obscured, as if by a darkening cloud, by all our desires that still turn toward the outer world. It is as if the dark demonic shadows rising from desires consumed by fire were mingling with a blissful world of spiritual experience. And not only shadows— these desires are real beings! This immediately becomes apparent when the I is stripped of physical organs and therefore becomes able to perceive things that are spiritual in character. These beings appear as distorted caricatures of what we formerly learned about through sense perception. Supersensible observation states that the world of the purifying fire is inhabited by beings whose appearance can be horrible and painful to the spiritual eye. They seem to take pleasure in destruction; their passion is intent upon an evil that makes the evil of the sense-perceptible world seem insignificant in comparison. When we bring desires of the sort described above into the supersensible world, they appear to these creatures as food that constantly nourishes and strengthens their powers.

This image of a world imperceptible to the senses can seem less incredible if we observe a portion of the animal kingdom without bias. To spiritual sight, what is a cruel, prowling wolf? What reveals itself in what the senses perceive in it? Nothing but a soul that lives in and acts out of desires. We can call the outward form of a wolf an embodiment of these desires. If we had no organs to perceive this form, we would still have to acknowledge the existence of the being in question if its invisible desires became visible through their effects—that is, if a power invisible to the eye were prowling around doing everything that can be done by a visible wolf.

Now it is true that the beings of the purifying fire are present only to supersensible consciousness and not to sense perception; however, their effects—namely the destruction of the I if it supplies them with nourishment—are clearly evident. These effects become visible when justifiable enjoyment escalates to the point of immoderation and excess, for sense-perceptible things would also only attract the I to the extent that enjoying them is somehow justified in the very nature of the I itself. Animals are driven to desire only through things in the outer world that their three bodies crave, but human beings have higher desires because a fourth element, the I, is added to their three bodily elements. But if the I seeks to satisfy such desires in a way that destroys its own being rather than maintaining and furthering it, this is a result, not of the effect of its three bodies or of its own nature, but of beings whose true form is concealed from our senses, beings who can assail the higher nature of the I and are capable of arousing desires in it that, although unrelated to sensory existence, can only be satisfied through it. The food of these beings consists of passions and desires that are worse than any animal passions because they are not played out in the sense world but take hold of the spiritual element and drag it down into the domain of the senses. Therefore, the forms of such beings appear much more hideous and gruesome to spiritual sight than the forms of the wildest animals, which only embody passions that are justifiable in the sense-perceptible world. The destructive forces of these beings are infinitely greater than any destructive fury that exists in the sense-perceptible animal kingdom. In this way, supersensible knowledge must expand our view to include a world of beings that are lower in a certain respect than any visible destructive animals.

[16]     Having passed through this world after death, we then find ourselves face to face with a world that contains the spiritual element. The only desire this world arouses in us finds satisfaction in the spirit alone. Here too, however, we distinguish between what belongs to our own I and what constitutes its surroundings, what we might also call the spiritual world outside of the I. Now, however, what we experience of these surroundings streams toward us in the same way that our perception of our own I streams toward us during life in the body. During life between birth and death, our surroundings speak to us through the organs of our bodies, but once we have discarded all our bodies the language of our new surroundings speaks directly to the "innermost sanctuary" of the I. Our entire surroundings are now filled with beings that are similar in nature to our I, for only an I has access to another I. Just

as we are surrounded in the sense-perceptible world by the minerals, plants, and animals that make up that world, after death we are surrounded by a world that is made up of beings of a spiritual nature.

However, something that is not part of our surroundings there comes with us into this spiritual world—that is, what the I has experienced in the sense-perceptible world. Immediately after our death and for as long as our ether body is still connected to the I, the sum total of these experiences appears temporarily in the form of a comprehensive memory-picture. The ether body itself is then discarded, of course, but something of this memory-picture remains behind as an imperishable possession of the I, as if we had made an extract or distillation of everything that happened to us between birth and death. This is life's spiritual yield, its fruits. Since this yield is of a spiritual nature, it contains everything spiritual that has been revealed through our senses; without life in the sense-perceptible world, it would not have come about. After death, the I feels this spiritual fruit of the sensory world to be its own inner world through which it enters the world of beings that manifest as only an I can become manifest to itself in its innermost depths. Just as a plant seed, which is the essence of the entire plant, can only develop when it is planted in a different world, namely the soil, what the I brings along from the sensory world now unfurls like a sprouting seed, and the spiritual environment that has received it begins to affect it.

It is true that the science of the supersensible can only use images to describe what happens in this "land of

spirits," but when supersensible consciousness investi-
gates the events—invisible to the physical eye—that
correspond to these images, it becomes evident that the
images represent a true reality. Comparisons with the
sensory world can illustrate what needs to be depicted,
since although this other world is completely spiritual in
character, it is similar to the sensory world in a certain
respect. For example, in the sensory world a color
appears when some object acts upon the eye. Similarly,
in the "land of spirits," an experience similar to the one
induced by a color is produced when the I is acted upon
by another being. During life between birth and death,
however, the inner self-perception of the I is the only
experience that is induced in the same way as this color-
like spiritual experience. This is not like light striking us
from outside; it is as if another being were acting directly
upon the I, causing it to imagine this activity as a colored
picture. Thus all the beings in the spiritual environment
of the I express themselves in a world radiant with color.

Since the way they come about is different, of course
these experiences of color in the spiritual world are also
of a somewhat different character than sense-perceptible
colors, and something similar must be said with regard to
the other impressions we receive from the sense-perceptible world. The sounds of the spiritual world are most
similar to impressions in the sensory world. The more we
live our way into the spiritual world, the more it appears
to us as a freely moving vitality that is comparable to
tones and harmonies in sense-perceptible reality. However, we do not sense these tones as something that

approaches a sense organ from outside, but rather as a force streaming through the I out into the world. We feel the tones the same way we feel our own speech or singing in the sense-perceptible world, but in the spiritual world we know that these tones that are streaming out of us are also manifestations of other beings who are pouring themselves out into the world through us.

A still higher manifestation takes place in the "land of spirits" when sound becomes the "spiritual word." Then not only the movement-filled vitality of another spiritual being but also the being itself communicates its own inner nature to the I. When this happens, when the "spiritual word" flows through the I, two beings live within each other without any of the separation that is a necessary part of togetherness in the sense-perceptible world. This is really what it is like for the I to be together with other spiritual beings after death.

Three distinct domains of the land of spirits appear to supersensible consciousness. They may be compared to three regions in the physical, sense-perceptible world. The first is the spiritual world's "land masses," so to speak; the second is its "bodies of water"; the third is its "atmosphere." *[17]*

In the first domain of the "land of spirits," everything that assumes a physical shape on Earth so that it can be perceived by means of physical organs is perceived according to its spiritual nature. For example, the force that gives a crystal its shape can be perceived in the "land of spirits," but its manifestation there is the opposite of what appears in the sense-perceptible world, so to speak.

To spiritual sight, the space occupied by a mass of rock in the physical world appears as a cavity of some sort, but the force that shapes the form of the stone is seen all around this cavity. The color the stone possesses in the sense-perceptible world appears as an experience of its complementary color in the spiritual world. Thus, from the viewpoint of the land of spirits, a red stone appears greenish and a green one is experienced as reddish. All other characteristics also appear in the form of their opposites. Just as things such as stones and masses of soil make up the sense-perceptible world's land masses or continents, the formations described above constitute the spiritual world's "land masses."

Everything that is life in the sense-perceptible world is the oceanic region in the spiritual world. To our physical eyes, life is evident in its effects in plants, animals, and human beings. To our spiritual eyes, life is a being that flows, permeating the land of spirits like seas and rivers. Better still, it can be compared to blood circulation in the body, because the distribution of seas and rivers in the sense-perceptible world is irregular, while a certain regularity, like that of the circulating blood, is the rule in the distribution of flowing life in the land of spirits. At the same time, this flowing life is also heard. It resounds spiritually, as it were.

The third domain of the land of spirits is its "atmosphere." Everything that appears in the sense-perceptible world as feeling exists in the spiritual realm as an all-pervading presence, just like the air on Earth. We must imagine it as a sea of flowing feeling. Sorrow and pain, joy and delight flow throughout this domain like winds and storms in the atmosphere of the sense-perceptible world. Let's imagine a battle being fought on Earth: Not only human figures with forms that can be seen with physical eyes confront each other here, but feelings confront feelings and passions confront passions. The battlefield is not only full of human figures, it is also full of pain. All the passions, the pain, and the joy of conquest that are active here not only manifest as sense-perceptible effects but also become perceptible to spiritual senses as an atmospheric process in the land of spirits. In the spirit, an event like this is like a thunderstorm in the physical world. Spiritual perception of such events can also be compared to hearing words in the physical world. This is why it is said that "wafting spiritual words" surround and permeate the beings and events of the land of spirits, just as air surrounds and permeates the beings of Earth.

Still other perceptions are possible in this spiritual world. Something comparable to the warmth and light of the physical world is also present here. The actual world of thoughts is what pervades everything in the land of spirits, like the warmth that pervades all earthly things and beings. Here, however, we must imagine these thoughts as living, independent beings. What we grasp as a thought in the manifest world is like a shadow of a thought being that is active in the land of spirits. Let's imagine that a thought is extracted from the human being in which it is present and is endowed with an inner life of its own as an active entity. We then have a feeble illustration of the content of the fourth domain in the land of

*[18]*

spirits. What we perceive as thoughts in our physical world between birth and death is merely a manifestation of the thought world, shaped as the instruments of our various bodies permit. But all the thoughts we cultivate that enrich the physical world have their origin in this spiritual domain. We need not think only of the thoughts and ideas of great inventors or geniuses in this regard. We can see how we all have ideas that suddenly occur to us—not merely ideas that are due to the outer world, but ideas we use to transform this outer world. To the extent that we speak of feelings and passions whose causes lie in the outer world, these belong in the third domain of the land of spirits, but everything that lives in our souls in a way that makes creators of us, everything that allows us to transform and fructify our surroundings, is evident in its primal, essential form in the spiritual world's fourth domain.

What is present in the fifth domain can be compared to physical light. It is *wisdom* revealing itself in its primal form. Beings belonging to this domain pour wisdom out into their surroundings like the sun that sheds light on physical beings. A thing that is illuminated by this wisdom shows its true significance and meaning for the spiritual world, just as a physical being shows its color when shone upon by light.

There are still higher domains of the land of spirits, but they will be described in a later part of this book.

[19]    After death, the I, along with what it brings with it from life in the world of the senses, is immersed in the spiritual world. What its past life yielded is still united with the

part of the astral body that is not discarded at the end of the purification period. As we have seen, only the part whose desires and longings are still directed toward physical life falls away after death. Immersing the I and its past life's yield in the spiritual world can be likened to planting a seed in fertile soil. The seed draws on substances and forces from its surroundings in order to develop into a new plant; similarly, development and growth are the very essence of the I that has been immersed in the spiritual world.

The force that creates an organ lies hidden within what that organ perceives. Our eyes perceive light, but without light there would be no eyes. Creatures that spend their life in darkness do not develop any organs of sight. Similarly, the whole bodily human being is created out of the forces lying hidden in what is perceived by the organs of our various bodies. The physical body is built up by the forces of the physical world, the ether body by those of the world of life, and the astral body out of the astral world. Now when the I is transported into the land of spirits, it encounters these forces, which are hidden to physical perception. In the first domain of the land of spirits, the spiritual beings that always surround human beings, building up our physical bodies, become visible to the I. In the physical world, what we perceive is nothing other than the manifestations of these spiritual forces that have shaped the human physical body. After death, we find ourselves surrounded by these same formative forces, but now they show themselves in their true forms, which were previously concealed.

Similarly, in the second domain we find ourselves in the midst of the forces that make up the ether body, while in the third domain the forces that stream toward us have organized the astral body. What the higher domains of the land of spirits send toward us is also what constitutes our makeup during life between birth and death.

[20]     From this point onward, these beings of the spiritual world work in conjunction with what we have brought with us as the fruit of our former life, which now becomes a seed. Through their interaction, we are first built up anew as spiritual beings. When we sleep, our physical and ether bodies persist; the astral body and the I, although outside of these two bodies, remain connected to them. Any influences the astral body and the I can receive from the spiritual world under these circumstances serve only to replenish the forces we have exhausted while awake. However, after the end of the purification period, when we have discarded not only the physical and ether bodies but also the part of the astral body that still clung to the physical world through its desires, everything flowing from the spiritual world toward the I serves not only to improve it but also to reconfigure it. And after a certain period of time (spoken of later on in this book) an astral body forms around the I and becomes capable of living in etheric and physical bodies of the sort appropriate to human beings between birth and death. Then we are ready to undergo birth again and to appear in a new earth existence which then incorporates the fruit of our previous life.

Up to the point of forming a new astral body, we witness our own rebuilding. Since the powers of the land of spirits, like our self-aware I, manifest from within rather than through outer organs, we are able to perceive their manifestations as long as our faculties are not yet directed toward an outwardly perceptible world. However, the moment the astral body has taken shape again, these faculties turn outward. From that point onward, the astral body again begins to demand an external ether body and physical body and turns away from the revelations of the inner world. For this reason, an interim period of sinking into unconsciousness now begins. Consciousness will be able to appear again only in the physical world, when the organs necessary for physical perception have been formed.

During this time when the consciousness illuminated by inner perception has come to an end, a new ether body begins to connect to the astral body, and we can then enter a physical body again. The only I that would be capable of taking part consciously in reconnecting to these two elements would be one that had succeeded in creating a life spirit and spirit body, the creative forces hidden in the ether and physical bodies. Until we reach this stage, beings that are further along in their development than we are must direct this process of reconnecting. These beings lead the astral body to a set of parents so that it can be given the appropriate etheric and physical bodies.

Before the connection to the ether body has been completed, something happens that is extremely significant for us as we enter physical existence again. As we have seen, each of us in our previous life created destructive forces that became evident during our journey backward after death. Let's look again at the example mentioned earlier: In the previous lifetime, the person in question, who was forty years old at the time, caused pain to someone else in an outburst of anger and later, after death, encountered that other person's pain as a force destructive to the develop- ment of his or her own I. The same is true of all similar incidents in this person's previous life. These obstacles to development then confront the person's I when it re-enters physical life. Just as the I saw a kind of memory-picture of the past life as death set in, it now has a preview of the life to come. Once again this person sees a picture of this sort, but this time it shows all the obstacles that need to be over- come in order to make progress along the path of self- development. What is seen in this way becomes the start- ing point for forces that this person must take along into his or her new life. The image of the pain inflicted on another becomes the force that motivates the I, on re- entering life, to make up for this pain. Thus our previous life has a determining effect on the new one. In a certain respect, our deeds in this new life are caused by ones in our previous life. We must see this lawful and regular connec- tion between an earlier existence and a later one as the *law of destiny*. We usually apply the term "karma," borrowed from oriental wisdom, to this law.

[21]    However, building up a new bodily organization is not the only activity that is required of us between death and a new birth. During this process, we live outside of the physical world. But meanwhile the physical world con- tinues to evolve. The face of the Earth changes within a relatively short period of time. A few thousand years ago,

what did the region look like that our country now occupies? As a general rule, when we appear on Earth in a new existence, it does not look the way it did during our last lifetime. All kinds of things have changed in our absence. Now, hidden forces are also at work changing the face of the Earth. They work out of the world we find ourselves in after death, and we, too, must help to transform the Earth. However, as long as we have not become clearly conscious of the relationship between the spiritual element and its physical expression by creating the life spirit and spirit body in ourselves, we require the guidance of higher beings if we are to assist in this transformation, but we do assist in it nonetheless. We can say that during the time between death and a new birth, we transform the Earth in a way that aligns its conditions with what is developing within us. If we observe some spot on Earth at a certain point in time and again after a long time has elapsed, we find it in a totally different condition. The forces that have brought about this change are present among human beings who have died. This is how they are connected with the Earth between death and rebirth.

Supersensible consciousness sees manifestations of the hidden spiritual element in all of physical existence.

To physical observation, what works at transforming the Earth is the light of the Sun, changes in climate, and so on. To supersensible observation, however, the forces of people who have died are active in the rays of sunlight falling on the plants. If we observe in this way, we become aware of human souls hovering around the plants, transforming the surface of the Earth, and so on. In death, our attention is not focused only on ourselves and on preparing our own new earthly existence. No, we are also called upon to work spiritually on the outer world, just as we are called upon to work physically during life between birth and death.

[22]     Not only does human life work on circumstances in the physical world from the land of spirits, but the reverse is also true—activity in physical existence has its effects in the spiritual world. An example can illustrate what happens in this connection: A bond of love exists between mother and child. This love arises out of an attraction between the two of them that is rooted in the sense world, but it changes over the course of time. The sensory bond becomes more and more spiritual. And this spiritual bond is fashioned not only for the sake of the physical world, but for the land of spirits as well. This is also true of other relationships. What is fashioned in the physical world by spiritual beings persists in the spiritual world. Friends who have become intimately connected during life also belong together in the land of spirits; after they have discarded their various bodies, their togetherness is much more intimate than it was during physical life, for as spirits they are there for each other in the same way that spiritual beings reveal themselves to others from the inside, as described above. Also, a bond that has formed between two people leads them together again in a new life. In the truest sense of the word, therefore, we must speak of people finding each other again after death.

This process that takes place with human beings between birth and death and then from death to a new birth repeats itself. We return to Earth again and again, whenever the fruit of one physical lifetime has ripened in the land of spirits. Yet this repetition does not go on without beginning or end. At one point we left different forms of existence for ones that run their course as described here, and in future we will leave these and move on to others. An overview of these changing stages will be presented later, when the evolution of the cosmos in its relationship to the human being is described from the viewpoint of supersensible consciousness.

Of course the processes that take place between death and a new birth are even more hidden from outer sensory observation than is the case with the spiritual element underlying our existence as it manifests between birth and death. Sense perception can see the effects of this part of the hidden world only where these effects enter physical existence. For sensory observation, the question is whether human beings entering existence through birth bring along something of the processes that supersensible knowledge describes between a death and the next birth. Even if we find a snail shell with no trace of an animal in it, we will acknowledge that the shell came about through the activity of an animal; we will not be able to believe that this form created itself by means of mere physical forces. Similarly, if we observe people during life and discover something that cannot have originated in *this* life, it is reasonable to admit that it originates in what the science of the supersensible describes, if this sheds clarifying light on something that is otherwise unexplainable. Thus it is also possible for rational sensory observation to understand invisible causes

*[23]*

through their visible effects. Any unbiased observer of our current life will find this more and more correct with each new observation. It is simply a question of finding the right point of view for observing effects in outer life. For example, where are the effects of what supersensible knowledge describes as processes belonging to the purification period? How do effects appear that belong to what we are supposed to experience after this period of purification in the purely spiritual realm, according to details provided by spiritual research?

[24]     If we reflect on life deeply and seriously, there are plenty of riddles that demand our attention in this particular area. We see one person born into poverty and misery, endowed with only meager talents and seemingly predestined for a pitiable existence because of the circumstances of his or her birth. Meanwhile, another person receives lavish care and attention from solicitous hands and hearts from the first moment of life, develops brilliant capabilities, and has all the potential for a fruitful and satisfying life. We can respond to such questions with one of two opposing points of view. The first one clings to what we can perceive with our senses and understand with our sense-bound intellect. This view does not question the fact that one person is born to happiness and another to misfortune. Even if it doesn't use the term *chance*, it will not think of assuming that there is some lawful interrelatedness that causes such disparities. And when it comes to potentials and talents, this way of looking at things will attribute them to what is "inherited" from parents, grandparents, and other ancestors. It will

refuse to look for causes in spiritual processes undergone by the person in question before birth, processes that shaped his or her potentials and talents, yet are quite independent of his or her line of descent.

However, there is also a second point of view that will feel unsatisfied with this interpretation, insisting that even in the manifest world we do not see things happen in specific places or under specific circumstances without needing to assume that there are reasons why they happen. Even though these causes remain undiscovered in many instances, they are present nonetheless. Alpine flowers do not grow on lowland plains; there is something in their nature that brings them together with Alpine surroundings. Likewise, there must be something in a person that causes him or her to be born into a particular environment. Causes that lie only in the physical world are not enough to explain this. To any more profound thinker, assuming that such causes are sufficient would be like assuming that the fact that one person hits another doesn't have to do with the feelings of the person doing the hitting, but only with the physical mechanism of his or her hand!

This second viewpoint is equally dissatisfied with any explanation of predispositions and talents as qualities that are merely "inherited." Nevertheless, it can be pointed out that certain abilities do run in families. Musical abilities were passed down in the Bach family for two hundred and fifty years.[3] The Bernoulli family produced

---

3. In the seventeenth and eighteenth centuries, this German family produced over fifty musicians.

eight mathematicians, some of whom were earmarked for quite different careers as children.[4] But their "inherited" talents always drove them into the family profession after all. Furthermore, it can be pointed out that exact investigation of someone's line of descent always demonstrates that in one way or another this person's talents were evident in his or her ancestors and are only an accumulation of inherited tendencies.

People who hold the second point of view will certainly not disregard such facts, but these cannot mean as much to them as they do to those who want to base their explanations purely on processes taking place in the sense-perceptible world. Adherents of the second view will point out that it is just as impossible for inherited predispositions to assemble themselves into a unitary personality as its is for metal clock parts to assemble themselves into a clock. To the objection that the parents working together can bring about this combination of predispositions and that this takes the place of the watchmaker, as it were, they will reply, "If you look at it impartially, you will find an element in each child's personality that is completely new. This cannot come from the child's parents simply because it was not present in them."

---

4. A prominent family of mathematicians in Basel during the seventeenth and eighteenth centuries. Jacob Sr. (1654–1705) studied theology, Johann Sr. (1667–1748) studied medicine, and Jacob Hermann (1678–1759) studied theology before turning to mathematics; Nicolaus Sr. (1687–1759) studied law, Nicolaus Jr. (1695–1726) studied mathematics and law, Daniel (1700–1782) studied medicine.

Unclear thinking can cause a great deal of confusion in *[25]* this area. The worst is if adherents of the first viewpoint see adherents of the second as opposing something that is based on "positive fact," while it may not even occur to the latter to deny the truth or value of such facts. They, too, see quite clearly that a particular cultural predisposition or spiritual direction is "passed down" within a family and that if certain predispositions are combined and accumulate, they can result in an outstanding personality. They are quite capable of agreeing that the most illustrious name almost always stands at the end of a bloodline rather than at the beginning. It should not be held against them, however, if they are forced to hold ideas that are quite different from those of people who choose not to go beyond sense-perceptible facts. These people can be rebutted by saying that individuals certainly do demonstrate certain characteristics belonging to their ancestors, because the element of spirit and soul that enters physical existence through birth derives its bodily nature from what heredity provides. However, this says nothing more than that a being shares the idiosyncracies of the medium in which it is immersed. Unbiased minds will not deny the justification for the comparison, although it is certainly a strange and trivial one, if we say that the fact that a human being appears clothed in the traits of his or her ancestors says just as little about the origin of this individual's personal characteristics as being wet from falling into the water says about the wet person's inner character. Furthermore, the fact that the most illustrious name stands at the end of a bloodline demonstrates that the bearer of this name needed that bloodline in order to fashion the body that was necessary for the development of his or her entire personality. This proves nothing about the "inheritability" of the personal element itself; in fact, it proves the exact opposite as far as healthy logic is concerned. If personal talents actually were passed down within a family, they would have to stand at the beginning of a bloodline to be transmitted to the descendants. The fact that they are present at the end, however, is evidence that they are *not* passed down.

[*]    Of course it would be easy to misunderstand the statement that if an individual's personal gifts were simply subject to the law of heredity, they would have to appear at the beginning of a bloodline. We might say: "Well, they cannot appear there, because they have to develop first." This is not a valid objection, because when we want to prove that something has been inherited from a predecessor, we have to demonstrate that the predecessor's previously existing trait becomes evident again in a descendant. If it is apparent that something is present at the beginning of a bloodline and reappears later on, it would be justified to speak of heredity, but we cannot do this if something that was not present earlier shows up at the end of a bloodline. The reversal of the sentence above was only intended to show that the idea of heredity is an impossible one.

[26]    This is not intended to deny the fact that those who speak of spiritual causation in life often add just as much to the confusion. They often speak in terms that are much too general and indefinite. If we say that an individual's

personality is an accumulation of inherited characteristics, that can certainly be compared to the statement that a number of metal parts have assembled themselves into a clock. But it must also be admitted that many statements about spiritual worlds are no different from the statement that the parts of a clock are incapable of putting themselves together so that the hands actually move, and that therefore something spiritual must be present to make sure this movement happens. Faced with such a statement, we actually have more reason to say, "I'm not going to bother any more with these 'mystical' beings that move the hands of the clock; I'd rather find out about the mechanical relationships that make this happen." It is not at all a question of merely knowing that there is something spiritual (the watchmaker) behind mechanical objects (such as clocks). The only significant thing here is to become familiar with the watchmaker's thoughts, which existed before the clock was assembled. We can rediscover these thoughts in the mechanism of the clock.

Merely dreaming or fantasizing about the supersensible *[27]* element never gives rise to anything except confusion because it is unable to satisfy the opponents of spiritual views, who are quite right when they say that such references to supersensible beings in the abstract do not help us understand the actual facts of the matter. Of course these opponents may also say the same thing about the statements of spiritual science, which are specific and definite. In that case, however, we can point to how the activity of a hidden spiritual element affects our outer life.

We can say, "Suppose it's true what spiritual research claims to have established by means of observation—that during the purification period we undergo after death, our souls experience how specific actions of ours in the previous life hinder our further development, and that while we are experiencing this, we develop an impulse to make up for the consequences of these actions. Let's assume that we bring this impulse with us into a new life, and that it then shapes character traits that put us in a position to make up for what we have done. If we look at the sum total of such impulses, we then have a reason why we are born into certain surroundings as a matter of destiny."

The same can be applied to a different assumption. Once again, let's assume that spiritual science is right in saying that the fruits of a bygone life are incorporated into an individual's spiritual "seed," and that in the land of spirits where we spend the time between death and a new life, these fruits ripen so that they can be transformed into predispositions and abilities that will appear in that new life, shaping our personalities to reflect the effects of what we have gained from a prior life. If we make these assumptions and use them to observe life in an unbiased way, we will see that they make it possible for us to acknowledge all the realities of the sense world in their full truth and significance. At the same time, they clarify everything that must always remain incomprehensible to those who base themselves strictly on sense-perceptible facts while turning their attention to the spiritual world. And above all, any illogical assumptions will disappear— for instance, the one to the effect that because the most illustrious name appears at the end of a bloodline, the bearer of that name must have inherited his or her talents. The supersensible facts communicated by spiritual science make life logically comprehensible.

However, conscientious truth-seekers who have no personal experience in the spiritual world but are attempting to chart a course among the facts will still be able to raise an important objection by claiming that it is inadmissible to assume the validity of any fact simply because it enables us to explain something that would otherwise be unexplainable. An objection of this sort is surely totally meaningless for anyone who knows the facts in question as a result of direct supersensible perception. And later sections of this book will indicate the path people can take to become personally familiar with the law of spiritual causation as well as with other spiritual facts that are described here. For those who do not choose to take this path, however, this objection can indeed be significant. Its refutation is also valuable for those who have decided on this path, and for them, accepting this objection in the right way is the best first step.

*[28]*

It is absolutely true that if we have no knowledge of something, we should not assume that the thing exists simply because it explains things that would otherwise remain unexplainable. However, in the case of the spiritual facts that have been presented here, the matter is actually quite different. If we assume that these facts are true, we experience not only the intellectual result that life becomes comprehensible, but also something quite different. Let's imagine that something happens to us that causes us considerable pain and embarrassment. We can react to this in one of two ways: We can be distressed about the incident and succumb to feeling embarrassed or even be overcome with pain, or we can relate to it quite differently, telling ourselves that in a previous life, we ourselves actually created the force that led us to this event; in fact, we've brought this thing upon ourselves. We can then kindle in ourselves all the feelings that are the results of a thought like this. Of course, for it to have such results for all our feelings and sensations, we have to experience this thought with the utmost sincerity and with all our strength.

If we manage to do this, we will have an experience that can best be illustrated by means of a comparison: Let's assume that two people get hold of a stick of sealing wax. One of them makes intellectual comments about its "inner nature." No matter how clever these comments are, people can easily retort that this "inner nature" is pure fantasy if it doesn't show itself in any way. But the other person rubs the sealing wax with a cloth and shows that it attracts small particles. There is a great difference between the thoughts that ran through the first person's mind and prompted his or her remarks and the thoughts of the second person. The first person's thoughts have no consequences for reality, but the second person's thoughts have lured a real thing, an actual force, out of hiding.

This is also the case with imagining that a former life has implanted in us the power to encounter a certain event. Simply imagining this arouses a real force in us that allows us to meet the event in a way that is very different from how we would have met it if we had not entertained this thought. The event's inherent necessity dawns on us, whereas otherwise we would only have been able to see it as a coincidence. We will immediately understand that since what we imagined was strong enough to show us the facts of the matter, we must have had the right idea. If we repeat inner processes like this, they begin to be a source of inner strength and their validity is confirmed by their fruitful consequences. This validity gradually becomes a force to be reckoned with. Such processes have a healing effect on spirit, soul, and body; they foster life in every respect. We become aware that while this allows us to take our place in the context of life in the right way, considering only a single life between birth and death means succumbing to delusion and falsehood. This knowledge makes our souls stronger.

Although people can only produce this purely inner proof of spiritual causation for themselves, through individual inner activity, it is possible for everyone to have such proof. However, those who have not produced it for themselves cannot evaluate its power to prove, while those who have produced it will no longer have any doubts about it. This need not surprise us at all. It's quite natural that such an intimate component of our innermost being, our personality, can only be adequately proved by means of the most intimate experience.

However, it is not legitimate to object that since such matters conform so closely to inner experience, each person must deal with them individually and that they [29] are therefore not an appropriate subject for spiritual science. Of course each person must have the experience for him or herself, just as each person must understand the solution to a mathematical equation. But the way to gain this experience holds good for all human beings, just as the method for solving a mathematical equation is valid for all.

Leaving aside supersensible observations, of course, we should not deny that the above-mentioned proof, which is based on the strength-generating force of the thoughts in question, is the only one that will stand up to any unbiased logic. All other considerations are certainly very important, but they all have aspects that leave them open to attack. If we have acquired a sufficiently unbiased view, however, the fact that human beings are educable will constitute logically effective proof for us that there is a spiritual being struggling for existence within the body that envelops it. We will compare animals to human beings, telling ourselves that an animal's normal characteristics and capabilities appear definitively at birth, clearly showing how the animal's heredity predetermines it and how it will develop under the influence of the outer world. We can see how a young chick carries out vital functions in a certain way from the very moment of its birth.

In human beings, however, upbringing and education establish a relationship between our inner soul activity and something that can exist without any connection to heredity. We are also capable of assimilating the effects of outer influences, and all educators know that such influences must be met by forces coming from within the person in question—if this is not the case, any attempt at education will be in vain. Unbiased educators are aware of a clear-cut boundary between inherited predispositions and the personal inner forces shining through them, which come from earlier lives. It is true that the proofs we can advance for such things are not as "weighty" as the proofs of certain facts of physics that can be demonstrated by means of a pair of scales. But then, these are subtle and intimate aspects of our lives, and if we have a sense for them, their intangible proofs are as conclusive or more so than tangible reality.

The objection that animals can also be trained and can acquire characteristics and faculties through education is not valid to those who are able to see the essentials. Aside from the fact that all kinds of intermediary states exist in the world, the results of training an animal do not fuse with its personal nature in at all the same way as this happens in humans. It has even been stated that the abilities domestic animals acquire through training and through living together with human beings are inheritable; that is, that they work directly on the level of the species rather than on the individual level. Darwin describes how dogs fetch and carry without being trained to do so or having seen it done. Who would make similar claims about human education?

There are thinkers whose observations have made them [30] go beyond the idea that human beings are put together from outside by means of purely hereditary forces. These thinkers have worked their way up to the idea that a spiritual being, an individuality, precedes and shapes our physical existence. Many of them, however, do not find it possible to grasp the existence of repeated earthly lives whose fruits are present in the interim as formative forces helping to build up the human being. Let's hear what one such thinker has to say. In his book *Anthropology*, Immanuel Hermann Fichte, son of the famous Fichte, cites the observations that led him to the following conclusion:[5]

> In the fullest sense of the word, the parents do *not* produce the child. They make not only the organic substance available but also the intermediate, sensory/soul element that is evident in the child's temperament, unique soul-coloring, specialization of impulses, and the like, whose common source is "fantasy" in that broader sense that we have already established. Since a unique mixture and union of the parents' souls is unmistakable in all these elements of the personality, it is completely justifiable to explain them as purely a product of procreation, especially if, as we have concluded, procreation is to be seen as an actual soul process. But precisely the crucial central point of the personality is lacking here, for a deeper and more penetrating observation reveals that even these

---

5. Immanuel Hermann Fichte (1796-1879), *Anthropologie*, Leipzig 1860, pp. 528 and 532. I.H. Fichte was a philosopher and edited the works of his father, philosopher Johann Gottlieb Fichte (1762-1814), a "transcendental idealist," who attempted to perfect Kant's ideas.

idiosyncrasies of mind and soul are only garments that cloak the child's real spiritual, ideal predispositions, instruments that are capable of furthering or hindering the development of these predispositions but in no way capable of creating them out of themselves.

Further on we read:

*Each person* existed previously in accordance with his or her fundamental spiritual form. Spiritually considered, no individual resembles another any more than one species of animal resembles another.

These thoughts go just far enough to permit a spiritual being to enter our physical bodily nature. However, since this being's formative forces are not derived from causes in previous lives, it would have to arise from a divine primal foundation each time a personality comes into existence. If we assume this to be true, there is no possibility of explaining the relationship that exists between predispositions that work their way out from inside us and what comes from our outer earthly surroundings and approaches our inner being in the course of life. The inner human being, springing anew for each individual out of a divine primal foundation, would have to be a total stranger to what confronts it in earthly life. For this not to be the case—as in fact it is not—the inner human being must have already been connected to the outer world; it must not be living in it for the first time. Unbiased educators can clearly perceive that they are introducing their students to results of earthly life that are indeed strange to their merely inherited traits of character, yet make them feel as if they had already taken part in the work that produces these results. If we consider the life of present-day humanity from all points of view, the only satisfactory explanation for it is provided by repeated earthly lives and the facts that spiritual research reveals about existence in the spiritual realm between these earthly lives.

The expression "present-day humanity" is used quite deliberately here. Spiritual research shows that when the cycle of earthly lives first began, the conditions facing spiritual beings entering their bodily garments were quite different from what they are at present. In the following chapters, we will go back to this primeval state of humanity. Once the results of spiritual science have demonstrated how human beings took on their present form in the context of the Earth's evolution, it will then be possible to point out more precisely how the human being's essential spiritual core comes from supersensible worlds and enters its bodily garments, as well as how "human destiny," the spiritual law of causation, develops.

# CHAPTER 4

# COSMIC EVOLUTION
# AND THE HUMAN BEING

## Introductory Thoughts

In previous chapters, we saw that our human makeup con-    [1]
sists of four parts: the physical body, the life body, the
astral body, and the vehicle of the I. The I works within
the other three elements to transform them. On a lower
level, this transformation results in the sentient soul, the
mind soul, and the consciousness soul; on a higher level,
in the spirit self, the life spirit, and the spirit body. Now,
these members of our human nature relate to the cosmos
as a whole in a great variety of ways, and their evolution
is linked to that of the cosmos. By considering cosmic
evolution, we gain insight into the deeper secrets of our
human makeup.

It is obvious that our life is connected in many ways to    [2]
our surroundings, to where it evolves. Even external science, through the facts available to it, has been forced to
see that the Earth itself—our dwelling in the most comprehensive sense of the word—has undergone an evolution. Science refers to stages of the Earth's existence
when human beings did not yet exist on this planet in

their present form, and it demonstrates how humankind slowly and gradually evolved from very basic stages of civilization to our present circumstances. Thus science, too, has come to believe that there is a connection between human evolution and the evolution of our celestial body, the Earth.

[3]     Spiritual science traces this connection by means of knowledge that derives its facts from perception enhanced by spiritual organs. (*Spiritual science* is used here to mean the same thing as "esoteric science," as should be evident from the context.) It traces the course of human evolution in reverse. In doing so, it becomes apparent that the actual inner spiritual beings of human individuals have gone through a series of lives on this Earth. In this way, spiritual research arrives at a point in time in the distant past when the inner essence of each human being first embarked on an outer life in the present sense of the word. This first earthly embodiment was when the I first began to be active within the three bodies (astral body, life body, and physical body) and to carry the fruits of this work over into a subsequent life.

[4]     If we shift our view back to this point in time, we will become aware that within the earthly conditions encountered by the I, the physical, etheric, and astral bodies were already developed and interconnected in a certain way. The I then united for the first time with the being consisting of these three bodies and began to take part in their further evolution. Until reaching this level where they first encountered an I, they had been evolving without one.

To answer our questions about how these three bodies *[5]* arrived at a stage of development where they were capable of receiving an I and about how this I itself came into existence and became capable of working within these bodies, spiritual scientific research must go still further back in time. We can only answer these questions by trac- *[6]* ing the development of the Earth itself by spiritual scientific means. Through such research, we arrive at this planet's beginning point. A view based solely on facts supplied by our physical senses is not far-reaching enough to come to conclusions that have anything to do with this beginning. One such view concludes that all of the Earth's substance formed out of a primeval mist. It cannot be the task of this book to go into such ideas in more detail, because spiritual research is more concerned with spiritual causes lying behind matter than with the mere material processes of Earth's evolution.

As an example, if there is a person in front of us who is raising a hand, this can suggest two different ways of looking at this action. We can either investigate the mechanism of the person's arm and the rest of his or her body and describe the process that is taking place as a purely physical one, or we can turn our spiritual attention to what is going on in the person's soul and to his or her inner motivation for raising a hand. In a similar way, researchers schooled in spiritual perception see spiritual processes behind all the processes of the physical, sense-perceptible world. To them, any transformation in the material aspect of the Earth is a manifestation of spiritual forces lying behind matter. But if we go further and further back in time in our spiritual observation of the life of the Earth, we eventually arrive at the point in evolution where matter first began to exist. This material element developed out of the spiritual. Before this point, only the spiritual element was present. Through further spiritual observation, we see how this spiritual element partially condensed into matter, so to speak. The process taking place before us is the same thing, on a higher level, as what would take place if we were observing a container full of water undergoing some ingenious cooling process so that lumps of ice gradually form. Just as we see ice condensing out of something that used to be all water, spiritual observation allows us to trace how material things, processes, and beings "condense" out of an element that was formerly completely spiritual in character.

This is how the Earth developed from a spiritual cosmic being into a physical planet: Everything materially connected to it condensed out of what was formerly spiritually connected to it. However, we must not imagine that the spiritual element is ever totally transformed into matter; matter is always only a transformed portion of the original spiritual element, which remains the actual guiding principle even while matter is evolving.

[7]     It is reasonable to state that a view restricting itself to sense-perceptible physical processes—and to what our intellect can conclude from them—is not able to inform us about the spiritual element in question here. Let's imagine a being with senses that are capable of perceiving ice, but not the finer state of water from which ice emerges by means of cooling. For this being, water would

simply not be present and could only be perceived when parts of it turned to ice. Likewise, the spiritual element that lies concealed behind earthly processes remains hidden from those who do not admit the existence of anything not present to the physical senses. If such people draw correct conclusions about earlier conditions on the Earth from current physical, perceptible facts, they will only be able to go back to the point in evolution when the preexisting spiritual element partially condensed into matter. Their method of observation perceives as little of the preexisting spiritual element as it does of the spiritual element currently at work behind matter.

Only in the last chapters of this book will we be able to speak about the paths we must follow in order to learn to use spiritual perception to look back on the earlier states of the Earth that are mentioned here. For the moment, it should only be mentioned that as far as spiritual research is concerned, facts about even the most distant past have not disappeared. Once a being has achieved physical existence, the material part of it disappears after the death of its body. However, the spiritual forces that have expelled this bodily element do not "disappear" in the same way. They leave their traces, exact reproductions of themselves, in the spiritual foundations of the world. If we are able to raise our perception from the level of the visible world to the invisible, we ultimately find ourselves face to face with something comparable to a mighty spiritual panorama that records all the bygone processes of the world. These imperishable traces of everything spiritual may be called the "Akashic record," *[8]* if we designate the spiritually lasting element in world events as their Akashic essence, in contrast to their transient forms.

Now at this point it must be said again that research into supersensible realms of existence can only be carried out with the help of spiritual perception, which in this case means reading the Akashic record. However, what has already been said in earlier parts of this book about similar instances also holds good here: Although supersensible facts can only be *discovered* by means of supersensible perception, once they have been discovered and communicated by the science of the supersensible, they can be *understood* by ordinary thinking, at least if it attempts to be truly unbiased. In the pages that follow, information on the Earth's evolutionary stages will be communicated from the standpoint of supersensible knowledge. The transformations our planet has undergone will be followed all the way down to its present-day state. If we consider what now actually confronts us as mere sense perception and then absorb what supersensible knowledge has to say about how what presently exists has been evolving since time immemorial, and if our thinking is truly impartial, we will be able to say: First of all, what this knowledge describes is thoroughly logical; secondly, when we accept what is communicated by supersensible research as true, we can understand how the things we encounter have become what they are.

Now, when we speak of logic in this context, of course, this doesn't mean that there is no possibility of logical error in any accounts of supersensible research. We will only speak of "logic" here in the same sense that we speak of it in ordinary life in the physical world. Just as we are challenged to present things logically in the physical world in spite of the fact that individuals presenting the facts of any given subject can fall into logical error, the same is true in supersensible research. It can even happen that researchers who are capable of perception in supersensible domains may succumb to error in presenting their results logically and may be corrected by someone who, although not capable of supersensible perception, has the capacity for sound thinking. Essentially, however, there can be no objection to the logic applied in supersensible research. It should be totally unnecessary to emphasize that nothing can be said against the facts themselves on purely logical grounds. Just as the existence of a whale in the physical world can never be proved logically, but only by seeing one, only spiritual perception can recognize supersensible facts as such.

However, it cannot be emphasized enough that before attempting to observe the spiritual world through our own perception, we must first acquire an overview of it both by means of logic, as was indicated earlier, and by realizing how universally understandable the sense-perceptible, manifest world becomes if we assume that the communications of esoteric science are correct. If we reject this path of preparation, all our experience in the supersensible world remains uncertain and even dangerous; we merely grope our way around. That's why this book presents the supersensible facts of Earth's evolution first, before discussing the actual path to supersensible knowledge.

We should also keep in mind that if we use thinking as our exclusive means of finding our way into what supersensible knowledge has to say, this is not at all comparable to simply listening to an account of some physical process we cannot see for ourselves. In itself, pure thinking is already a supersensible activity. To the extent that it is a sense-oriented process, thinking cannot lead to supersensible processes all by itself, but if we apply it to the supersensible processes reported by supersensible perception, it then grows into the supersensible world on its own. In fact, one of the very best ways of achieving perception in the supersensible domain is to grow into the higher world by thinking about the information supersensible knowledge conveys. If we do it this way, we enter the higher world with greatest possible clarity. This is why a certain trend in spiritual scientific research considers this type of thinking to be the best possible first step in any spiritual scientific training.

It should seem quite understandable that this book does not describe how the outer world confirms the supersensible with regard to every detail of Earth's evolution as perceived in the spirit. That was not what was intended when it was said that the hidden element can be detected everywhere in its manifest effects. What was meant was that everything we encounter can gradually be illuminated and become understandable if we see manifest events in the light provided by spiritual science. In the following pages, the manifest element's confirmation of the hidden element will be referred to in only a few characteristic instances in order to show how this can be done at any point in the course of practical life, wherever we choose to do so.

## An Overview of Planetary Incarnations

If we follow the Earth's development in reverse in the sense of the above-mentioned spiritual scientific method of research, we arrive at a stage when our planet existed in a spiritual state. If we continue researching still further back in time, however, we find that this spiritual element previously existed as a physical embodiment of a sort. That is, we encounter a bygone physical planetary state that was later spiritualized; still later, it rematerialized and was transformed into our Earth. The Earth as we know it thus appears as the reincarnation of an ancient planet. But spiritual science can go still further back, and when it does, it finds that this whole process was repeated two more times. This Earth of ours has undergone three prior planetary stages with intervening stages of spiritualization. The further back we trace these incarnations, the more subtle and delicate in character the physical element becomes. [9]

When faced with the descriptions that follow, it's natural to wonder how anyone of sound mind can possibly assume the existence of cosmic evolutionary stages lying so far back in the past. It must be said in response that for those who are now able to see and understand the spiritual element hidden in what is perceptible to the senses, insight into earlier stages of evolution, no matter how distant, is not an impossibility. Talking about [10] evolution in the sense intended here is meaningless only for those who do not acknowledge this hidden spiritual element in the present. For those who do, previous stages of evolution are present in their perception of the present one, just as the one-year-old child is still present in their perception of a fifty-year-old person. You may object that in this example, in addition to the fifty-year-old, one-year-old children and all the stages in between are actually there for us to see. That's true, but it is equally true of the evolution of the spiritual element in the sense intended here. Anyone who has come to an objective conclusion on this matter will also see that in any comprehensive observation of the present that also includes its spiritual element, past evolutionary stages really are present along with the perfected stages of present-day evolution, just as one-year-old babies are present along with fifty-year-olds. If we can simply distinguish between the different successive stages of evolution, it is possible to see primeval events within the earthly events of the present.

[11]    Now, in the form in which we are currently evolving, human beings appeared for the first time in the fourth of the above-mentioned planetary incarnations, the actual Earth itself. The essential feature of our current human makeup is that it comprises four parts, the physical body, the life body, the astral body, and the I. However, this composite figure would not have been able to appear if it had not been prepared by the circumstances of prior evolution. Within the previous planetary incarnation, beings developed that already possessed three of the present four

components of the human being—the physical body, the life body, and the astral body. These beings, who could be called the predecessors of human beings in a certain respect, still had no I, but they had developed the three other parts and their interrelationships to the point of becoming mature enough to then receive the I. Thus, our predecessors on the planet in its previous incarnation achieved a certain degree of maturity in the three parts they possessed. This planetary incarnation then passed over into a spiritual state, out of which a new physical planetary state then developed, namely that of the Earth. In this Earth our matured human predecessors were present in a seminal state, so to speak. The entire planet, having undergone spiritualization and reappearance in a new form, was able to offer these embryonic humans with their physical, etheric, and astral bodies not only the possibility of developing to their previous level again, but also the possibility of moving beyond it by receiving the I.

The Earth phase of evolution, therefore, fell into two parts. In the first period, the Earth itself appeared as a reincarnation of the previous planetary stage. This recapitulation period, however, took place on a higher level than that of the previous incarnation because of the intervening stage of spiritualization. And at this point the Earth contained the seminal stages of our predecessors from the previous planet. These first developed to their previous level; once they had achieved it, the first period was over. Because of its own higher level of evolution, however, the Earth could then develop these seminal human beings still further by making them capable of receiving the I. The second period in this Earth phase of evolution is characterized by the unfolding of the I within the physical, etheric, and astral bodies.

[12]    Just as humankind is being brought to a higher level by the Earth phase of evolution, this was also the case in each of the earlier planetary incarnations, since a human element was already present even during the first of these incarnations. This is why we can shed light on the essential nature of present-day human beings by tracing our evolution back to the very distant past, to the first planetary incarnation.

Now, supersensible research gives names to these planetary incarnations, calling the first *Saturn*, the second *Sun*, the third *Moon*, and the fourth *Earth*. We must keep clearly in mind, however, that these classifications must not immediately be associated with the use of the same names for the components of our present-day solar system. *Saturn*, *Sun*, and *Moon* are intended as names for evolutionary forms the Earth went through in the past. The relationship between these worlds of the ancient past and the celestial bodies that make up our present solar system will become clear in the course of the descriptions that follow. It will then also become clear why these names were chosen.

[13]    Conditions during these four planetary incarnations will now be described, but only in brief outline. The processes, beings, and destinies on *Saturn*, *Sun*, and *Moon* were truly as varied as on Earth itself, so only a few individual characteristics of these conditions will be emphasized in order to illustrate how earthly conditions

developed out of earlier ones. We must also keep in mind that the further back we go, the less similar these conditions are to the present day, and yet, in order to describe them at all, we have to characterize them by using mental images derived from present-day earthly circumstances. Thus, when we use words such as *light* or *heat* with regard to these earlier stages, we must not forget that they do not mean exactly the same thing as what we now call light and heat. And yet this terminology is correct, because what light and heat developed out of is apparent to observers of the supersensible at earlier stages of evolution. By following the descriptions given here, we will be able to gather from the context what mental images we need in order to arrive at illustrations and comparisons that characterize events that took place in the far distant past.

This difficulty in finding suitable descriptions becomes especially significant with regard to planetary conditions prior to the Moon incarnation. The conditions prevailing during the Moon incarnation itself still showed a certain similarity to earthly conditions, so when we attempt to describe them, their similarity provides certain clues about how to express supersensibly acquired perceptions in clear ideas. It is a different matter when the Saturn and Sun phases of evolution are described. What is accessible to clairvoyant observation there is very different from the objects and beings belonging to our present sphere of life, and this makes it extremely difficult to bring these ancient realities into the scope of supersensible consciousness. But since our present makeup cannot be understood without going back as far as the Saturn state, these realities must be described. These descriptions will certainly not be misunderstood by anyone who keeps this difficulty in mind and is aware that much of what is said is more of an allusion to actual realities than an exact description of them.

[14]     A contradiction might be found between what is said here and on the following pages and what is said in the paragraph beginning on page 125 about the past continuing to exist in the present. We might imagine that an earlier Saturn, Sun, or Moon state, or even a human form such as is described here as having existed during those bygone stages, does not exist anywhere alongside the current state of our Earth. It is true that there are no Saturn, Sun, and Moon humans running around among earthlings in the same way that there are little children running around among fifty-year-olds. However, humankind's earlier states are supersensibly perceptible *within* earthly human beings. In order to recognize this, we must only have acquired a power of discrimination that includes the full scope of life's circumstances. Just as the little child is present along with the fifty-year-old, the corpse, the sleeper, and the dreamer are also present along with the living, waking, earthly human being. Even if these various manifestations of the present-day human being are not the *direct* equivalents of the various stages of evolution, an objective observer will nonetheless see these stages in them.

. . . . . . . .

The physical body is the oldest of the present four elements of our makeup, and in its own way it is also the one
that has achieved the greatest degree of perfection. Supersensible research shows that this physical human element
was already present during the Saturn phase of evolution.
However, as will become evident in the course of this
description, the form it had on Saturn was something completely different from the present physical human body. It
is inherent in the nature of this present physical body that it
can only survive in connection with the life body, astral
body, and I, as has been described earlier in this book. This
connection did not yet exist on Saturn. At that time the
physical body was undergoing its first evolutionary stage
and did not incorporate these other elements. It matured
enough to receive a life body only in the course of the Saturn phase of evolution, but in order for it to actually do so,
Saturn first had to spiritualize and then reincarnate as Sun.
During the Sun incarnation, what the physical body had
become on Saturn had to develop all over again, as if from
a residual embryo, before it could imbue itself with an ether
body. Incorporating an ether body changed the character of
the physical body, raising it to a second level of perfection.

Something similar took place during the Moon phase of
evolution, when our predecessors, having evolved from
the Sun to the Moon, incorporated the astral body. This
transformed the physical body for a third time, raising it
to a third level of perfection. The life body was similarly
transformed and was then at its second level of perfection.
During the Earth phase, the I was incorporated into our
human predecessors, who consisted of physical, etheric,

and astral bodies at that point. Through this process, the physical body achieved its fourth level of perfection, the life body its third, and the astral body its second, while the I is still only in its first stage of existence.

[16]     If we can devote ourselves to taking an unbiased look at the human being, we will have no difficulty imagining these elements' different degrees of perfection in the right way. All we need to do is to compare the physical body with the astral body in this respect. Obviously the astral body, as a soul component, is at a higher level of evolution than the physical body, and in future, when it has been perfected, it will be much more significant for our overall makeup than the present physical body. In its own way, however, the physical body has reached a certain climax in its evolution. Just think of the structure of the heart, which is organized in harmony with the greatest possible wisdom, or of the wonderful construction of the brain or even of a single part of a bone such as the upper end of the thigh bone. Within the end of this bone we find a regularly structured network or trellis-like pattern of delicate rods. The whole thing is arranged so as to yield the best possible results for the surface of the joint—for example, the best distribution of friction—so that it achieves the right kind of mobility while using as little material as possible.

We find wisdom-filled arrangements such as this in all parts of the physical body. And if we then go on to observe the harmonious interaction between the parts and the whole, we will certainly agree that this member of our human makeup is complete and perfect in its own way. Any apparent ineffectiveness in certain parts of the body or disturbances in its structure or functioning seem unimportant in comparison. We will even discover that in a certain respect, such disturbances are only the necessary shadow side of the wisdom-filled light that illumines our entire physical organism.

Now let's compare this to the astral body as the vehicle of our pleasure and pain, desires and passions. What insecurity prevails there with regard to joy and sorrow; what frequently meaningless desires and passions are played out, often running counter to our higher aims! The astral body is only beginning to achieve the harmony and internal consistency that we already find in the physical body. Similarly, it is possible to show that the ether body, although more perfect in its own way than the astral body, is less perfect than the physical body. If we consider the I in the right way, it will also become evident that it is currently only at the very beginning of its evolution. To what extent, for example, has it already accomplished its task of transforming the other components of our makeup into manifestations of its own nature?

For those familiar with spiritual science, the results of outer observations in this area are underscored by something else. We might point out that the physical body is subject to illness. But spiritual science is in a position to demonstrate that a great percentage of all illness originates in errors and aberrations of the astral body that destroy the perfect harmony of the physical body in a roundabout way, through being transmitted to the ether body. Both this deeper connection (which can only be touched on here) and the actual reason for many disease processes elude any scientific method of observation that chooses to confine itself to physical, sense-perceptible facts. Since in most cases this connection results in damage to the astral body that does not produce pathologies in the physical body during the lifetime in which this damage occurs, but only in the following one, the laws governing this process are meaningful only for those who acknowledge the existence of repeated human lives. But even if we do not choose to acquire this deeper knowledge, looking at life in the usual way will also show us that human beings indulge in far too many gratifications and desires that undermine the harmony of the physical body. And gratification, desire, passion, and so on have their seat in the astral body rather than in the physical body. In many respects, the astral body is still imperfect enough to destroy the perfection of the physical body.

It should be pointed out again at this point that discussing these things does not constitute an attempt to prove spiritual scientific statements about the evolution of the four members of our human makeup. Any proof is taken from spiritual research itself, which shows that the physical body has undergone four transformations toward higher degrees of perfection, while our other members have undergone fewer, as already described. Here, we are simply attempting to show that spiritual research communicates facts whose effects are also evident in the varying degrees of perfection of the physical body, life body, and so on, and that these different levels of perfection are also outwardly perceptible.

*Saturn*

If we want to form an approximately accurate idea of     *[17]*
conditions during the Saturn phase of evolution, we must
consider the fact that during that period, none of the
things and creatures currently belonging to the Earth and
its mineral, plant, and animal kingdoms were present as
such. The beings of these three kingdoms developed only
during later evolutionary periods. Of all the earthly beings
that are now physically perceptible, human beings were
the only ones existing at that time, and of these human
beings, the physical body was the only part already
present, as described above. However, the beings of the
mineral, plant, animal, and human kingdoms are not the
only beings that belong to the Earth at present. There are
also other beings that do not reveal themselves in physical
bodies. Such beings were also present during the Saturn
phase of evolution, and their activity in this Saturn setting
resulted in the later evolution of human beings.

In looking at the middle evolutionary period of the Sat-     *[18]*
urn incarnation, although not at its beginning or end, spiritual perception can discern a state consisting primarily of
warmth. No gaseous, liquid, or solid elements are to be
found; these all appear only in later incarnations. Let's
imagine that human beings with present-day sense organs
were to approach this Saturn world as observers. With the
exception of the sensation of warmth, they would experience none of the sensory impressions humans can have.
On entering the space occupied by Saturn, they would
perceive only that its condition of warmth is different
from the rest of the surrounding space. However, they

would discover that this space is not uniformly warm throughout but has warmer and colder areas that alternate in a great variety of patterns. Warmth would be perceived radiating along certain lines that are not straight but form irregular shapes produced by variations in heat. Our observers would be confronted by something like a structured cosmic being that appears in constantly changing states and consists only of heat.

[19]     It is difficult for modern individuals to imagine something that consists only of warmth, since we are accustomed to perceiving warmth only in association with hot or cold gaseous, liquid, or solid bodies, rather than thinking of it as something in itself. Especially those of us who have absorbed the ideas of modern physics will find it ridiculous to talk about warmth or heat in the way just described, and we might say this: While there are solid, liquid, and gaseous bodies, heat only indicates a condition of one of these three types. When the smallest particles of a gas are in motion, this motion is perceived as heat, so where there is no gas, there can be no such movement and therefore no heat.

Spiritual scientific researchers see this subject in a quite different light. For them, heat is something that they can speak of in the same sense that they speak of a gas, a liquid, or a solid body. It is a substance still more delicate than a gas, and a gas is nothing other than condensed heat in the same sense that a liquid is a condensed vapor or a solid a condensed liquid. So spiritual scientists speak of bodies of heat just as they also speak of bodies of gas or vapor.

In order to follow spiritual researchers into this domain, it is only necessary to admit that soul perception is possible. In the world that is presented to our physical senses, heat certainly does exist as a condition of solids, liquids, and gases. However, this is only an external aspect or effect of heat. Physicists speak only about heat's effect, not about its inner nature. Let's try to disregard all the effects of heat we receive through external objects and simply picture the inner experience we have when we say "I feel warm" or "I feel cold." Only this inner experience can give us an idea of what Saturn was like in the evolutionary period described above. We would have been able to run right through the space it occupied; there would have been no gas to exert any pressure, no solid or liquid bodies to reflect any impressions of light. But at every point within this space, we would have had the inner feeling of a particular degree of warmth, yet without receiving any impression from outside.

Conditions in a cosmic body like this are not suitable for [20] the animals, plants, and minerals of the present time. (It should, therefore, hardly be necessary to say that what was described above could never actually take place. It is not possible for a modern human being as such to actually confront Old Saturn as an observer; the description was only intended as an illustration.) The beings that supersensible perception becomes aware of while observing Saturn are at a very different stage of evolution than present-day sense-perceptible earthly beings. The first beings to appear to this supersensible perception do not have physical bodies like those of present-day human beings. When we speak of a "physical body" in this context, we must be careful to avoid thinking about human physical bodies as they exist today. Rather, we must distinguish carefully between the physical body and the mineral body. A physical body is one that is governed by the physical laws we observe today in the mineral kingdom. However, our present-day physical bodies are not only governed by such physical laws but are also imbued with mineral substance. There can be no talk of physical/mineral bodies like this on Saturn.

The physical corporeality that existed on Saturn was governed by physical laws, but these laws expressed themselves only in the effects of warmth, so the physical body was a delicate ethereal body of heat. All of Saturn consisted of warmth bodies like this, which laid the first foundations for present-day physical/mineral human bodies. Our present bodies developed when the gaseous, liquid, and solid states of matter that later came into existence were incorporated into these warmth bodies.

Among the other, non-human beings perceived by supersensible consciousness when it becomes aware of the Saturn state, there are some, for example, who have no need for a physical body. The lowest component of their makeup is an ether body; in addition, however, they have a part that is higher than any belonging to human beings. The highest member of the human being is the spirit body, but these other beings have something that is higher still. Between the ether body and the spirit body they also have all the other components described in this book as belonging to human beings: the astral body, the I, the spirit self, and the life spirit.

Saturn, like our Earth, was surrounded by an atmosphere, but instead of being a sphere of air, Saturn's atmosphere was of a spiritual character. To precisely express this inner experience that occurs in spiritual research, instead of saying "Saturn *is surrounded* by an atmosphere," we would have to say, "While supersensible cognition is becoming aware of Saturn, an atmosphere that belongs to Saturn also *presents itself* to consciousness." Similarly, we would have to say "other beings"—or "beings of this sort"—"present themselves." Transforming this into the expression that something "is present" must be permitted, because this also takes place in the expressions we use for actual soul experience in the case of sensory perception. This is evident from the context of the discussion; however, it must kept in mind in reading the descriptions that follow.

Saturn consisted entirely of beings, those just described and still others. There was a constant interaction between the warmth bodies on Saturn and these beings, who allowed the elements of their makeup to sink down into Saturn's physical warmth bodies. So while there was no life in these warmth bodies themselves, the life of their surroundings was expressed in them. They could be compared to mirrors, but instead of reflecting images of the beings in question, they reflected their state of life. We would not have been able to discover anything living on Saturn itself, and yet Saturn had an enlivening effect on the surrounding celestial space because, like an echo, it radiated back the life sent down to it. Saturn seemed like one big mirror of celestial life.

Certain exalted beings whose life was reflected by Saturn may be called the *Spirits of Wisdom*. (In Christian esotericism, they are known as *kyriotetes* or "dominions.") Their activity on Saturn did not begin with the middle evolutionary period described above; in fact, in a certain sense it had already come to an end by then. Before they could become conscious of how the warmth bodies of Saturn were reflecting their own life, the Spirits of Wisdom first had to bring these bodies to the point of being able to carry out this reflecting process. For this reason, their activity commenced shortly after the beginning of the Saturn phase of evolution, when Saturn's bodily nature still consisted of chaotic substance that would not have been capable of reflecting anything.

In observing this chaotic substance, we are making use of spiritual perception to transport ourselves back to the beginning of the Saturn phase. What can be observed at this point has not yet acquired the character of heat that it will later possess. In trying to characterize it, we can only speak of a quality that can be compared to human willing. It is will and only will, through and through. At this point, therefore, we are dealing with a state that is all soul. If we trace this element of will back to its source, we find that it originally emanated from certain exalted beings. Through stages we can only guess at, these beings had brought their evolution to the point where, at the beginning of the Saturn phase, they could pour forth will out of their own essence. After they had been doing this for some time, the activity of the above-mentioned Spirits of Wisdom united with this outpouring of will. Thus this will, previously wholly without attributes, gradually acquired the ability to reflect life back into celestial space. The beings who experienced bliss in pouring forth will out of themselves at the beginning of the Saturn phase of evolution can be called *Spirits of Will*. (In Christian esotericism, they are called "thrones.")

After a certain stage in Saturn's evolution had been reached through this interaction between will and life, other beings present in Saturn's surroundings became active. They can be called *Spirits of Motion*, the Christian *dynamis* or "virtues." They have no physical body and no life body. Their lowest element is the astral body. Once the Saturn bodies had acquired the ability to reflect life, this reflected life was ready to be imbued with characteristics that had their seat in the astral bodies of the Spirits of Motion. As a result, it seemed as if feelings, manifestations of sensation, and other soul forces were being hurled outward from Saturn into celestial space. Saturn as a totality appeared to be an ensouled being demonstrating sympathies and antipathies. However, these manifestations of soul were certainly not its own; it was only flinging back soul activities belonging to the Spirits of Motion.

After this had been going on for some time, still other beings, which can be called the *Spirits of Form*, became active. Their lowest part was also an astral body, but it was at a different stage of evolution than that of the Spirits of Motion. Whereas the Spirits of Motion imparted only general expressions of sensation to the life Saturn was reflecting, the astral activity of the *Spirits of Form* (the Christian *exousiai*, or "powers") was such that their expressions of sensation were flung out into space as though from individual beings. It could be said that the Spirits of Motion allowed Saturn as a whole to appear as an ensouled being, while the Spirits of Form divided this life into individual living beings, so that Saturn then appeared as a conglomerate of soul beings. To get a picture of this, imagine how a mulberry or a blackberry is made up of small individual fruits. To those with supersensible perception, Saturn at this period in its evolution was likewise made up of individual Saturn beings which, although they did not yet possess individual lives and souls, reflected the lives and souls of the beings that lived in them.

In the next order of beings to intervene in this state of Saturn, the astral body was also the lowest element, but these beings had brought the astral body to a stage of development where it functioned like a present-day human I. Through these beings, the I looked down upon Saturn from its surroundings and conveyed its own nature to Saturn's individual living beings. As a result, what was sent out from Saturn into space appeared similar to the activity of human personalities in our present cycle of life. The beings bringing this about may be called the *Spirits of Personality*, the Christian *archai* or "principalities." They granted a semblance of the character of personality to the little Saturn bodies. However, personality as such did not exist on Saturn, but only its reflection, as it were, an empty shell of personality. The Spirits of Personality had their real personality out on the periphery, in Saturn's surroundings. The delicate substance described earlier as *heat* was bestowed on the Saturn bodies through the fact that the Spirits of Personality allowed their essence to be reflected back by these bodies in the way that has been described. There was no inwardness in anything on Saturn, but the Spirits of Personality recognized the image of their own inwardness as it streamed back to them from Saturn in the form of heat.

While all this was going on, the Spirits of Personality [21] were at the level of present-day human beings; they were going through their human phase. If we want to take an unbiased look at this state of affairs, we must imagine that a being can be "human" in a form different from the form we presently possess. The Spirits of Personality were "human" on Saturn. Their lowest component was not the physical body, but the astral body with the I. Although they had no physical or ether body such as ours in which to express the astral body's experiences, they not only possessed the I but were also aware of it because the heat of Saturn made them conscious of it by reflecting it back to them. They were "human beings" under circumstances different from those of Earth.

The events in the further course of Saturn's evolution [22] were different in character from the previous ones. Previously, everything had been a reflection of outer life and sensation, but at this point an inner life of a sort began. Here and there within the Saturn world light began to stir, flaring up and then darkening again. Flickers and glimmers of light appeared in some places, while in others lightning-like flashes appeared. Saturn's warmth bodies started to flicker and glow and eventually to shine.

The fact that this stage of evolution had been reached made it possible once again for certain beings to become active. These beings can be called *Spirits of Fire*, the Christian *archangeloi* or archangels. They did have astral bodies, but at that stage of their existence they were unable to stimulate them by themselves; they would have had no feeling or sensation if they had not been able to work on the warmth bodies that had reached the Saturn stage that has just been described. Acting on these bodies gave the Spirits of Fire the possibility of recognizing their own existence through the influence they exerted. They could not say to themselves: I exist, but only something like: My surroundings permit me to exist. They did perceive, and their perceptions consisted of the activities of light on Saturn that have been described above. These are, in a certain sense, their I. This granted these beings consciousness of a very particular sort that can be described as pictorial consciousness. We can imagine it as similar in nature to human dream consciousness, but it possessed a much greater degree of vitality than our dreaming does, and we must realize that its images were no mere insubstantial dream images surging in and out but bore an actual relationship to Saturn's stirrings of light.

In this interplay between the Spirits of Fire and Saturn's warmth bodies, the germinal form of human sense organs were incorporated into evolution. We see the first glimmering, the first delicate ethereal beginning, of the organs we currently use to perceive the physical world. Phantom human beings, who at this point exhibit only light-archetypes of sense organs, are recognizable to clairvoyant perception within the Saturn world.[1] Sense organs, therefore, are the fruit of the activity of the Spirits of Fire, but these spirits were not the only ones involved in bringing these organs about. At the same time, other beings entered the field of Saturn. These beings were so far advanced in their evolution that they were able to use these embryonic senses to perceive the cosmic events taking place in life on Saturn. These beings may be called the *Spirits of Love*, the Christian *seraphim*. Without them, the Spirits of Fire could not have had the consciousness described above. The Spirits of Love looked at events on Saturn with a consciousness that enabled them to convey these events in image form to the Spirits of Fire. They themselves renounced any benefits, any gratification or pleasure, that they might have derived from perceiving events on Saturn. They renounced all of this so that the Spirits of Fire could have it.

---

1. Regarding the nature and development of human perception and the sense organs, see Rudolf Steiner, *Anthroposophy (a Fragment) A New Foundation for the Study of Human Nature,* Anthroposophic Press, Hudson, NY, 1996.

Regarding the *phantom*, see for example Rudolf Steiner, *From Jesus to Christ*, Rudolf Steiner Press, London, 1991, lecture 6; "...the physical forces and substances laid aside [at death] are not the whole physical body, because its complete configuration could never derive from them alone. Something else belongs to these substances and forces, which is best called the 'phantom' of the human being. This phantom is the form-shape that, as a spiritual texture, builds up the physical substances and forces so that they fill out the form we encounter as a human being on the physical plane" (p. 113).

[23]    These events were followed by a new period in Saturn's existence. Something else was added to the stirrings of light. It may seem sheer folly to many when we speak of what then reveals itself to supersensible cognition. Saturn's interior was like surging, intermingling sensations of taste. Sweet, bitter, sour, and so on could be observed at various points within Saturn, while outwardly all of this reverberated into celestial space as sound and was perceived as music of a sort.

Once again, certain beings found it possible to become active in these processes taking place on Saturn. We will call them *Sons of Twilight* or *Sons of Life,* the Christian *angeloi* or angels. They interacted with the surging forces of taste that were present in Saturn's interior. Through this, their ether body or life body became active in a way that can be described as a type of metabolism. They brought life into Saturn's interior, and processes of nutrition and elimination began to take place there. The activity of these beings brought about these processes indirectly rather than directly. This internal life made it possible for still other beings to enter, beings who can be called *Spirits of Harmony*, the Christian *cherubim*. They transmitted a dim type of consciousness to the Sons of Life. It was even dimmer and more dusk-like than our present-day dream consciousness, similar to our consciousness during dreamless sleep, which is of such a low order that we never become conscious of it at all, so to speak. Nonetheless, it is present. It is different from our day consciousness in kind as well as in degree. At present, plants also have this dreamless sleep consciousness.

Although it does not convey perceptions of an outer world in the human sense, it does regulate the life processes and bring them into harmony with the processes of the outer cosmos. At the Saturn stage in question, the Sons of Life were not able to perceive this regulating process, but the Spirits of Harmony did perceive it and were therefore the actual regulators.

All this life-activity was played out in phantom human beings described earlier; as a result, spiritual sight perceived them as enlivened. Their life was only a semblance of life, however. It actually belonged to the Sons of Life, who made use of these phantom human beings, as it were, in order to express their own life.

Now let's turn our attention to these phantom humans *[24]* with their semblance of life. During the Saturn period described, their forms were ever-changing, resembling now this figure, now that. As they continued to evolve, these forms became more defined and lasted somewhat longer as they began to be imbued with the effects of spirits that we have already mentioned with regard to the beginning of the Saturn phase of evolution, namely the *Spirits of Will,* or thrones. As a result, these phantom humans themselves appeared with the simplest, dullest form of consciousness. We must imagine this consciousness as even duller than that of dreamless sleep. Under present conditions, minerals have this form of consciousness, which brings the inner being into harmony with the outer physical world. On Saturn the Spirits of Will regulated this harmony. As a result, human beings appeared as reproductions of the life of Saturn itself. What Saturn was on a large scale, human beings were on a small scale. This provided the initial nucleus of something that is still only in a seminal state in present-day human beings, namely the spirit body or *atma*. Within Saturn, the dull will of these ancient human beings was evident to supersensible perception through effects that can be compared to smells. What manifested outwardly, moving out into celestial space, was something similar to a personality, but instead of being directed by an internal I, it was regulated from outside like a machine. The regulating agents were the Spirits of Will.

[25]     If we survey the descriptions above, it becomes evident that, starting from the middle stage of the Saturn phase described first, the stages of this evolutionary phase can be characterized by comparing their effects to present-day sense impressions. We said that the Saturn phase manifested first as heat, followed by stirrings of light and then by stirrings of taste and sound; finally something arose that revealed itself within Saturn like sensations of smell and, on the outside, like a mechanically acting human I.

What were Saturn's manifestations prior to the state of warmth? What had existed before that cannot be compared to anything accessible to outer sensory perception. Saturn's warmth state was preceded by a state that we now experience only in our inner being. If we give ourselves up to ideas that we form voluntarily in our souls, without being impelled to do so by outer impressions, we have within us something that no physical senses can perceive, something that can only be perceived by higher sight. Saturn's warmth state was preceded by manifestations that exist only for those who perceive supersensibly. We can list three such states: pure soul warmth that is not outwardly perceptible, pure spiritual light that is darkness for everything outside, and finally a state of spiritual essence that is complete in itself and needs no external being in order to become conscious of itself. Pure inner warmth accompanies the appearance of the Spirits of Motion; pure spiritual light, the Spirits of Wisdom; pure inner essence is connected to the first outpourings of the Spirits of Will.

With the appearance of Saturn's warmth, therefore, *[26]* our evolution made the step from a purely spiritual inner life to an existence that manifested outwardly. It will be especially difficult, no doubt, for present-day consciousness to accept the statement that what we call "time" first appeared during Saturn's warmth stage, since preceding states were not temporal at all but belonged to a domain that spiritual science can call "duration." Therefore, it must be understood that all references in this book to temporal relationships with regard to conditions in the "domain of duration" are used only as comparisons and aids to understanding. In fact, what precedes time can only be described in human language by using expressions that include the concept of time, so we must be aware that although the first, second, and third Saturn periods really did not take place "one after the other" in the present meaning of the phrase, we cannot avoid describing them in succession. And in spite of their duration or simultaneity, they were dependent on each other in a way that actually can be compared to a sequence in time.

[27]     Pointing to Saturn's first evolutionary states also sheds light on all further questions about where these states came from. From a purely intellectual standpoint, of course, it is entirely possible to inquire about the origin of any origin, and so on, but this won't do when we are faced with facts. An illustration is enough to make this clear: If we find tracks on a road somewhere, we can ask where they came from. The answer may be, "From a wagon." We can then continue, asking, "Where did the wagon come from, and where did it go?" Again, it is possible to give an answer based on facts. We can then still ask, "Who was sitting in the wagon? What were that person's intentions, and what did he or she do?" Eventually, however, we get to a point where the facts put an end to the questioning quite naturally. If we continue questioning after that, we are getting away from the purpose of the original question and simply go on asking questions mechanically. In instances such as the one just cited for purposes of comparison, it is easy to tell where the facts put an end to the questioning. This is not so easy when it comes to great questions about the cosmos. If we look closely, however, we will still be able to see that all questions of where things came from must end in the Saturn states described above, because there we come to a place where beings and processes derive their justification from themselves rather than from their origins.

[28]     As a result of the Saturn phase of evolution, germinal human beings evolved to a certain stage, reaching the low-grade, dull consciousness we talked about earlier. We must not imagine that it began to develop only in the

last Saturn period. The Spirits of Will worked during all of Saturn's stages, but to supersensible perception the result of their activity is most conspicuous in the last period. There is no fixed dividing line between the activities and effects of the different groups of beings. When it is said that the Spirits of Will were active first, and then the Spirits of Wisdom, that does not mean that they were active only at that time. They were active throughout the entire evolution of Saturn, but their activity can be observed best during the periods specifically mentioned with regard to each group, when the beings in question took over the leadership, as it were.

The entire Saturn phase of evolution, therefore, appears as a reworking of what emanated from the Spirits of Will by the Spirits of Wisdom, Movement, Form, and so on. In this process, these spiritual beings were also undergoing an evolution of their own. For example, after having their life reflected back to them from Saturn, the Spirits of Wisdom were at a different level than they were before. The fruits of their activity enhanced their own intrinsic capabilities. As a result, when the activity was completed, something similar to human sleep set in for them. The periods when their activity was directed toward Saturn were followed by periods when they lived in other worlds, so to speak, and their activity was turned away from Saturn. Therefore, clairvoyant perception sees an ascent and a descent in the Saturn evolution described above. The ascent continued until the state of warmth had been formed; with the first stirrings of light, the ebbing had already begun. By the time phantom human beings

*[29]*

had acquired form through the Spirits of Will, the spiritual beings had gradually withdrawn. The Saturn phase of evolution died away and disappeared as such, and a period of rest set in. It was as if the incipient human beings entered a state of dissolution—not one in which they disappeared, but one similar to what happens to the seed of a plant, which rests in the earth as it prepares to mature into a new plant. Similarly, germinal human beings rested in the bosom of the cosmos and awaited a new awakening.

When the time came for these germinal human beings to awaken, the spiritual beings described above had acquired, under different circumstances, the capacity to work on them once more. The ether bodies of the Spirits of Wisdom had acquired a capacity not only for enjoying the reflection of life as they did on Saturn, but also for allowing life to stream out from themselves, endowing other beings. At this point the Spirits of Motion were as far advanced as the Spirits of Wisdom had been on Saturn. Previously, the lowest member in their makeup had been the astral body, but then they acquired the ether body or life body. The other spiritual beings, too, had arrived at correspondingly higher levels of evolution and could therefore work differently to evolve the germinal human beings than they could on Saturn.

However, the germinal human beings had dissolved at the end of the Saturn evolutionary phase. In order for the spiritual beings who had evolved further to pick up where they had left off, the germinal human beings first had to briefly recapitulate what they had gone through on Saturn.

(This is visible to supersensible perception.) Incipient human beings emerged from concealment and began to develop through their own capacity, through forces that had been implanted in them on Saturn. They emerged from the darkness as beings of will and advanced through the stages of seeming alive and seeming ensouled to the mechanical manifestation of personality they had possessed at the end of the Saturn phase.

## Sun

The second of the great evolutionary phases we mentioned, the Sun stage, raised human beings to a higher state of consciousness than had been achieved on Saturn, although in comparison to our present-day consciousness, this Sun state might well be described as "unconsciousness," since it approximates the state we now find ourselves in during completely dreamless sleep. Or we could also compare it to the low-grade consciousness in which the present-day plant world slumbers. To supersensible perception, there is no such thing as "unconsciousness," only various degrees of consciousness. Everything in the world is conscious.

*[30]*

In the course of the Sun phase of evolution, the human essence attained a higher degree of consciousness, because the etheric body or life body was incorporated into its makeup. Before this could happen, the Saturn stages had to be recapitulated, as described earlier. This recapitulation had a very specific purpose. Once the period of rest came to an end, the former Saturn emerged from "cosmic sleep" as a new cosmic being, as the Sun.

But as a result, the circumstances of evolution had changed. The spiritual beings whose activity on Saturn has been described had moved on to different states of being. To begin with, however, germinal human beings appeared on the newly formed Sun just as they were at the end of the Saturn phase. They first had to transform the various stages of development they went through on Saturn so that these stages would correspond to circumstances on the Sun. For this reason, the Sun phase began with a repetition of events on Saturn, adapting them to the changed circumstances of the Sun's life.

When human beings had gone far enough in adapting the level of development it had acquired on Saturn to the Sun's circumstances, the Spirits of Wisdom mentioned earlier began to allow the etheric body or life body to stream into the physical body. The higher level that human beings achieved on the Sun can be characterized by saying that the physical body, already seminally formed on Saturn, was lifted to a second level of perfection by becoming the vehicle for an etheric or life body. This etheric body or life body itself achieved its first level of perfection during the Sun phase of evolution. In order for the physical body to reach its second level of perfection and the life body its first, however, still other spiritual beings had to intervene during the further course of the Sun's life, just as was already described with regard to the Saturn phase.

[31]     When the Spirits of Wisdom began to pour the life body into the germinal human beings, the Sun, dark until then, began to shine. With the life body, the first signs of inner

vitality also entered the germinal human being. Life began. What still had to be described as a mere semblance of life on Saturn then became actual life. The period of pouring the life body into the human being lasted for a certain length of time, after which an important change took place in the germinal human being. It separated into two parts. Whereas previously the physical body and the life body were intimately connected and formed a whole, at this point the physical body began to detach itself as a separate part. However, it also continued to be permeated by the life body. Now we are dealing with a twofold human being. One part is a physical body permeated by a life body working within it, the other part is pure life body. This separation, however, took place during a rest period in the life of the Sun. During this period the shining that had already begun was extinguished, and the separation took place during a "cosmic night," as it were. However, this interval of rest was much shorter than the above-mentioned one between the Saturn and Sun phases. Once this rest period was over, the Spirits of Wisdom continued to work for a time on the twofold human being, just as they had formerly worked on the unitary human being. Then the Spirits of Motion began their activity. They suffused the human life body with their own astral body. Within the physical body, the human life body then acquired the ability to carry out certain inner movements that can be compared to the movements of sap in a present-day plant.

Bodies on Saturn had consisted solely of heat substance. *[32]* During the Sun phase of evolution, this heat substance condensed into a state that can be compared to the present state of gas or vapor, a state that can be described as *air*. The first beginnings of this state became evident after the Spirits of Motion had begun their activity. The following scene presents itself to supersensible consciousness: Within the substance of heat, something resembling delicate structures appeared and began to make rhythmical movements by means of the forces of the life body. These structures represented the human entity's physical body at that stage of evolution. They were totally permeated with warmth and wrapped in a mantle of warmth. Physically speaking, we can call them warmth structures that incorporated regularly moving shapes of air. If we want to retain the earlier comparison to the present-day plant, we must keep in mind that we are not dealing with a compact plant formation, but with a gaseous or airy structure whose movements are comparable to the movements of sap in the present-day plant. This gaseous or airy substance becomes visible to supersensible consciousness through the effect of the light that it emits, so we could also speak of figures of light that present themselves to spiritual vision.

The evolution we have characterized then continued. After a certain time, another rest period ensued, after which the Spirits of Motion continued their activity until it was supplemented by that of the Spirits of Form, whose effect was to allow the formerly constantly changing gaseous shapes to assume permanent forms. This also took place through the fact that the Spirits of Form allowed their forces to flow in and out of the human life body. Previously, when only the Spirits of Motion were working on them, the gaseous shapes were in constant motion, retaining their form only for an instant. At this point, however, they took on temporarily distinguishable forms.

After a certain length of time, a rest period again ensued, after which the Spirits of Form resumed their activity. Then, however, entirely new conditions appeared within the Sun's evolution. We have reached the midpoint of the Sun phase of evolution. This is the time when the Spirits of Personality, who had reached the human stage on Saturn, transcended this stage and rose to a higher level of perfection. They acquired a consciousness that present-day human beings have not yet acquired in the ordinary course of evolution. We will acquire it when the Earth—that is, the fourth of the planetary stages of evolution—arrives at its goal and enters the next planetary phase. Then we will not only perceive what our senses convey to us about our surroundings but will also be capable of perceiving in image form the inner soul states of the beings around us. We will possess pictorial consciousness while retaining full self-awareness. There will be nothing dream-like or dull in the pictures we see. We will perceive the soul element in images, but in images that express realities in the same way that physical colors and sounds do now. At present we can only rise to this kind of vision through spiritual scientific training, which will be discussed later on in this book.

Midway through the Sun phase, the Spirits of Personality acquired this vision as a gift of their normal evolution. It made them capable of working on the newly formed human entity's life body in a way that was similar

*[33]*

to how they had worked on the physical body during the Saturn phase, when warmth reflected their own personality back at them. At this point, the gaseous shapes were reflecting the images of these beings' pictorial consciousness back at them in resplendent light. They beheld supersensibly what was taking place on the Sun, and their vision was no mere observing. It was as if something of the power that human beings call "love" were asserting itself in the images that streamed toward them from the Sun. If we observe this more closely with our soul powers, we discover the reason for this phenomenon. Exalted beings were mingling their activity with the light streaming out from the Sun. These were the *Spirits of Love*, the Christian *seraphim* that were mentioned earlier. From this point onward, they acted on the human etheric body, or life body, along with the Spirits of Personality. This activity caused the life body itself to advance one stage further in its course of evolution. It acquired the ability not only to transform the gaseous shapes within it, but also to adapt them so that the first signs of reproduction appeared in the living human being. Secretions were driven out of the gaseous structures—sweated out, so to speak—and assumed forms similar to their maternal structures.

[34]    In characterizing the Sun's further evolution, we must point to a fact that is all-important in cosmic evolution— namely, that not all beings reach their goals in the course of an evolutionary epoch. Some fall short of their goal. Thus, during the Saturn phase, not all of the Spirits of Personality actually reached the intended human level that

was described earlier. Likewise, not every human physical body that developed on Saturn attained the degree of maturity necessary to become the vehicle of an independent life body on the Sun. As a result, there were beings and formations on the Sun that were not adapted to the circumstances there and had to use the Sun phase to make up for what they had missed on Saturn. Therefore, spiritual observation of the Sun stage shows that when the Spirits of Wisdom began pouring into the life body, the body of the Sun grew dark, as it were. Intermingled in it were formations that would actually still have belonged to Saturn. These were warmth structures that were not able to condense into air in the right way—human beings who had remained behind at the Saturn stage. They could not become vehicles for normally developed life bodies.

This Saturn warmth substance that remained behind then divided into two parts on the Sun. One part was sucked up, so to speak, by human bodies and formed a certain internalized lower human nature from then on. This means that human beings on the Sun absorbed something into their bodily nature that actually corresponded to the Saturn phase. Just as the human Saturn bodies had made it possible for the Spirits of Personality to rise to the human level, this Saturn element in human beings did the same for the Spirits of Fire on the Sun. They raised themselves to the human level by allowing their forces to stream in and out of this Saturn element, just as the Spirits of Personality had done on Saturn. This, too, happened in the middle of the Sun phase of evolution. At this point, the Saturn element in human beings was mature enough so that with its help, the Spirits of Fire (*archangeloi*) were able to pass through their human stage.

Another part of Saturn's warmth substance separated off and achieved an independent existence alongside and among human beings of the Sun phase. It constituted a second kingdom alongside the human kingdom, a kingdom that developed a completely independent but purely physical warmth body on the Sun. Consequently, it did not include independent life bodies that could be worked on by the fully developed Spirits of Personality in the way described earlier. However, some of the Spirits of Personality had also remained behind at the Saturn stage, not reaching the level of humanity. A bond of attraction existed between them and the second, newly independent Sun kingdom. These spirits then had to work on this underdeveloped kingdom in the same way that their more advanced counterparts had worked on the human beings who first developed physical bodies on Saturn. On the Sun itself, however, it was not possible for the underdeveloped Spirits of Personality to do this, so they withdrew from the body of the Sun and formed a separate and independent cosmic body outside of it. From there, they were able to work back on the beings of the second Sun kingdom. Thus, the single cosmic formation of the former Saturn split into two. From this point on, the Sun had a second cosmic body in its surroundings, a body that constituted a rebirth of Saturn, after a fashion—a new Saturn. From there, the quality of personality radiated into the second Sun kingdom. In this second kingdom, we are dealing with beings that had no personality of their own on the Sun itself. However, they reflected the personality of the Spirits of Personality on the new Saturn back to them. Supersensible consciousness can observe warmth forces at work among the human beings on the Sun, forces that played into the Sun's normal evolution. In these forces we can see the influence of these new Saturn spirits.

We must keep in mind that during the middle of the Sun    [35] phase, the human being was organized into a physical body and a life body in which the more advanced Spirits of Personality worked in conjunction with the Spirits of Love. Part of the underdeveloped Saturn nature, in which the Spirits of Fire were active, mingled with the physical body. Everything the Spirits of Fire produced in this Saturn nature must be seen as a precursor of present-day human sense organs. We have seen how the Spirits of Fire had already worked on rudimentary forms of our senses in the warmth substance on old Saturn. And in what the Spirits of Personality accomplished in conjunction with the Spirits of Love (*seraphim*), we can recognize the seminal stages of our present-day glandular system.

However, the work of the Spirits of Personality dwelling on new Saturn was not exhausted in what was described above. They not only extended their activity to the second Sun kingdom, as has been mentioned, but also created a certain connection between this kingdom and the human senses. The warmth substances of this kingdom flowed in and out through the seminal human senses, enabling human beings on the Sun to achieve a certain perception of this lower kingdom that was outside of themselves. Of course this was only a dim perception in keeping with the dullness of the Saturn consciousness we talked about earlier. It consisted essentially of various impressions of heat.

[36]     Everything described here as belonging to the middle of the Sun phase of evolution lasted for a certain amount of time, and then another period of rest began. After that, evolution continued along the same lines for a while until the human ether body was mature enough to permit the beginning of a joint effort between the Sons of Life (*angeloi*) and the Spirits of Harmony (*cherubim*). Within the human being, manifestations comparable to perceptions of taste (but expressing themselves outwardly as sounds) became apparent to supersensible consciousness. As you recall, we already had to describe something similar with regard to the Saturn phase of evolution. On the Sun, however, this development was more inward; it was full of a life that was more independent.

In this process, the Sons of Life achieved the dim pictorial consciousness that the Spirits of Fire had achieved on Saturn. This was done with the help of the Spirits of Harmony (*cherubim*), who actually beheld spiritually what was taking place at that point in the Sun's evolution, but renounced all the fruits of this perception, all feeling for the wisdom-filled images that came about, and allowed these to flow into the dream consciousness of the Sons of Life in magnificent supernatural disclosures, as it were. In turn, the Sons of Life worked the figures of these visions of theirs into the human ether body, which could then go on to achieve ever higher levels of development.

Once again a period of rest set in; once again everything arose out of "cosmic sleep," and after a time human beings matured to the point where they began to rouse forces of their own. These were the same forces that had streamed into them through the activity of the thrones during the last part of the Saturn phase. These human beings now developed an inner life that presents itself to consciousness in a way comparable to an inner perception of smell. Toward the outside, however, toward celestial space, these human beings revealed themselves as personalities that were not, however, directed by any internal I, but seemed more like plants giving the impression of personality. We have already seen machine-like manifestations of personality at the end of the Saturn phase. And just as the initial nucleus of something that is only seminally present even in present-day human beings—namely, the spirit body or *atma*—developed on Saturn, a similar initial nucleus of the life spirit (*buddhi*) was formed on the Sun.

After all this had been going on for a while, another period of rest ensued, after which—just as in previous similar instances—human activity proceeded for a certain time. The conditions that then set in entailed a new intervention on the part of the Spirits of Wisdom. Through this, human beings became capable of feeling the first traces of sympathy and antipathy for their surroundings. They still had no real feeling, but they did have a forerunner of feeling, because the inner life activity whose manifestations might be characterized as perceptions of smell expressed itself outwardly as a kind of primitive speech.

*[37]*

Having inwardly perceived a sympathetic smell—or a taste or a glimmer of light—the human being in question expressed this outwardly through a sound, and this also occurred in the appropriate fashion in the case of inwardly unsympathetic sensations.

As far as human beings were concerned, the actual purpose of the Sun phase of evolution was accomplished through all the processes that have been described: Human beings had achieved a sleep consciousness, a level of consciousness higher than what they had possessed on Saturn.

After a while, the point in evolution was reached when the higher beings associated with the Sun stage had to move on to other spheres in order to assimilate the potentials they had laid down in themselves through their work on the human being. A major period of rest ensued, like the one that had taken place between the Saturn and Sun phases. Everything that had developed on the Sun passed over into a state comparable to that of a plant when its growth forces lie dormant in the seed. Just as these forces of growth come to light again in a new plant, however, all of the Sun's life emerged from the womb of the cosmos again when the rest period was over, and a new planetary existence began. We will be able to grasp the significance of this pause, this "cosmic sleep," if we direct our spiritual view to one of the orders of beings mentioned above, such as the Spirits of Wisdom, for example. On Saturn they had not yet advanced to the point of being able to allow an ether body to stream out of them. They only became ready to do so through the experiences they had on Saturn. During the rest period, they transformed what had been prepared in them into actual capacities, so that on the Sun they were sufficiently advanced to allow life to stream forth from them, endowing human beings with ether bodies of their own.

## Moon

After the rest period, what had formerly been the Sun [38] emerged from "cosmic sleep." That is, it became perceptible to the forces of spiritual vision once again, as it had been before becoming invisible during the rest period. However, a twofold aspect then appeared in the newly emerging planetary being that will be called the Moon (not to be confused with the part of it that is the Earth's moon at present). The first thing we must note is that what had separated off during the Sun phase as "new Saturn" had been reabsorbed into this new planetary being. That is, new Saturn had reunited with the Sun during the period of rest. To begin with, everything that had been present in the first Saturn reappeared as a single cosmic formation. The second thing we must note is that during the period of rest, the human life bodies that had developed on the Sun had been absorbed by something that constituted a certain spiritual covering for the planet. At this point, therefore, these life bodies did not appear in union with the corresponding physical human bodies, which appeared separately for the time being. Although these physical bodies carried with them everything that had been created in them on Saturn and Sun, they lacked ether bodies or life bodies. They were not able to absorb ether bodies immediately, because they had not yet adjusted to the evolution these ether bodies had undergone during the rest period.

In order to accomplish this adjustment, a repetition of the Saturn state once again took place at the beginning of the Moon phase of evolution. Physical human beings again recapitulated the periods of Saturn's evolution, but under totally changed circumstances. On Saturn, as we know, the only forces at work in human beings had been the forces of a warmth body, but at this point the forces of the gaseous body acquired on the Sun were also active. However, they did not appear at the very beginning of the Moon phase of evolution, when it was as if human beings consisted only of heat substance with the gaseous forces lying dormant within them. Then a time came when the first signs of these gaseous forces appeared. Finally, in the last stage of the Saturn recapitulation, human beings again appeared as they had done while in a living state on the Sun. Their life, however, again proved to be only a semblance of life.

First a period of rest ensued, similar to the short periods of rest during the Sun phase of evolution. Then the influx of the life body into the physical body—which had meanwhile become mature enough to receive it—began again. Like the Saturn recapitulation, this influx took place in three distinct epochs. During the second of these epochs, human beings adjusted to the new Moon circumstances to the extent that the Spirits of Motion were able to transform the ability they had acquired into deeds and were able to allow the astral body to flow out of their own essential nature into the human being. The Spirits of

Motion had prepared themselves for this work during the Sun phase and transformed what they had prepared into the above-mentioned ability during the rest period between the Sun and Moon incarnations.

The influx of the astral body continued for a while, and then one of the shorter rest periods ensued, after which the influx continued until the Spirits of Form began their activity. The astral body acquired its first soul characteristics through the fact that the Spirits of Motion were allowing it to stream into human beings. Processes that took place in the astral body because it possessed a life body—processes that had still been plant-like in character during the Sun phase of evolution—began to be accompanied by sensation, and the astral body began to experience pleasure and displeasure because of these processes. Until the intervention of the Spirits of Form, however, this remained an ever-changing inner ebb and flow of pleasure and displeasure. But these ever-changing feelings were, at that point, transformed in such a way that the first trace of longing and desire appeared in human beings, who then attempted to repeat what had once given them pleasure and to avoid what they had experienced with antipathy. However, since the Spirits of Form did not surrender their own being to humans, but simply allowed their forces to stream in and out of them, human desires lacked inwardness and independence. They were guided by the Spirits of Form and appeared instinctive in character.

On Saturn, the human physical body was a body of warmth. On the Sun, it condensed into the gaseous state; [39]

that is, into air. During the Moon phase of evolution, at a certain point when the astral element was streaming in, the physical body achieved a further degree of condensation and entered a state comparable to present-day liquids. We can call this state *water*, meaning not water as we understand it today, but any fluid form of existence. The human physical body then gradually assumed a form consisting of three structures composed of different states of matter. The densest, a *water body*, had currents of air running through it, and both water and air were also permeated by warmth in various manifestations.

[40]     Once again, not all the bodies that had existed at the Sun stage had achieved the full maturity corresponding to that stage. On the Moon, therefore, there were some bodies that were only at the Saturn stage and others that had only reached the Sun stage, so two other kingdoms came about alongside the kingdom of normally developing human beings. One of these kingdoms consisted of beings that had remained behind at the Saturn stage and thus had only physical bodies that were not ready to become vehicles for independent life bodies on the Moon. This was the lowest Moon kingdom. The second kingdom consisted of beings that had remained behind at the Sun stage and, therefore, did not become mature enough on the Moon to incorporate independent astral bodies. These beings formed an intermediary kingdom between the kingdom just mentioned and the kingdom of normally developing human beings.

However, something else also took place: Since substances composed merely of forces of heat and those composed merely of air also permeated human beings at this stage, humans also carried a Saturn and a Sun character within themselves. As a result, a certain rift developed in human nature, calling up something very significant in Moon evolution after the activity of the Spirits of Form began. A cleft started to form in the cosmic body of the Moon, and part of its substances and beings separated from the rest. Two cosmic bodies were formed out of one. One of them became the dwelling place of certain higher beings who had formerly been more closely linked to the unitary cosmic body. In contrast, the other was occupied by human beings, the two lower kingdoms described above, and certain higher beings who did not move over to the first cosmic body. The first cosmic body with its higher beings appeared like a reborn but refined Sun, while the other was the actual new formation of this phase, the "old Moon," the third (after Saturn and Sun) planetary incarnation of our Earth.

The reborn Sun took only warmth and air with it from the substances that had come about on the Moon, while the watery element was present on what remained of the Moon in addition to these two other substances. As a result of this separation, the beings who had departed with the reemerging Sun were not hampered in their further development by the denser Moon beings and were able to proceed unhindered in their own evolution. This made it possible for them to achieve an even greater power in working down on the Moon beings from outside, from their Sun. In turn, these Moon beings also received new evolutionary possibilities. The Spirits of Form, in particular, had remained united with these Moon beings and proceeded to firmly establish the character of their passions and desires. This was gradually expressed in a further condensation of the human physical body. Its formerly merely watery consistency became viscous, and its air and warmth formations become correspondingly denser. Similar processes also took place in the two lower kingdoms.

*[41]*　As a result of the separation of the Moon body from the Sun body, the Moon related to the Sun in the same way that the Saturn body had once related to the entire surrounding cosmos and its evolution. The Saturn body had been formed out of the body of the Spirits of Will, or thrones. Its substance reflected back into cosmic space everything experienced by the spiritual beings living in the surroundings, and through events that followed, this reflection gradually awoke to independent life. The basis of all evolution lies in this gradual separation of independent being from the life of its surroundings. As though by reflection, these surroundings then imprint themselves on this separate being, which then continues to evolve independently.

The Moon body also separated from the Sun body in this way, first reflecting back the life of the Sun. This is the cosmic process that would have taken place if nothing else had happened: There would have been a Sun body where the beings adapted to it would have experienced certain things in the elements of warmth and air. Opposite this Sun body, there would have been a Moon body where other beings living in warmth, air, and water would have evolved. The progress from the Sun embodiment to the

Moon would have consisted in the fact that the life of the Sun beings was mirrored for them by Moon processes, as it were, allowing them to enjoy it in a way that was not possible for them during the Sun embodiment.

In fact, however, the process of evolution did not continue in this way. Something then happened that was profoundly significant for all subsequent evolution. Certain beings adapted to the Moon body took possession of the element of will (the legacy of the thrones) that was available to them and used it to shape a life of their own, independent of the life of the Sun. Alongside Moon experiences that were fully under the influence of the Sun, other independent Moon experiences developed, causing a state of rebellion or revolt against the Sun beings. The different kingdoms that had come about on Sun and Moon, especially the kingdom of incipient human beings, were drawn into this revolt. As a result, the Moon body contained two sorts of life, both spiritually and materially speaking—one that was intimately connected to the life of the Sun and one that broke away from all this and went its own independent way. This division into two kinds of life was then expressed in all subsequent events of the Moon embodiment.

What this evolutionary period presents to supersensible consciousness can be characterized in the images that follow. The entire surface of the Moon consisted of a semi-living substance that was sometimes sluggish and sometimes animate in its movement. There was still no mass of minerals in the sense of the rocks and soil we walk around on today. We could say that a kingdom of

*[42]*

plant-minerals was present. However, we must imagine that the entire surface of the Moon consisted of this plant-mineral substance, just as the Earth now consists of rocks, soil, and so on. Just as nowadays we have towering masses of rock, on the Moon there were harder portions comparable to hard, woody structures or horn formations. Just as plants now rise out of the mineral soil, Moon-soil was covered and permeated by the second kingdom, which consisted of certain plant-animals whose substance was softer and more inherently mobile than that of the surface mass. This kingdom spread out over the other one like a viscous sea.

Human beings themselves can be described as animal-humans whose nature included the components of the two other kingdoms. However, each human being was totally permeated by a life body and an astral body that were worked on by forces emanating from the higher beings on the detached Sun. This ennobled the human form. While the Spirits of Form had given human beings a form that adapted them to life on the Moon, the Sun spirits made them into beings that transcended that life. They then had the strength to ennoble their own nature by means of the abilities bestowed on them by these spirits; in fact, it was possible for even the aspect of human nature that was related to the lower kingdoms to be raised to a higher level.

[43]    Perceived spiritually, the processes involved here can be described like this: The predecessors of human beings had been ennobled by beings who had broken away from the Sun kingdom. This ennobling process especially affected everything that could be experienced in the element of

water, since the Sun beings who governed the elements of warmth and air had less influence on this element. For our predecessors, the result of this was that two types of beings exerted influence on their makeup. One part of it was totally imbued with the effects and activities of the Sun beings, while the break-away Moon beings worked in the other part, making it more independent than the first. In the first part, the only states of consciousness that could come about were those in which the Sun beings lived, while in the second a type of cosmic consciousness similar to that of the Saturn state prevailed, only on a higher level. Our predecessors thus felt themselves to be an image of the cosmos, while their Sun portion experienced itself only as an image of the Sun.

Within human nature, a certain conflict then arose between these two types of beings. It was resolved by the Sun beings making the material organism, which allows independent cosmic consciousness to come about, frail and perishable so that it would need to be cast off from time to time. While shedding this material organism and for some time afterward, our predecessors were dependent solely on the Sun's influence. Their consciousness became less independent and they surrendered completely to the life of the Sun. Their independent Moon part was then renewed, and after a while this whole process repeated itself. On the Moon, then, our predecessors lived in alternating states of clearer and duller consciousness, accompanied by transformations in the material aspect of their being. From time to time they cast off their Moon bodies and put them on again later.

[44]     Seen physically, great variations appeared in the Moon
kingdoms described here. The mineral-plants, plant-animals, and animal-humans were differentiated into groups.
We can easily understand this if we consider the fact that
because certain structures had remained behind at each of
the earlier stages of evolutions, their forms were endowed
with the most varied characteristics. Some still displayed
characteristics of the beginning of the Saturn phase, while
others were typical of its middle and final periods, and the
same was true of all the stages of the Sun's evolution.

[45]     In the cosmic body's evolution through successive
planetary incarnations, some of the structures associated
with it fell behind, and so did some of the beings involved
in its evolution. A number of levels of such beings had
already come about in the evolution leading up to the
Moon. There were Spirits of Personality who had still not
reached their human level on the Sun, but there were also
others who had caught up to the stage of humanity there.
The Spirits of Fire should have been human on the Sun,
but a number of them also fell behind. During the Sun
phase, certain underdeveloped Spirits of Personality had
withdrawn from the main body of the Sun to reconstitute
Saturn as a separate cosmic body. Similarly, in the course
of the Moon phase the beings mentioned above also withdrew to separate cosmic bodies. Up to this point, we have
only spoken of the separation of Sun and Moon, but for
the reasons described above, still other cosmic formations
split off from the Moon body that appeared after the great
pause between Sun and Moon evolutions. After some
time, a system of cosmic bodies came into existence. It is

easy to see that the most advanced of these must be called the *new Sun*. Just as a bond of attraction existed between the underdeveloped Saturn kingdoms and the Spirits of Personality on new Saturn, as described earlier, a similar bond now formed between each of these cosmic bodies and the corresponding Moon beings. It would take us too far afield to follow up all these cosmic bodies in detail, so we must be content with indicating why a whole series of cosmic bodies gradually separated from the unitary cosmic formation that appeared as Saturn at the beginning of human evolution.

After the Spirits of Form became active on the Moon, evolution continued for a while in the way already described. After this time, a pause again ensued, and the coarser portions of the three Moon kingdoms entered a certain state of rest, but the finer portions—specifically human astral bodies—separated from these coarser formations and entered a state in which the higher forces of exalted Sun beings were able to work on them especially strongly. When the rest period was over, they reentered the parts of the human being composed of coarser substances. Through having assimilated these strong forces during the rest period—in a state of freedom—they were then able to make these coarser substances mature enough to receive the influence that was soon to be exerted on them by the normally advancing Spirits of Personality and by the Spirits of Fire. [46]

Meanwhile, these Spirits of Personality had arisen to the level of consciousness of *Inspiration*, where they were not only able to perceive the inner states of other beings [47] in image form, as they did in their earlier pictorial consciousness, but could also perceive the actual inner nature of these beings as if in a spiritual language of sounds. The Spirits of Fire, however, had risen to the level of consciousness occupied by the Spirits of Personality on the Sun. Therefore, both types of spirits were able to intervene in the matured life of human beings. The Spirits of Personality worked on the astral body, the Spirits of Fire on the human ether body.

This gave the astral body the character of personality. From this point onward, it not only experienced pleasure and pain but also related them to itself. It did not yet achieve a full I-consciousness that would allow it to say, "I exist," but felt that it was being carried and protected by other beings in its surroundings. Looking up to them, it could say, "These surroundings of mine maintain my existence."

From this point onward, the Spirits of Fire worked on the ether body. Under their influence, the movement of forces within this body increasingly became an inner life activity. What happened there found physical expression in the movement of fluids and in phenomena of growth. Since gaseous substances had been condensed into watery ones, it was now possible to speak of a certain process of nourishment in the sense that what was taken in from outside was transformed and assimilated within. If we think of something halfway between digestion and breathing as we know them now, this will give us an idea of what was going on in this direction. Human beings were taking nourishing substances from the kingdom of the plant-animals. We must imagine these plant-animals as swimming or floating in, or lightly attached to, the element that surrounded them, just as present-day lower aquatic animals live in water or land animals live in air. However, this element was neither water nor air as we know them now, but something halfway between the two, a kind of dense vapor in which various substances moved to and fro in various currents, as if in solution. The plant-animals simply seemed to be like regular, condensed forms of this element and were frequently only slightly different from their surroundings. Alongside the process of digestion, respiration existed, not as we know it now, but as a process of drawing warmth in and allowing it to stream out again.

To supersensible observation, this was as if the organs involved in these processes were opening and closing again, allowing a stream of warmth to flow in and out and drawing in and expelling gaseous and water-like substances. Because human beings already possessed an astral body at this stage of their evolution, these processes of respiration and digestion were accompanied by feelings, so that a certain pleasure came about when the substances absorbed from outside were favorable to development. Displeasure was aroused when harmful substances flowed in, or even when they appeared nearby.

As has already been described, the processes of breathing and digestion were very closely related. Likewise, the process of forming mental images was very close to reproduction. The things and beings in the Moon humans' surroundings did not exert a direct effect on senses of any kind. The character of mental image-forming was such that the presence of these things and beings stimulated pictures in the dull, dusk-like consciousness of human beings. These images were much more intimately connected with the actual nature of the surroundings than our present-day sense perceptions, which only reveal the outer aspect of things and beings through colors, sounds, odors, and so on.

To get a clearer idea of the consciousness of the Moon human, let's imagine it as being embedded in the vapor-like surroundings described above. A great variety of processes were taking place in this vapor-like element. Substances were combining and separating; certain parts were becoming denser, others less dense. All this was taking place in such a way that although human beings did not see or hear the process directly, it did call up images in their consciousness. These images can be compared to those of our present-day dream consciousness. For example, when something falls to the ground, someone who is sleeping does not perceive the actual event but may imagine that a shot has been fired. However, the images of Moon consciousness were not arbitrary like our dream images today. Although they were symbols rather than exact reproductions, they did correspond to outer processes. A particular outer process gave rise to only one specific picture. Moon humans were therefore in a position to adapt their actions to these images, just as we adapt ours to our perceptions. We must keep in mind, however, that our perception-based actions are subject to personal choice, while Moon humans under the influence of such images were impelled to action by some unclear impetus.

This pictorial consciousness made it possible not only to have an image of outer physical processes but also to picture the spiritual beings and their activities that were in effect behind the physical facts. Thus, the Spirits of Personality became visible, so to speak, in the objects of the plant-animal kingdom; the Spirits of Fire appeared in and behind mineral-plant beings, and the Sons of Life appeared as beings that could be mentally pictured without connection to anything physical, as etheric-soul formations, so to speak.

Even though the mental images of Moon consciousness were symbols rather than exact reproductions of outer things, their effect on the inner human being was much more significant than that of present-day mental images transmitted through perception. They were capable of setting the whole inner being in motion and rousing it to action. Inner processes took shape in accordance with them; they were true formative forces. Human beings became what these formative forces fashioned; they became copies of the processes of their own consciousness, so to speak.

The more evolution proceeded in this direction, the more [48] profoundly and incisively human beings changed as a result. Gradually the force emanating from the images of this consciousness became unable to extend to all of human physical nature, which then divided into two parts that were different in character. Certain elements formed that were subject to the formative influence of this pictorial consciousness; to a great extent, these became a copy of the human image-forming activity described above. Other organs, however, withdrew from this influence. In one part of their being, human beings were too dense, so to speak, too much determined by other laws to act in accordance with the images of consciousness. These images withdrew from human influence but became subject to that of the exalted Sun beings themselves. This stage of evolution, however, was preceded by a period of rest while the Sun spirits summoned the strength to work on Moon beings under totally new circumstances.

After this rest period, the makeup of the human being was clearly separated into two different aspects. One of them, not subject to the independent activity of pictorial consciousness, took on a more definite form and came under the influence of forces which, although emanating from the Moon body, came about there only under the influence of the Sun beings. This part of the human being participated increasingly in the life inspired by the Sun. The second part grew up out of the first part like a kind of head. It was inherently mobile and plastic, taking shape as the expression and vehicle of dimly active human consciousness. These two parts, however, were intimately connected and exchanged fluids with one another. Some of their organs also stretched from one into the other.

[49]     During the time when all this was happening, a significant harmony was achieved through the development of a relationship between Sun and Moon that was in line with this evolution. It has already been mentioned that because of their stages of evolution, advancing beings

pull their celestial bodies out of the general cosmic mass (see page 151). They radiate the forces, as it were, and the substances separate accordingly. This was how Sun and Moon separated in order to create the right dwelling places for the corresponding beings.

The spirit's role in regulating substance and its forces, however, is much greater than this. The beings involved also determine certain motions of the heavenly bodies, such as how they revolve around each other. Thus these bodies come into varying positions in relation to each other, and when their relative positions change, the effects the corresponding beings have on each other also change.

This is what happened with Sun and Moon. With the beginning of the Moon's movement around the Sun, there were times when human beings moved more into the influence of the Sun's activity, and other times when they were able to turn away from it and be more independent. The Moon's movement was the result of certain Moon beings breaking away, as described earlier, and of the resolution of the ensuing conflict. It was only the physical expression of the spiritual relationship of forces created by the secession of these beings. The consequence of one celestial body revolving around another is that alternating states of consciousness set in, as described earlier, in the beings occupying these bodies. We can say that the Moon turned its life alternately toward the Sun and away from it. It had a Sun period, but also a planetary period when the Moon beings developed on the side of it that was turned away from the Sun. As far as the Moon was concerned, however, something else was involved in addition to the movement of these celestial bodies. Looking back by means of supersensible consciousness, we can see how the Moon beings themselves moved around their own cosmic body at regular intervals. At certain times they sought out the places that would expose them to the influence of the Sun, while at other times they migrated to places where they would not be subject to this influence and would have the possibility for self-reflection, so to speak.

[50]     To complete our understanding of the picture that is being drawn of these processes, we must also consider that the Sons of Life reached their human stage during this time period. On the Moon, the human senses, which had already begun in seminal form on Saturn, were still not available for human beings to use for their personal perception of outer objects. At the Moon stage, however, these senses became instruments for the Sons of Life, who made use of them in order to perceive through them. These senses, which belonged to the physical human body, thus entered into a reciprocal relationship with the Sons of Life, who not only made use of them but also perfected them.

[51]     As has already been described, a change also took place in the circumstances of human life through human beings' changing connections to the Sun. Things took shape in such a way that each time human beings became subject to the Sun's influence they became more devoted to the Sun and its phenomena than to themselves. At such times, they experienced and absorbed, so to speak, the

grandeur and glory of the cosmos as expressed in the existence of the Sun. In this case, the exalted beings who had their dwelling on the Sun were working on the Moon, which in turn worked on human beings. However, this influence did not extend to the whole human being, but primarily to the parts that had withdrawn from the influence of personal pictorial consciousness. In particular, the physical body and life body achieved a certain size and form, but on the other hand manifestations of consciousness declined. However, when the life of human beings was turned away from the Sun, they were occupied with their own nature. An inner activity began, especially in the astral body, while the outer human figure became less attractive and less perfect in its form.

Thus, during the Moon phase of evolution there were two distinctly different, alternating states of consciousness—a duller consciousness during the Sun period and a clearer state during the time when life was left to depend more on itself. The first state was the duller one, but it was also the more selfless. In this state, human beings were more devoted to the outer world, to the cosmos as it was reflected in the Sun. This alternation in states of consciousness can be compared both to our present-day alternation between sleep and waking and to our life between birth and death, on the one hand, and our more spiritual existence between death and a new birth, on the other. Waking up on the Moon, as the Sun period gradually drew to a close, could be characterized as something halfway between ordinary morning awakening and being born, as we now know them. Similarly, the gradual dimming of consciousness as the Sun period approached resembles a state halfway between falling asleep and dying, because on the Moon, human consciousness of birth and dying was not yet what it is today.

During a kind of Sun life, human beings gave themselves up to enjoying that life and were withdrawn from their own life for the duration, living more spiritually. It is only possible to attempt an approximate and figurative depiction of what human beings experienced during these times. They felt as if the causative forces of the cosmos were streaming into them and pulsating through them. They felt as if intoxicated with the cosmic harmonies they took part in. During these times, the astral body was as though freed from the physical body, and a part of the life body also withdrew from it. This formation consisting of astral body and life body was like a marvelous, delicate musical instrument, and the mysteries of the universe resounded from its strings. The elements of the physical/ etheric part of the human being that was less influenced by consciousness were shaped according to the harmonies of the universe, because the Sun beings were at work in these harmonies. In this way, that part of the human being was shaped by the spiritual tones of the cosmos.

At this time, the alternation between clearer and duller states of consciousness was by no means as abrupt as our present-day alternation between waking and deep, dreamless sleep; although human pictorial consciousness was not as clear as our present waking consciousness, the other state of consciousness was also not as dull as our present dreamless sleep. Thus, human beings did have some idea, although a subdued one, of the play of cosmic harmonies in the physical body and the part of the ether body that had remained united with it.

During the time when the Sun was not shining on human beings, so to speak, pictorial ideas took the place of these harmonies in the consciousness; in the physical and ether bodies, especially the organs that were directly under the authority of consciousness flourished during that time. In contrast, the other parts of the human being, which were no longer being worked on by formative forces from the Sun, underwent a kind of hardening and desiccating process. When the Sun period approached again, the old bodies disintegrated and separated from the human being, who then arose, inwardly reconfigured if still unsightly, as if from the grave of the old bodily nature. The processes of life had been renewed. Through the workings of the Sun beings and their harmonies, the form of the newborn body was then perfected and the process described above repeated itself.

To human beings, this renewal was like putting on new clothes. Their essential nuclei had not passed through an actual birth or death but had simply shifted from a state of spiritual tone-consciousness, where they were devoted to the outer world, to a state of turning inward to a greater extent. They had "shed their skins." Their old bodies had become unusable, so they were cast off and renewed. This is also a more precise characterization of what was mentioned earlier as a kind of reproduction closely related to the process of mental image-forming. Human beings were reproducing their own kind with regard to certain parts of the physical and ether bodies. What came about, however, was not a child totally distinguishable from the parent. Instead, the essential nucleus of the parent-being shifted over into the child. The parent-being did not produce a new being, but reproduced itself in a new form.

This was how Moon humans experienced changes in consciousness. When the Sun period was approaching, their pictorial ideas grew dimmer and dimmer. They were filled with a blissful sense of surrender, and cosmic harmonies resounded within the stillness of their inner being. Toward the end of this period, the images in their astral bodies were re-enlivened, and they began to feel and sense themselves to a greater extent, experiencing something like an awakening out of the peace and bliss they had been immersed in during the Sun period.

However, there is still another important experience that appears in this connection. As the images of their consciousness became clear again, human beings had the experience of feeling wrapped in a being-like cloud that had descended from the cosmos. Each of them experienced one such being as complementing and belonging to them personally. It was experienced as an I, as something that granted them their existence. This being was one of the Sons of Life. The individual human being's feelings for that being were something like this: "Even during the Sun period, when I was given over to the glory of the cosmos, I dwelled in this being. It was invisible to me then, but now it is becoming visible." These Sons of Life were also the source of the strength that allowed human beings to work on their own bodily nature during the Sunless period. And then, as the Sun period approached again, human beings felt themselves becoming one with their Sons of Life. Although they did not see them then, they still felt intimately connected to them.

This connection to the Sons of Life was such that individual human beings did not each have a personal Son of Life, but a whole group of human beings experienced one such being as belonging to them. Moon-humans lived in separate groups like this, and each group experienced one Son of Life as their collective I. The difference between groups was made apparent by the fact that the ether bodies of each group's members shared a distinctive form. Since their physical bodies took shape in accordance with their ether bodies, the characteristics of the ether bodies were imprinted on the physical bodies and the individual groups of human beings appeared as so many different human types. When the Sons of Life looked down on the groups of human beings belonging to them, they saw multiplications of themselves in these individual human beings. This was their experience of being an I; they were mirrored in human beings, so to speak. This was also the task of the human senses at that time. It has already been shown that these senses did not yet transmit any perceptions of objects. However, they did reflect the essence of the Sons of Life. What the Sons of Life perceived through this reflection provided them with their I-consciousness. And in human astral bodies, this reflection aroused the images typical of their dull and dusk-like Moon consciousness.

The human being's own activity and interaction with the Sons of Life brought about the first seminal beginnings of

*[52]*

the nervous system in the physical body. The nerves represent an extension of the senses into the interior of the human body, as it were.

*[53]*     From this description, it can be seen how three types of spirits—the Spirits of Personality, the Spirits of Fire, and the Sons of Life—worked on Moon humans. If we look at the main time period in the Moon evolutionary phase, its middle period, we can say that this is when the Spirits of Personality implanted independence and the character of personality in the human astral body. This made human beings capable of turning inward and working formatively on themselves during the times when the Sun was not shining on them, so to speak. The Spirits of Fire were actively at work on the ether body to the extent that this body imprints the independent form of the human being on itself. These spirits were responsible for human beings feeling that they were still the same beings after each bodily renewal. Thus, through the Spirits of Fire, the ether body was given memory of a sort. The Sons of Life worked on the physical body so that it could become the expression of the newly independent astral body. They also made it possible for this physical body to become a physiognomic copy of its astral body.

In contrast to this, at times when the physical body and ether body were developing independently of the autonomous astral body during the Sun periods, higher spiritual beings intervened in them, specifically the Spirits of Form and the Spirits of Motion. They worked down from the Sun to accomplish this intervention, as was described above.

Human beings matured under the influence of these circumstances, gradually developing in themselves the seminal nucleus of the spirit self, just as they had developed
the nucleus of the spirit body on Saturn and that of the life
spirit on the Sun. This brought about a change in conditions on the Moon. In the transformations and renewals
that followed, human beings became ever nobler and
more refined, but they also gained in strength. As a result,
their image-consciousness was increasingly maintained
during the Sun periods and began to influence the formation of the physical and etheric bodies, which had formerly been accomplished totally through the activity of
the Sun beings. What was happening on the Moon by
means of human beings and the spirits associated with
them was becoming increasingly similar to what had formerly been accomplished by the Sun and its higher
beings. As a result, these Sun beings became more and
more able to apply their forces to their own development.
Because of this, after a certain time passed, the Moon
became ready to reunite with the Sun.

Perceived spiritually, these processes appear like this:
The "break-away" Moon beings were gradually overcome
by the Sun beings and had to adapt so as to incorporate
their undertakings into those of the Sun beings to whom
they had become subject. However, this happened only
after long epochs had gone by in which the Moon periods
became ever shorter and the Sun periods ever longer. During the evolutionary period that followed, Sun and Moon
were again a single cosmic formation. During this time,
the physical human body became completely etheric.

Having said this, we must not imagine that we cannot speak of the existence of a physical body in this state. What had been formed as the physical body during the Saturn, Sun, and Moon phases was still present. In this case, it's important to recognize the physical element even when it does not manifest in an outer physical way. The physical element still exists even when it outwardly displays the form of the etheric or even of the astral element. We must simply distinguish between outer appearances and inner laws. It is possible for a physical entity to etherize or astralize, yet still retain its physical laws. This is what happened when the physical human body had reached a certain degree of perfection on the Moon—it became ether-like. However, when supersensible consciousness, which can observe things like this, looks at an ether-like body of this sort, this body appears imbued with the laws of the physical element instead of those of the etheric element. In such cases the physical element has been absorbed into the etheric in order to rest and be cared for there as if in the womb of a mother. Later it reemerges in physical form, but on a higher level. If Moon humans had kept their physical bodies in a crudely physical form, the Moon would never have been able to reunite with the Sun. By assuming an etheric form, the physical body became more closely related to the ether body and could therefore also be more intimately imbued with the parts of the ether and astral bodies that had to withdraw from it during the Sun periods of the Moon phase of evolution. Human beings, who had appeared in the form of dual beings while Sun and Moon were separated, became unified beings again. Although their physical element became more soul-like, their soul element was more united with the physical.

These unitary human beings had now entered the immediate sphere of the Sun beings, who were then able to work on them in a way that was quite different from when their activity had been directed toward the Moon and its human beings from outside. Human beings were now in surroundings that were more soul-like and spiritual in character, which made it possible for the Spirits of Wisdom to have a significant effect on them—specifically, to imprint wisdom on them, to ensoul them with wisdom. This allowed them to become independent souls in a certain sense. The influence of the Spirits of Wisdom was then augmented by the Spirits of Motion, who worked primarily on the astral body, which developed a soul-like mobility and a wisdom-filled life body under the influence of these two orders of beings. The wisdom-filled ether body constitutes the first seminal beginnings of what was described in an earlier chapter as the mind soul in present-day human beings, while the astral body stimulated by the Spirits of Motion is the seminal nucleus of the sentient soul. And because all this was brought about when human beings were in a state of heightened independence, these seminal nuclei of the mind and sentient souls appeared as the expression of the spirit self. We must not make the mistake of thinking of the spirit self at this stage in evolution as something independent of the mind and sentient souls. They are only the expression of the spirit self, which signifies their higher unity and harmony.

*[55]*     It is especially significant that the Spirits of Wisdom intervened during this epoch in the way just described. They did so not only with regard to human beings, but also with regard to the other kingdoms that had developed on the Moon. When Sun and Moon were reunited, these lower kingdoms were absorbed into the sphere of the Sun, and everything physical about them was etherized. From that point on, therefore, mineral-plants and plant-animals existed in the Sun alongside human beings. However, these other beings remained endowed with laws of their own that made them feel like strangers in their new surroundings. Their character had little in common with that of their environment. Since they had been etherized, however, the effect of the Spirits of Wisdom was able to extend to them as well. In fact, everything that entered the sphere of the Sun from the Moon was imbued with the forces of the Spirits of Wisdom. For this reason, what the Sun-Moon formation became during this period in evolution can be called the *cosmos of wisdom.*

After a period of rest, our Earth's solar system appeared as the successor to this cosmos of wisdom. When that happened, all the beings that came to life again on Earth, emerging from their Moon nuclei, appeared filled with wisdom. This is why we present-day Earth humans, if we observe closely, can discover wisdom in the nature of the things around us. We can admire the wisdom in every leaf of every plant, in every human or animal bone, and in the marvelous structure of the brain and heart. When human beings need wisdom in order to understand things—that is, when we extract wisdom from them—this shows that wisdom is inherent in the things themselves, for no matter how hard we might try to understand things with wisdom-filled ideas, we would not be able to extract wisdom from these things if it were not present in them to begin with. If we want to use wisdom to grasp things that we think have not received wisdom themselves, we might as well believe that we can get water from a glass that has not had any poured into it. As will be shown later on in this book, the Earth is the resurrected "old Moon." It appears as a wisdom-filled formation because the Spirits of Wisdom imbued it with their forces during the period just described.

It should be understandable that this book's descrip- [56] tion of conditions on the Moon necessarily emphasized only some of their transitory evolutionary forms. In this flow of events, certain things had to be selected and emphasized for the sake of the description, so to speak. Naturally, such a description of evolution yields only separate images and may therefore seem the worse for not being incorporated into a context of fixed and definite concepts. In response to this objection, let it be said that this description was deliberately given in the form of less concise concepts, because the point here is not so much to build constructs of speculative concepts and ideas as to give an idea of what can actually present itself when spiritual sight turns to these facts. And with regard to the Moon phase of evolution, what presents itself in this way simply does not have the clear and definite contours that earthly perceptions reveal. During the Moon epoch, we are dealing with very changeable, vacillating impressions, with mobile, fluctuating images and the transitions between them. In addition, we must consider the fact that the evolution in question took place over long, long periods of time and that we can only select certain momentary images to emphasize when describing it.

[57]     Essentially, the high point of the Moon phase of evolution was reached when, thanks to the astral bodies implanted in them, human beings had advanced far enough so that their physical bodies made it possible for the Sons of Life to achieve their human stage. At that point human beings had also achieved everything that this phase could give them for themselves and the progress of their inner development. What followed, the second half of the Moon phase of evolution, could therefore be described as a period of abatement. Nonetheless, something important happened during this period with regard to human beings themselves and their surroundings. Wisdom was implanted into the Sun-Moon body. As we have seen, the seminal nuclei for the mind and sentient souls were laid down during this period of abatement. Not until the Earth phase of evolution, however, did they unfold, together with the consciousness soul, so that the birth of the I, of independent self-awareness, could take place. At the Moon stage, the mind and sentient souls were not yet actual expressions of human beings themselves; rather, these soul elements appeared as instruments for the Sons of Life who belonged to these human beings. What human beings on the Moon felt with regard to this would have to be described as follows: The Son of Life lives in me and through me, sees the Moon environment through

me, and thinks in me about the things and beings of this environment. Moon humans felt themselves overshadowed by their Son of Life; they felt like tools for this higher being. During the separation of Sun and Moon, at times when the Moon was turned away from the Sun, they felt a greater degree of independence, but they also felt as if the I belonging to them, which disappeared from their pictorial consciousness during the Sun periods, then became visible to them. For Moon humans, what we described as a change in their state of consciousness gave them the feeling that during the Sun periods, their I drifted away with them into higher regions to sublime beings, and that it descended with them into lower worlds when the Sun disappeared.

The actual evolutionary phase of the Moon had been [58] preceded by preparatory periods during which the Saturn and Sun phases were repeated in a certain way. Similarly, we can distinguish two epochs within the time of abatement after the reunification of Sun and Moon. During these epochs, things even condensed physically to a certain degree. Thus, the Sun-Moon formation alternated between states that were soul-like or spiritual in character and states that were physical. In the physical epochs human beings, and also the beings of the lower kingdoms, appeared as stiff figures that were not independent but seemed to foretell what they were meant to become later, during the Earth phase, in a more independent way. We can thus speak of two preparatory epochs in the Moon phase and two different ones during the time of abatement. Epochs such as these can be called "cycles." In what followed the two preparatory epochs but preceded those of the abatement—that is, the time of the Moon's separation from the Sun—we will also be able to distinguish three epochs. The middle one is the time when the Sons of Life became human. This was preceded by an epoch whose circumstances were all focused on this main event, and it was followed by another in which the beings in question found their way into and developed their new creations. Thus, the middle portion of the Moon phases is divided into three epochs; along with the two preparatory epochs and the two epochs of abatement, this makes a total of seven Moon cycles. We can therefore say that the entire Moon phase of evolution ran its course in seven cycles. The periods of rest between these cycles have already been described several times.

We only arrive at an accurate idea of this state of affairs, however, if we imagine that there were no abrupt transitions between periods of rest and periods of activity. For example, the Sun beings withdrew gradually from their activity on the Moon. For them, an apparent period of rest began while there was still lively independent activity taking place on the Moon. The active period of one order of beings often overlaps with the rest period of others. If we take this into account, we can talk about a rhythmic, cyclical rising and falling of forces. Similar divisions can be observed even within the seven Moon cycles that were pointed out above. We can call the entire Moon phase of evolution one great cycle, one planetary cycle, in which case the seven divisions within it constitute smaller cycles, and their parts still smaller cycles.

This division into seven times seven sections was already noticeable during the Sun phase and a suggestion of it was even present during the Saturn phase. However, we must consider the fact that the boundaries between sections were already blurred on the Sun and even more so on Saturn. These boundaries became ever clearer as evolution continued toward the Earth phase.

### Earth

After the conclusion of the Moon phase of evolution as outlined above, all of the beings and forces involved in it entered a more spiritual state of existence that was at a totally different level from either the Moon phase itself or the Earth phase that followed. This means that a being whose faculties of cognition were highly developed enough to perceive all the details of the Earth and Moon phases would still not be in a position to view what happened between them. As far as such a being is concerned, at the end of the Moon phase the cosmic beings and forces would have disappeared as if into nothingness, so to speak, and would reappear out of the darkness of the cosmic womb after a certain interim period had elapsed. Only a being with far higher faculties would be able to trace the spiritual events taking place in the interim.   *[59]*

At the end of the interim period, the beings who had been involved in evolutionary events on Saturn, Sun, and Moon appeared with new abilities and faculties. Through their previous actions, the beings who were more advanced than human beings had acquired the ability to bring humans to the point of being able to develop   *[60]* a consciousness one level higher than the pictorial consciousness that belonged to them during the Moon phase. This was to take place during the subsequent Earth phase. However, these human beings first had to be prepared to receive what was to be given to them. During the Saturn, Sun, and Moon phases of evolution, they had incorporated the physical body, the life body, and the astral body into their nature, but these parts of their makeup had only received abilities and forces that enabled them to support pictorial consciousness. They still lacked the organs and the overall form that would permit perception of a world of outer sense-perceptible objects in a way appropriate to the Earth stage. Just as a new plant can unfold only the inherent predispositions that are present in the seed of the old plant, at the beginning of this new evolutionary phase, the three members of human makeup appeared in forms and with organs that would only allow them to develop pictorial consciousness. They required a certain preparation in order to develop to a higher level of consciousness.

This happened in three preliminary stages. During the first stage, the physical body was raised to a level where it was possible to make the necessary transformations to support object consciousness. This first preliminary stage in the Earth phase of evolution can be described as a repetition of the Saturn phase on a higher level, because during this period, as was the case during the actual Saturn phase, higher beings worked only on the human physical body. When this body had advanced far enough in its development, all the beings in question first had to shift into a higher form of existence before the life body could also advance. The physical body had to be recast, so to speak, so that when it unfolded again it would be able to receive the more highly developed life body. After this interim period devoted to a higher form of existence, a certain repetition of the Sun phase of evolution ensued, but on a higher level, in order to develop the life body. After another interim period, something similar happened to the astral body in a repetition of the Moon phase of evolution.

Let's now turn our attention to events in evolution after *[61]* the conclusion of the third repetition described above. All of the beings and forces in question had spiritualized again and had ascended into higher worlds during this time. Something of these beings and forces was still perceptible in the lowest of these worlds, which is the same world where present-day human beings dwell between death and a new birth. It consists of the various regions of the land of spirits. Before the physical evolutionary phase of the Earth began, the beings in question once again descended to a point where their lowest manifestations could be seen in the astral or soul world.

All aspects of the human being that were present during *[62]* this period were still in their astral form. In order to understand this state of humankind, we should note that although, at that point, human beings each contained a physical body, a life body, and an astral body, the physical body was not present in physical form, nor the life body in etheric form. Both of them were present in astral form. What made the physical body physical was not a physical form, but rather the fact that it still contained physical laws in spite of having taken on an astral form. It was a being governed by physical laws but appearing in soul form. Something similar was true of the life body.

*[63]*     At the beginning of this stage of evolution, spiritual sight is confronted with the Earth as a cosmic being that is all soul and spirit. That is, its physical and life forces still appeared in soul form. This cosmic formation included, in seminal form, everything that would later be transformed into the creatures of the physical Earth. This being was luminous, but its light was not yet such that it could have been perceived by physical eyes even if any had been present. It shone with a soul light perceptible only to the receptive eye of the seer.

*[64]*     Within this being, something we can call "condensation" then took place. After some time, this resulted in the appearance of a fiery form in the midst of this soul formation. This form was similar to Saturn in its densest condition and was interwoven with the effects of various beings involved in evolution. As we observe the interaction between these beings and the celestial body, they seem to emerge from the Earth's fiery sphere at some times and to immerse themselves in it at others. Thus, this fiery sphere was not a uniform substance but resembled an organism imbued with soul and spirit. The beings destined to assume the present-day form of human beings on Earth were still not in a position to participate much in this process of immersion in the body of fire. They remained almost exclusively in its uncondensed surroundings, in the bosom of higher spiritual beings. At this

stage only one spot on each of their soul-shapes touched the fiery Earth, whose heat was therefore able to condense a portion of the astral form of each one. This kindled Earth life in them, but the greater part of their being still belonged to soul-spiritual worlds. The warmth of life played around them only to the extent that they were in contact with the Earth's fire.

In order to form an image of the supersensible human being at the beginning of the physical Earth period, we must imagine an egg-shaped soul form existing in the surroundings of the Earth. Its lower surface was enclosed in a cup, like that of an acorn, but the substance of this cup consisted purely of heat or fire. As a result of being encased in heat, not only was life kindled in the human being, but the astral body also underwent a change at the same time, incorporating the seminal beginnings of what would later become the sentient soul. Thus, we can say that at this level of existence, the human being consisted of a sentient soul, an astral body, a life body, and a physical body woven of fire. The spiritual beings involved in human existence surged up and down in the astral body, while the sentient soul made the human being feel bound to the body of the Earth. Human consciousness at this stage was primarily a pictorial consciousness in which spiritual beings disclosed themselves. The human being lay in the bosom of these spiritual beings, and the sensation of a personal body appeared only as a point within this consciousness. The human being looked down from the spiritual world on an earthly possession, so to speak, and had the feeling, "This is yours."

As the Earth continued to condense, the characteristic divisions within human beings became more distinct. After a certain point in time, the Earth became condensed enough so that only one part of it was still fiery, while another part took on a material form that we can describe as *gas* or *air*. A change then took place in human beings, too. Not only were they touched by Earth's heat, but air substance was incorporated into their bodies of fire. Just as heat kindled life in human beings, the air that then played around them aroused an effect in them that can be described as (spiritual) sound. The human life body began to resound. At the same time a portion of the astral body split off from it, forming the first beginnings of the mind soul that would appear later.

In order to form an image of what was taking place within the human soul at this time, we must realize that higher beings were surging up and down within the Earth's body of air and fire. Within the fire body of the Earth, the Spirits of Personality were of primary significance for human beings. When heat roused human beings to life, their sentient souls acknowledged the presence of these spirits. Similarly, the beings that were called *archangels* (in terms of Christian esotericism) earlier on in this book disclosed themselves in the air body. Their effects were what human beings experienced within themselves as sounds when the air played around them. When this happened, their mind souls acknowledged the presence of the archangels. Thus, what human beings perceived at this stage through their connection to the Earth was not yet a collection of physical objects. Instead, they lived in sounds and in sensations of warmth that rose up in them, and in these currents of warmth and surging sounds they perceived the Spirits of Personality and the archangels. However, they were not able to perceive these beings directly, but only through a veil of heat and sound, as it were. While their souls were being penetrated by these perceptions that came from the Earth, human beings still experienced themselves as resting in the bosom of higher beings, and their souls were still filled with ebbing and flowing images of these beings.

Earth's evolution continued, again expressing itself in a condensation. Watery substance was incorporated into the Earth body, which then consisted of three elements—the fiery element, the airy, and the watery. Prior to this, however, an important event took place. An independent cosmic body separated from the Earth of fire and air. In the course of further evolution, this developed into our present-day Sun. Previously, Earth and Sun had been one body, and at this point the Earth still contained everything that is included in our present-day Moon. The Sun separated from the Earth because certain higher beings could no longer continue to tolerate the presence of condensed watery matter in their own evolution and in what they had to accomplish for the sake of the Earth. From the general Earth body, they extracted the substances that were suited only to their purposes and withdrew from the Earth to form a new dwelling place for themselves on the Sun. They then worked down upon the Earth from outside, from the Sun (see page 168). Humankind's own further evolution, however, required a setting where matter continued to condense.

*[65]*

*[66]*     Human beings also underwent a change as a result of
the incorporation of liquid substance into the Earth body.
From this point on, not only did fire stream into human
beings and the air play around them, but their physical
bodies incorporated liquid substance. At the same time,
the etheric part of them changed and became perceptible
to them as a delicate body of light. Formerly, human
beings had felt streams of warmth rising up toward them
out of the Earth and had sensed the air pressing in on them
through sound, but now the watery element also permeated their bodies of air and fire, and they saw its ebbing
and flowing as brightening and dimming light. A change
took place in their souls, too. The first beginnings of the
consciousness soul were added to those of the sentient
and mind souls. The angels, or Sons of Life, work in the
element of water, and it is they who also actually generate
light. For human beings, it seemed as if the angels
appeared to them in the light.

     Certain higher beings formerly present within the Earth
body itself were now working on it from the Sun. This
changed all their effects on the Earth. Earth-bound human
beings would not have been able to feel the Sun beings'
effects any more if their souls had been constantly turned
toward the Earth that supplied their physical bodies, so an
alternation in human states of consciousness developed.
The Sun beings pulled human souls away from their
physical bodies at certain times, and as a result humans
began to alternate between a purely spiritual existence in
the bosom of the Sun beings and a state of being united
with the body and receiving Earth's influences. When

human beings occupied physical bodies, currents of warmth streamed toward them, air masses surrounded them with sound, and liquids flowed in and out of them. When they were outside of these bodies, they rested in the bosom of higher beings and images of these beings surged through their souls.

At this stage of its evolution, the Earth experienced two different periods. During one, it was allowed to surround human souls with its substances and clothe them in bodies. During the other, these souls deserted it and only the bodies remained, and both the Earth and its human beings were in a state of sleep. We can state quite objectively that at this point in the distant past, the Earth was going through periods of day and night. (This was expressed physically and spatially in the fact that the Earth moved in relationship to the Sun, bringing about the alternation between daytime and nighttime. This movement was caused by the interaction of Sun beings and Earth beings. The day period occurred when the surface of the Earth where humans were evolving faced the Sun; night—that is, the time when human beings led a purely soul existence—occurred when this surface was turned away from the Sun. We must not imagine, however, that the Earth's movement around the Sun in those ancient times was already similar to what it is today. Circumstances were still quite different then. However, even at this point, it may be useful to hint that the interrelationships of spiritual beings inhabiting celestial bodies are a cause of these bodies' movement. Causes that are soul-like and spiritual in character move these celestial bodies into position and set them in motion in ways that allow spiritual circumstances to be played out in the physical realm.)

[67]     Turning our gaze toward Earth during its nighttime, we would see its body in a corpse-like state, since it consisted, for the most part, of the disintegrating bodies of human beings whose souls were in a different state of existence. The differentiated fluid and gaseous structures that made up human bodies were disintegrating and dissolving into the rest of the Earth's mass. Only outwardly unattractive seminal nuclei remained, the parts of physical human bodies that the interaction of fire and the human soul had been building up ever since the beginning of the Earth phase of evolution. These nuclei had been growing increasingly dense.

As we can see, what is said here about day and night should not be thought of as being too similar to what these terms mean when applied to our present-day Earth. At the beginning of its day period, when the Earth again began to experience the direct effect of the Sun, human souls again made their way into the realm of physical life. They made contact with the above-mentioned nuclei, causing them to germinate and take on outer forms that seemed to be images of their soul-beings. What took place between the human soul and the bodily nucleus was something like a gentle impregnation. Now these embodied souls also began to attract masses of air and water and incorporate them into their bodies. Air was forced out of the differentiated body and drawn in again—the first beginnings of what later became the process of respiration. Water was also taken in and expelled; the process of digestion began in its earliest form. These were not yet perceived as external processes, however. A kind of outer perception took place through the soul only in the case of the above-mentioned impregnation-like process, when the soul dimly felt its own awakening to physical existence as it contacted the seminal nucleus extended toward it by Earth. It heard something that can be approximately expressed in the words, "This is my form." The resulting feeling, which we might call a dawning of the I feeling, persisted in the soul throughout its connection with the physical body.

In contrast, the soul still experienced the assimilation of air in a purely soul-spiritual way, as a pictorial process appearing in the form of ebbing and flowing images of sound that supplied the germinal nucleus with forms as it was differentiating. The soul felt surrounded by surging sounds on all sides and sensed how it shaped its body in accordance with these sound-forces. This was how human figures took shape at that stage. To present-day consciousness, they would not have been perceptible in any external world. They took shape as plant-like or flower-like shapes of delicate substance, but since they were inwardly mobile, they seemed like fluttering flowers. During their Earth or day period, human beings experienced the blissful feeling of being shaped into forms such as these.

The soul experienced the assimilation of watery parts as an influx of strength, an inner strengthening. Outwardly, it appeared as the growth of the physical human structure.

As the direct influence of the Sun waned, the human soul also lost its ability to control these processes, and they were gradually discarded. The only aspects remaining were the ones that permitted the above-mentioned nucleus to mature. Meanwhile, human beings left their bodies and returned to the spiritual state of existence.

Since not all parts of the Earth's body were used in building up human bodies, we must not imagine that the Earth during its night period consisted only of disintegrating corpses and nuclei waiting to be awakened. These were all embedded in other structures that took shape out of the Earth's substances. What was happening with these structures will be described later.

[68]      The process of condensing the Earth's substance, however, continued. The solid element, which we can call "earthy," was added to the liquid. At this point, human beings also began to incorporate the earthy element into their bodies during their times on Earth. As soon as this began, the forces their souls brought with them from their body-free times no longer had the same power as before. Prior to this, each soul had shaped its body out of the fiery, airy, and watery elements in accordance with the tones that resounded around it and the images of light that played around it. The soul was no longer able to do this when it was confronted with a solidified figure, so from this point onward other powers intervened in the process of fashioning the body. What remained of the human being when the soul slipped out of the body was no longer a mere nucleus that was roused to life by the returning soul. It had become a formation in which the

force necessary for its own re-enlivening was inherent. When the soul departed, it left behind something more than a mere afterimage of itself; it also sank part of its enlivening power into that image. When the soul reappeared on Earth, it could no longer merely rouse its image to life; the re-enlivening had to take place within the image itself. The spiritual beings working down upon Earth from the Sun now maintained this enlivening power in human bodies, even when the human beings in question were not present on Earth.

When the soul incarnated during this period, it not only felt surrounded by surging sounds and light-images in which it sensed the presence of the next higher beings; through receiving the earthy element, it also experienced the influences of still higher beings who had chosen the Sun as their sphere of activity. Formerly, human beings had experienced themselves as belonging to spirit-soul beings, with whom they were united during their body-free state, and the I of each human being still existed in the bosom of these spirits. Now, however, how the I confronted human beings during physical embodiment was no different from how everything else around them appeared during that time. From this point onward, independent likenesses of soul-spiritual human beings were present on Earth. Compared to present-day human bodies, these likenesses were formations of a very delicate material nature, since earthy portions were intermingled in them only in the very finest state, comparable to how present-day human beings use their organ of smell to take in very finely dispersed substances coming from an object.

Human bodies were like shadows. However, since they were distributed over the entire Earth, they came under certain influences of the Earth that are different in character on different parts of its surface. Previously, bodily likenesses had corresponded to the human soul-being that enlivened them and had therefore been essentially similar everywhere on Earth, but now differences appeared among these human forms, preparing the way for what later appeared as racial differences.

While bodily human beings were becoming increasingly independent, the formerly intimate connection between Earth humans and the world of spirit and soul was loosening to a certain extent. At this point, when souls left their bodies, these bodies continued to live a life of a sort.

If evolution had continued in this direction, the Earth would have become petrified under the influence of its solid element. To supersensible cognition looking back on these circumstances, it becomes evident that when human bodies were abandoned by their souls, they were solidifying more and more. After a while, human souls returning to the Earth would not have found any usable material to unite with, since all the substances that could have been utilized by human beings would have been used up in filling the Earth with the hardened remains of earlier embodiments.

[69]     At this point, however, something happened that gave the whole process of evolution a different direction. Everything that would have contributed to permanently hardening the Earth's solid substance was expelled. At that point our present-day Moon withdrew from the

Earth, and everything that had previously contributed directly to fashioning lasting forms on Earth now worked down from the Moon, indirectly and in a weakened form. The higher beings responsible for this form-fashioning had decided that they were no longer going to contribute their effects from within the Earth, but were going to work on it from outside. As a result, a distinction appeared among human bodily structures that must be regarded as the beginning of gender separation into male and female.

The previous inhabitants of the Earth, human figures composed of finely dispersed substance, had brought forth their offspring— new human forms—through the interaction of the two forces within each individual: the force of the seed and the enlivening force. These offspring were now transforming themselves. In some of them, the germinal force of the element of spirit and soul worked more strongly, while in the other group the force that enlivened the germinal nucleus was stronger. This was brought about by the weakening of the solid element's power through the withdrawal of the Moon. The interaction of these forces became more delicate than it was previously, when it took place within a single body. As a result, the offspring were also finer and more delicate. They entered the Earth in a fine material state and only gradually incorporated the finest solid particles. This made it possible for human souls returning to the Earth to unite with bodies once again. Since these bodies were now being enlivened on the Earth itself, souls no longer enlivened their bodies from outside, but they united with them and caused them to grow. Certain limits were imposed on this growth, however. As a result of the Moon's separation, human bodies became flexible for a while, but the more they continued to grow on Earth, the more the forces of solidification gained the upper hand. Ultimately, souls grew less and less able to participate in the organization of their bodies, which disintegrated when these souls ascended into spiritual and soul modes of existence.

*[70]*    It is possible to trace how the forces that human beings gradually acquired during the Saturn, Sun, and Moon phases of evolution became increasingly involved in humankind's continued progress as the Earth took shape through the processes described above. First the astral body, which also still contained the life body and the physical body within it in a state of dissolution, was kindled by the Earth's fire. Then it separated into a finer astral portion, the sentient soul, and a coarser etheric portion that could then be affected by the Earth element. At this point, the ether body or life body, which already existed in prototype, made its appearance. While the mind and consciousness souls were developing in the astral human being, the coarser portions of the ether body that were sensitive to sound and light were separating off.

At the point in time when the ether body condensed still further, changing from a body of light into a body of fire or warmth, evolution had reached the stage of incorporating particles of the solid earth element into the human being, as described above. Because the ether body had condensed to the level of fire, it was then also able to unite with substances of the physical Earth that were diluted to the level of fire. This also had the effect of utilizing forces of the physical body that had been implanted into the ether body at an earlier stage. Meanwhile, the physical body had become more solid, however, so if the ether body had been acting on its own, it would no longer have been able to introduce gaseous substances into it. As indicated earlier, the higher beings that lived on the Sun made their appearance at this point and breathed air into the body. Higher beings guided the living breath of air into human beings; however, thanks to their past, human beings possessed the necessary forces for imbuing themselves with Earth's fire. Prior to solidification, the human life body, as the receptor of sound, had guided this stream of air, imbuing the physical body with life, but once this life was received from outside, it consequently became independent of the soul portion of the human being.

At this point, human beings leaving the Earth left behind not only seminal nuclei of their forms, but also living likenesses of themselves. The Spirits of Form remained united with these likenesses; having bestowed life on them, they also transferred it to the next generation after these human souls had left their bodies. This is how what is known as heredity developed. When a human soul then returned to the Earth, it found itself in a body whose life had been transferred to it from that soul's ancestors. The soul felt especially drawn to just such a body; as a result, it developed a certain memory of these ancestors with whom it felt at one. This memory passed like a common consciousness through a succession of descendants. The I flowed down through the generations.

*[71]*     At this stage of evolution, human beings experienced themselves as independent beings during their time on Earth. They felt the inner fire of their life bodies uniting with the outer fire of the Earth. They felt that the warmth that flowed through them was their I. These currents of warmth, interwoven with life, were the first beginnings of blood circulation. However, in the air that streamed into them, human beings did not feel that they were quite their own beings, since the forces of the above-mentioned higher beings were active in this air. But some of the active forces in the air streaming through human beings already did belong to them, thanks to their previously developed etheric forces, and they retained this portion, so they did control some of these currents of air. To the extent that this was the case, they themselves were active in their own formation alongside the higher beings. They shaped their own airy parts according to the images of their astral bodies. While air was streaming into their bodies from outside, becoming the basis of respiration, part of the internal air separated and developed into an organism that was then imprinted onto human beings, forming the basis for what would later become the nervous system. Thus, at this time warmth and air connected human beings to the external world of the Earth.

In contrast, they sensed nothing of the solid element that was being introduced. Although it was involved in their incarnation on Earth, they could not perceive its introduction directly, but only in a dull state of consciousness and in the form of images of the higher beings at work in this element. At an earlier stage, they had also perceived the introduction of liquids in the form of such images of superior beings. By now these earlier images had undergone a transformation within human consciousness due to the densification of the human earthly figure. The liquid element was suffused with the solid, so the addition of solids also had to be experienced as something coming from higher beings acting from outside the human being. In their souls, human beings were no longer able to possess the power to guide this process of incorporation, because it now had to serve the human body that was built up from outside. They would have destroyed the form of this body if they had tried to guide the process themselves. Thus, what they took in from outside seemed to them to be commanded by the higher beings who were working on fashioning the human body.

The human beings of this time did feel that they were I-beings; each had a mind soul as part of the astral body and used it to experience inwardly, in the form of images, what was happening outside, and also to penetrate the delicate nervous system. Thanks to the life that flowed from generation to generation, they felt themselves to be the descendants of their ancestors. They breathed and felt their breathing to be the effect of the higher beings described earlier as the Spirits of Form, and they also obeyed the Spirits of Form in taking in the nourishment that these beings' impulses brought them from the outer world.

Human beings were least aware of their origin as individuals, feeling only that they had been influenced by the Spirits of Form who expressed themselves in the Earth's forces. Their relationship to the outer world was guided and directed. This was expressed in the fact that they were somewhat conscious of the soul-spiritual activities taking place behind their physical world. It is true that they did not perceive these spiritual beings in their actual form. Instead, they experienced sounds, colors, and so on in their own souls and knew that the deeds of spiritual beings were active in this world of mental images. Communications from these beings resounded toward human beings, who received their manifestations in images of light. The most inward feelings of Earth humans came from the images they received through the element of fire or warmth. They already distinguished between their own internal warmth and the currents of warmth in their earthly surroundings. The Spirits of Personality disclosed themselves in these currents, but human beings were only dimly conscious of what stood behind these currents of outer warmth, perceiving in them only the influence of the Spirits of Form. When heat exerted powerful effects on their surroundings, human souls felt that spiritual beings were inflaming the surroundings of the Earth, and that a spark given off by these beings was warming the inner being of each soul through and through.

Human beings did not yet make this same distinction between outside and inside with regard to the effects of light. The feelings produced in the souls of Earth humans by light images appearing in their surroundings were not always the same. There were times when human beings experienced these images as external ones, specifically during their period of growth on Earth, shortly after having descended from the body-free state into incarnation.

As the time approached when the nucleus of a new Earth human formed, these images faded, leaving behind only something like inner memory images of themselves. These light images contained the deeds of the Spirits of Fire or archangels; to human beings, they appeared to be the servants of the warmth beings who sent the spark into their inner nature. When the outer manifestations of these Spirits of Fire were extinguished, human beings experienced them inwardly as mental images or memories and felt united with their forces. This was indeed the case, because what they received from these spirits allowed human beings to work on the surrounding atmosphere so that it began to shine. At this time, natural and human forces were not yet separated from each other to the extent that they would be later. A great deal of what was happening on Earth still originated in forces belonging to human beings. At that time, someone looking down from outside at natural processes taking place on the Earth would have perceived not only effects that were independent of human beings, but human effects as well.

For Earth humans, perceptions of sound took shape differently and were perceived as outer sounds ever since the very beginning of the Earth lifetime. Whereas light images were perceived from outside only until the middle period of human existence on Earth, outer sounds could still be perceived after this midpoint. It was only toward the end of their life that Earth humans were no longer sensitive to sounds. They were left with memory-images of these sounds, which contained the manifestations of the Sons of Life, or angels. Toward the end of their lives, human beings felt inwardly united with these forces and, by imitating them, were also able to produce powerful effects on the Earth's water element. The waters in and above the Earth surged in great waves under their influence.

Human beings had a notion of taste only during the first quarter of their Earth life, and even then their souls experienced these impressions like memories of experiences in the body-free state. As long as human beings had these sensations, their bodies continued to densify by taking in outer substances. In the second quarter of their Earth life, although their growth continued, human forms were already completely developed. During this time, human beings were not yet capable of forming a mental image of the solid element and could therefore perceive living beings other than themselves only through the effects these beings produced in warmth, light, and sound. In the first quarter of their lives, human beings received the above-mentioned impressions of taste only from the watery element.

*[72]*   The outer form of the human body was a copy of the inner soul state of the human being. The parts containing the potential for what would later form the head were the most completely developed, while the other organs gave the impression of appendages and were shadowy and indistinct. However, Earth humans varied with regard to their forms. Their appendages were developed to a greater or lesser extent, depending on the earthly circumstances of their lives. These circumstances varied from place to place on the Earth. The appendages were more

prominent in areas where human beings were more entangled in the earthly world. The human beings whose previous development made them most mature at the beginning of the Earth's physical evolution and who had therefore been able to experience contact with the element of fire right at the beginning, when the Earth had not yet condensed into air, were then able to develop their potential heads to the greatest degree of perfection. These were the human beings who were most harmonious in themselves.

Others had only been ready for contact with the element of fire once the Earth had already developed air. They were more dependent on outer circumstances than humans of the first type, who experienced the Spirits of Form clearly in the element of warmth; in earthly life, humans of the first type felt that they retained a memory of togetherness with these spirits in the body-free state. Human beings of the second type were less aware of this memory of the body-free state; they experienced their fellowship with the spiritual world primarily through the light impressions of the Spirits of Fire or archangels.

There was also a third type of human beings who were even more entangled in Earth existence. These were the ones who had only been able to come into contact with the element of fire after the Earth separated from the Sun and assimilated the watery element. Their feeling of belonging to the spiritual world, particularly at the beginning of the Earth phase, was especially weak. They experienced this connection only when human beings began to feel the effects of the archangels and especially those of the angels in their inner conceptual life. In contrast, at the beginning of the Earth period these human beings were full of active impulses for deeds that could be accomplished under earthly circumstances. Their appendage organs were especially strongly developed.

[73]     Before the Moon's separation from the Earth, the Moon forces in the Earth had led to increasing densification, and as a result human souls returning from the body-free state were no longer able to incarnate into some descendants of the nuclei left behind on the Earth by human beings. The forms of these descendants had become too solidified, and the Moon forces had made them too dissimilar to human forms to receive human souls. Under these circumstances, some human souls no longer found it possible to return to Earth. Only the strongest and most mature human souls felt up to the task of transforming growing earthly bodies so that they could blossom into human figures. And only some of the bodily descendants of human beings became the vehicles of earthly human beings. Others, because of their densified forms, were only capable of receiving souls that were on a lower level than human souls.

Meanwhile, some human souls were forced not to participate in the Earth phase of evolution at that time and had to embark on a different course. There were souls who found no place on Earth already at the time when the Sun separated from the Earth. They were removed to another planet to develop further. Under the guidance of cosmic beings, this planet detached itself from the general mass of the cosmos that was still united with the Earth at the beginning of its physical evolution. (The Sun had already disconnected itself.) This planet is the one whose physical expression is known to outer science as Jupiter. (The names of celestial bodies and planets are used here in exactly the same sense that a more ancient science spoke of them. The intended meaning becomes clear from the context. Just as the physical Earth is only the physical expression of an organism of spirit and soul, this is also the case with every other celestial body. And just as observers of the supersensible do not use the name "Earth" to mean merely the physical planet or the name "Sun" to mean merely the physical fixed star, they also have broad spiritual contexts in mind when they speak of "Jupiter," "Mars," and so on. Of course the shapes and functions of the celestial bodies have changed since the times described here. In a certain respect, even their locations in space have changed. We can only recognize the connection between our present-day planets and their ancestors if we are able to trace their evolution back into the far-distant past by means of supersensible cognition.)

The souls described above continued to develop on "Jupiter." Later, as the Earth continued to solidify, another dwelling place had to be created for other souls who had been able to inhabit these solidifying bodies for a while but were no longer able to do so when the solidification advanced too far. An appropriate place for their further evolution was created for them on "Mars." Even while the Earth was still united with the Sun and was incorporating its airy elements, it had become evident that some souls were not fit to participate in the Earth phase of evolution at that time because they were too strongly affected by the body's earthly configuration. Already at that point, they had to be withdrawn from the direct influence of the Sun forces; they needed the Sun to work on them from outside. A place was made for them to continue their evolution on "Saturn."

So we see that in the course of the Earth's evolution the number of human bodies decreased, while bodies appeared that were not capable of embodying human souls but only of receiving astral bodies of the sort that human physical and life bodies had received on the old Moon. Figures of this sort colonized the Earth as it grew too desolate for human beings. Ultimately, human souls would have had to leave the Earth entirely if the Moon's separation had not made it possible for any human figure still capable of receiving a human soul to remove its human nucleus from the influence of the Moon forces coming directly from the Earth, allowing it to mature within itself until it could be safely surrendered to these forces. As long as this nucleus was taking shape within the human being, it was under the influence of beings who had separated the Moon from the Earth (under the guidance of their mightiest member) in order to help the Earth's evolution over a critical point.

[74]     When the Earth had developed the element of air within itself, the astral beings described above were present on it, remnants from the old Moon who had fallen further behind in their evolution than the lowest human souls. They ensouled the figures that had already been abandoned by human beings before the Sun's detachment. These beings were the ancestors of the animal kingdom.

Over the course of time they developed especially those organs that were present in human beings only as appendages. Their astral bodies had to work on the physical and life bodies in the same way that humans had done on the old Moon. The animals that came about in this way had souls that could not dwell in individual animals. The being of each soul expanded to include all the descendants of one ancestral figure. Thus all animals that were essentially descended from a single figure had a common soul. A new animal soul was embodied only when specific influences made the descendants too different from the figure of their ancestor. In this sense, therefore, spiritual science can speak of a group soul belonging to the animal species (or genus).

Something similar happened at the time when Sun and   [75]
Earth separated. Forms emerged from the watery element that were no further along in their evolution than human beings had been prior to the old Moon phase. They could only receive the effects of an astral element if it influenced them from outside. This was only possible after the Sun had left the Earth. Each time the Earth's Sun period commenced, the Sun's astral element stimulated these figures to form their life bodies out of the Earth's etheric element. When the Sun turned away from the Earth, however, these life bodies dissolved into the general body of the Earth. Thus, as a result of cooperation between the Sun's astral element and the Earth's etheric element, the physical forms that were the ancestors of the present-day plant kingdom emerged from the waters.

*[76]*     On Earth, human beings became individualized soul beings. The astral bodies that the Spirits of Motion had poured into them on the Moon divided into sentient, mind, and consciousness souls on Earth. When their consciousness souls had advanced far enough to be able to shape bodies fit to receive them, the Spirits of Form endowed each of these with a spark of their own fire, kindling the I in each one. After this point, each time human beings left their physical bodies, they were in the spiritual world where they met the beings who had given them their physical bodies, their life bodies, and their astral bodies during the Saturn, Sun, and Moon phases of evolution and had brought them to the level of the Earth phase. The body-free state also underwent a change once the spark of the I had been kindled in earthly life. Prior to this point in evolution, human beings had no independence with regard to the spiritual world. They never felt like individual beings in this world, but more like organs in an exalted organism made up of beings superior to themselves. At this point, however, their experience of the I on Earth began to carry over into the spiritual world. From this point onward, human beings felt themselves to be independent entities in this world, but they also felt constantly connected to it. In the body-free state, they encountered a higher manifestation of the Spirits of Form whose earthly manifestation they had perceived on Earth through the spark of the I.

*[77]*     In conjunction with the Moon's separation from the Earth, body-free souls began to have certain experiences in the spiritual world. Reproducing human bodies that

were capable of receiving soul-individualities was possible on Earth only because some formative forces had been transferred from the Earth to the Moon. This brought human individualities into the domain of the Moon beings. Lingering echoes of earthly individuality were possible in the body-free state only because souls in this state also remained in the domain of the mighty spirits who had brought about the Moon's separation. This process developed in such a way that immediately after leaving their earthly bodies, souls could see the exalted Sun beings only in the reflected radiance of the Moon beings, as it were. Souls were able to see these exalted Sun beings directly only after having been sufficiently prepared by beholding this reflection.

The Earth's mineral kingdom also came about through [78] expulsion from the general evolution of humankind. Its structures are what remained solidified when the Moon separated from the Earth. The only portion of the soul element that felt drawn to these structures had remained at the Saturn stage and was therefore only suited to shaping physical forms.

All events mentioned here and in what follows took place over the course of vast periods of time. We cannot go into a discussion of the time frame here.

The processes described here present the Earth phase of [79] evolution from the external side. Considered from the spiritual side, it looks like this: The spiritual beings that pulled the Moon out of the Earth and united their own existence with it, thus becoming Earth-moon beings, brought about a specific configuration of the human organism through the forces they sent down to Earth from that cosmic body. Their effect was directed at the newly acquired human I and made itself felt in the interplay between this I and the astral body, ether body, and physical body. As a result, it became possible for human beings to consciously reflect the wisdom-filled configuration of the cosmos in themselves, to reproduce it as if in a mirror of knowledge.

Let's recall our earlier description of how human beings during the old Moon period achieved a certain degree of independent organization through the separation of the Sun at that time. They achieved a more independent level of consciousness than they could have derived directly from the Sun beings themselves. This free and independent consciousness, which reappeared during this particular period of the Earth phase of evolution as the legacy of the old Moon phase, could now be brought into harmony with the cosmos again through the influence of the above-mentioned Earth-moon beings, who shaped it into a copy of the cosmos. That is, this is what would have happened if no other influences had taken effect. In the absence of other influences, human beings would have become beings with a consciousness whose content reflects the world in the images of cognitive activity as a matter of natural necessity, rather than through their own independent intervention.

However, this is not what happened. Just at the time of the Moon's separation, certain spiritual beings intervened in human evolution. These beings had retained too much of their Moon character to be able to take part in the Sun's separation from the Earth, so they were also excluded from the activity of the beings who directed their effects down upon the Earth from the Earth's moon. These beings with their old Moon character had been condemned to an abnormal evolution on the Earth, so to speak. Something in their Moon character had rebelled against the Sun spirits during the old Moon phase of evolution. At that point, this was a blessing to human beings in that it led them to a free and independent state of consciousness. The consequences of these beings' idiosyncratic evolution during the Earth period meant that they then became the opponents of the beings who were working down from the Moon and trying to shape human consciousness so that its cognitive processes would inevitably reflect the cosmos. What had helped human beings achieve a higher level on the old Moon proved contrary to adaptations that had become possible through the Earth phase of evolution. The old Moon character of the opposing powers gave them the ability to work on the human astral body—specifically, in the sense of the descriptions above, to make it independent. They exercised this ability by giving the astral body a certain independence for the duration of the Earth phase, in contrast to the involuntary and unfree state of consciousness that would have been brought about by the Earth-moon beings.

It's difficult to find expressions that can be employed to describe how the above-mentioned spiritual beings affected human beings in this period of the primeval past. We must not imagine their effects to be like present-day natural influences, nor are they like the effect one person now has on another by using words to awaken inner forces of consciousness, allowing the other person to learn to understand something or to be stirred to moral or immoral actions. In this primeval period, the effect of these beings was not a natural influence but a spiritual one working in a spiritual way and transferring itself from the higher spiritual beings to human beings in accordance with the state of human consciousness at that time. We totally miss the essence of this if we imagine it as an effect of nature. But on the other hand, if we say that beings with old Moon character approached human beings in order to "seduce" them and win them over to their own goals, we are using a symbolic expression that holds good only as long as we remain aware of its symbolic character and are quite clear about the spiritual reality behind the symbol.

[80]     The effect of the spiritual beings who had remained at the Moon stage had two consequences for human beings. Because these beings aroused the possibility of independently regulating and mastering the images of consciousness in the astral body, human consciousness was stripped of the character of merely mirroring the cosmos. Human beings became masters of their knowledge. However, this control originated in the astral body, and so the I, which was actually superior to this body, became constantly dependent on it. This meant that in the future, human beings would be exposed to the ongoing influence of a lower element in their nature and would therefore be able to sink below the level specified for them by the Earth-moon beings in the course of cosmic events. In the

time that followed, the abnormally developed Moon beings exerted a continual influence on human nature. We can contrast these old Moon beings, who can be called the Luciferic spirits, to the others who worked down from the Earth's moon to shape human consciousness into a mirror of the cosmos but gave it no free will. They gave human beings the possibility of unfolding free activity in their consciousness, but at the same time they gave them the possibility of error and of evil.

As a result of these processes, human beings' relationship to the Sun spirits was different from the one predestined for them by the Earth-moon spirits, who strove to develop the mirror of human consciousness in such a way that the influence of the Sun spirits would have dominated all of human soul life. These processes were thwarted, and a conflict came about in human beings between the influence of the Sun spirits and that of the spirits who had developed abnormally during the Moon phase of evolution. This conflict made it impossible for human beings to recognize the physical effects of the Sun as such; these remained concealed behind earthly impressions of the outer world. The human astral element, filled with these impressions, was drawn into the domain of the I. From that point onward, this I, which would otherwise only have felt the spark of fire bestowed on it by the Spirits of Form and would have subordinated itself to their commands in everything pertaining to outer fire, worked on outer phenomena of warmth through the astral element injected into it, creating a bond of attraction between itself and the Earth's fire. This meant that human beings

*[81]*

became entangled in earthly matter to a greater degree than had been predestined for them. Previously, each human being had a physical body consisting primarily of fire, air, and water with only a trace of solid earth substance, but now the solid body grew denser. And whereas previously human beings had been more delicate in their organization and had hovered above solid ground in a sort of floating, swimming movement, they now had to descend from the surroundings of the Earth onto parts that were already more or less solidified.

[82]    The character of the spiritual influences described above—the fact that they were neither natural influences nor ones that work between human beings on a soul level—explains how they could have such physical effects. Soul effects that human beings have on each other do not work as deeply into the bodily element as the spiritual forces that we are considering here.

[83]    Because human beings were exposing themselves to the outer world's influences through their own mental images, which were subject to error, and because they were living their lives in accordance with desires and passions that they did not allow higher spiritual influences to control, the possibility of illness appeared. One particular effect of the Luciferic influence, however, was that human beings could no longer experience a given earthly lifetime as a continuation of body-free existence. From this point onward, they assimilated earthly impressions that could be experienced by the astral element injected into them. These impressions united with the forces that destroyed the physical body. Human beings experienced

this as a dying-off of their earthly life, and so death made its appearance, brought about by human nature itself. This points to a significant mystery of human nature—the human astral body's connection to disease and death.

At this point, conditions set in that specifically affected   *[84]* the human life body. It was incorporated into a relationship between the physical body and the astral body that freed it in some respects from the effect of abilities human beings had acquired through the Luciferic influence. One part of this life body remained outside of the physical body so that it could only be governed by higher beings and not by the human I. These higher beings were the ones that had left the Earth at the time of the Sun's separation in order to occupy a new dwelling place under the leadership of one of their exalted fellows. If this part of the life body had remained united with the astral body, human beings would have used previously acquired supersensible powers for self-serving purposes and would have extended the Luciferic influence to these powers. This means that they would have gradually freed themselves from the Sun beings, and the human I would have become a completely earthly I. After the death of the physical body, or even as soon as it started to deteriorate, this earthly I would have moved into another physical body, the body of a descendant, without first undergoing a connection to higher spiritual beings in a body-free state. In this way, human beings would indeed have become aware of the individual I, but only as an earthly I.

This was averted by the process that involved the life body and was brought about by the Earth-moon beings.

The actual individual I was released from the merely earthly I so that human beings identified only partially with this individual I during life on Earth, but at the same time felt the earthly I to be a continuation of the earthly I of their ancestors down through the generations. During life on Earth, each human soul felt the presence of a kind of group I extending back to its distant ancestors, and human beings felt themselves to be members of such groups. Only in the body-free state was the individual I able to feel that it was a single and separate being. However, the fact that the I was encumbered with the memory of earth consciousness, of the earthly I, interfered with this individualized state by dimming the view of the spiritual world, which was beginning to be veiled between death and birth in a way similar to how it was obscured to physical vision on Earth.

[85]    All the changes taking place in the spiritual world while human evolution was passing through these conditions were expressed physically in the gradual regulation of interrelationships between the Sun, the Moon, and the Earth, and in a broader sense those of other celestial bodies as well. We will emphasize a single consequence of these interrelationships—alternating days and nights. (The movements of celestial bodies are regulated by the beings that inhabit them. The movement of the Earth that caused day and night was brought about by the interrelationships of various spirits superior to human beings. The movement of the Moon came about in a similar way so that the Spirits of Form could work on the physical human body in the right way and in the right rhythm

through the Moon's revolution around the Earth after their separation.) At this point, the human I and astral body were working in the physical body and the life body by day. At night this working ceased, and the I and the astral body left the physical and ether bodies and were totally in the domain of the Sons of Life (angels), the Spirits of Fire (archangels), the Spirits of Personality, and the Spirits of Form. In addition to the Spirits of Form, the Spirits of Motion, the Spirits of Wisdom, and the thrones also included the physical and life bodies in their field of activity. In this way, damage to the human being from the effects of astral body's mistakes during the day could be corrected.

Now that the number of human bodies on Earth was increasing again, there was no longer any reason for them not to receive human souls. Because of how the forces of the Earth's moon were now working, the human bodies taking shape under their influence were fully fit to embody human souls, so the souls that had previously moved to Mars, Jupiter, and so forth were led back down to Earth. This meant that there was a soul available for each human descendant born over the course of the generations. This continued over a long period of time, so the movement of souls back to Earth corresponded to the increase in the number of human beings. At this time, souls undergoing earthly death and leaving their bodies retained a memory-like echo of earthly individuality during the body-free state. The effect of this memory was that these souls reincarnated whenever bodies appropriate for them were born again on Earth. As time went on,

*[86]*

human offspring came to include both people with souls that came from outside—those who were appearing on Earth for the first time since its very earliest stages—and others with souls reincarnating on Earth. During the period that followed, there were fewer and fewer of the young souls that were appearing for the first time and more and more reincarnated souls, but for a long time the human race did consist of these two types of human beings as a result of this state of affairs.

During this period, human beings felt more united with their ancestors through their common "group-I" during life on Earth, while the experience of the individual I was correspondingly stronger in the body-free state between death and a new birth. The souls coming from celestial space to enter human bodies were in a different situation from the ones who already had one or more Earth lives behind them. The new souls brought with them into physical life on Earth only the conditions they had been subjected to by the higher spiritual worlds and by their own experiences outside the earthly domain. The others had added conditions themselves during earlier lifetimes. At this point, the destiny of the new souls was determined by things that lay outside their new earthly circumstances, while the destiny of the reincarnated souls was determined also by what they themselves had done in earlier lifetimes under earthly circumstances. Along with reincarnation, individual human karma also appeared.

The fact that the human life body had been withdrawn from the astral body's influence, as described above, meant that the circumstances of reproduction did not fall within the scope of human consciousness but were subject to control by the spiritual world. When a soul was meant to descend into the earthly sphere, the impulse to reproduce appeared in Earth humans. To a certain extent, this whole process was shrouded in mysterious darkness as far as earthly consciousness was concerned.

But the consequences of this partial separation of the life body from the physical body also appeared within earthly life. The life body's abilities could be very much enhanced through the influence of the spirit. As far as human soul life was concerned, this was expressed in the exceptional degree to which memory developed. In the human beings of this time, independent logical thinking was only at its earliest beginning stages. In contrast, their capacity for memory was almost boundless. It was also outwardly apparent that human beings had a direct, feeling-like knowledge of the working forces in all living things. The forces of life and reproduction of the animal kingdom and especially those of the plant kingdom were at their disposal. For example, they could extract and apply what rouses a plant to growth, just as we now extract the forces of lifeless nature such as those lying dormant in anthracite and apply them to making machines move. (More details on this subject may be found in my booklet *Our Atlantean Ancestors.*[2])

2. This first appeared as a chapter in *"Aus der Akasha-Chronik"* ("From the Akashic Chronicle") in the magazine *Lucifer-Gnosis* (nos. 14–16, July–September, 1904), which Rudolf Steiner founded and edited. It is contained in *Cosmic Memory: Prehistory of Earth and Man*, Steinerbooks, Blauvelt, NY, 1990 (GA 11) pp. 38–41.

The inner soul life of human beings also changed in a great many ways because of the Luciferic influence. It would be possible to describe many types of feelings and sensations that resulted from this, but only a few of them will be mentioned here. Before this influence took effect, everything human souls shaped and did was carried out in the sense intended by higher spiritual beings. There was a predetermined plan for everything that was supposed to be done. To the extent that human consciousness had already developed, it could predict how things would have to develop in future according to this preconceived plan. This awareness of what the future would bring was lost as the veil of earthly perceptions was woven over the manifestations of higher spiritual beings. The actual forces of the Sun beings were concealed in these perceptions. From this point onward, the future became uncertain. Along with this uncertainty, the possibility of fear was implanted in the human soul. Fear is a direct consequence of error. But we also see how human beings, formerly involuntarily subject to certain forces, became independent of them under the Luciferic influence. From this point onward, they were capable of making decisions on their own. Freedom is the result of this influence, and fear and similar feelings are simply concomitants of human evolution toward freedom.

[87]    Human beings had fallen under the influence of earthly forces through the Luciferic powers. Seen spiritually, the appearance of fear indicates that still other powers were at work within the earthly forces. These other powers had become abnormal much earlier in the course of evo-

lution than the Luciferic powers. Human beings absorbed their influence along with the earthly forces. They contributed the character of fear to feelings whose effect would otherwise have been quite different. These beings can be called "Ahrimanic," or, in the Goethean sense, "Mephistophelian."

Although the Luciferic influence first made itself felt    [88] among the most advanced human beings, it soon spread to others as well. The descendants of advanced human beings intermingled with the less advanced ones described above, allowing the Luciferic force to reach them too. But the life bodies of souls returning from the planets could not be protected to the same extent as those belonging to the descendants of souls that had remained on Earth, who were protected by an exalted being whose leadership in the cosmos was in effect when the Sun separated from the Earth. In the domain under consideration here, this being appeared as the ruler of the Sun kingdom. The exalted beings who had attained sufficient maturity through their cosmic evolution moved with this being to a dwelling place on the Sun.

However, there were also beings who had not ascended to such heights at the time of the Sun's separation, and they had to look for different settings for their activity. These were the beings who brought about the withdrawal of Jupiter and the other planets from the common cosmic substance that was originally included in the physical organism of the Earth. Jupiter became the dwelling place of some of the beings who had not matured to the level of the Sun. The most advanced among them became the leader of Jupiter. Just as the leader of the Sun's evolution became the higher I that worked in the life body of the descendants of human beings who had remained on Earth, this Jupiter leader became the higher I that spread like a common consciousness through the human beings who had their origins in the interbreeding of Earth offspring with humans who first appeared on Earth during the period of the air element and then moved to Jupiter. In the sense of spiritual science, we can call these the "Jupiter humans." They were descended from beings who had still embodied human souls at a certain time in the distant past, but had not been mature enough to participate in the first contact with fire at the beginning of the Earth phase of evolution. These were souls that fell between the human and animal kingdoms.

There were also beings who had detached Mars from the common cosmic substance and made it their dwelling place under the leadership of their most advanced member. A third type of human beings fell under their influence. These were "Mars humans," who also came into existence through interbreeding. (This information sheds light on the origins of the planets of our solar system. All of the celestial bodies in this system came about because of the various stages of maturity of the beings inhabiting them. However, it is not possible to go into all the details of these cosmic divisions here, of course.)

Human beings who perceived the presence of the exalted Sun-being in their life bodies can be called "Sun humans." The being who lived in them as their higher I— only in the generations, of course, not in individuals—is one who was later given various names as human beings acquired conscious knowledge of him. To present-day human beings, the Christ's relationship to the cosmos is revealed in this being.

We can also distinguish "Saturn humans." The being who appears as their higher I had to leave the common cosmic substance along with his associates already before the Sun's separation from the Earth. In human beings of this type, both the life body and the physical body had portions that remained untouched by the Luciferic influence.

Now, in the case of the lower types of human beings, *[89]* the life body was too unprotected to be able to withstand the Luciferic influence. These human beings were capable of capriciously extending the free will of the I spark within themselves to the point where it caused mighty and destructive fires in their surroundings, resulting in a tremendous catastrophe on Earth. A large part of the inhabited Earth was destroyed by firestorms, and with it the human beings who had succumbed to error. Only a small number who had remained partially untouched by error were able to escape to an area of the Earth that had been protected from the corrupting influence of humans up to that point.

### Atlantis

The land in the area presently covered by the Atlantic Ocean proved to be an especially appropriate dwelling place for this new breed of humanity. The human beings who were most untouched by error retreated to this area.

Only scattered groups occupied other areas of the Earth. In the sense of spiritual science, the part of the Earth that once existed between present-day Europe, Africa, and America can be called "Atlantis."[3] (The relevant literature makes references of a sort to the pre-Atlantean stage of humanity's evolution that is described in the preceding section of this chapter. It is called the Lemurian age of the Earth, and it is followed by the Atlantean age. However, the time when the Moon forces had still not unleashed their primary effects can be called the Hyperborean age. This is preceded by still another age that coincides with the very earliest period in the physical evolution of the Earth. In the biblical tradition, this time prior to the intervention of the Luciferic beings is called the Age of Paradise, and human beings' descent to Earth and their entanglement in the world of the senses is known as the expulsion from Paradise.)

*[90]*     The Atlantis period of evolution was the period of the actual division of the human race into the Saturn, Sun, Jupiter, and Mars groups. This division had only been prefigured prior to that time. The separation of the waking and sleeping states also had specific consequences that became especially evident among humankind on Atlantis. The human astral body and the I spent the night in the domain of superior beings, up to and including the Spirits of Personality. Part of the life body was not bound up with the physical body, and because human beings were able to remain united with this part during sleep,

---

3. See Plato's *Timaeus*, 24-25e and Kritias 112e-121c.

they were able to have perceptions of the Sons of Life or angels and the Spirits of Fire or archangels. Because of the Luciferic influence, however, their perception of the Spirits of Personality remained unclear. But in addition to the angels and archangels, human beings in this state were able to perceive the beings who, as a result of having remained behind on Sun or Moon, were incapable of entering Earth existence and therefore had to remain in the world of soul and spirit. The Luciferic principle, however, made it possible for human beings to draw these beings into the domain of souls separated from their physical bodies. This meant that human beings came in contact with beings who had a very strong seductive effect on them and increased the soul's leanings toward error, especially with regard to misusing the forces of growth and reproduction, which had come under human control through the separation of the human physical and ether bodies.

During the Atlantean age, some individuals were [91] granted the possibility of being entangled in the world of the senses to the least possible extent. This transformed the Luciferic influence from an obstacle to human evolution into a means of further advancement that put these individuals in a position to develop their knowledge of earthly things earlier than would have been possible otherwise. In this process, these people attempted to eliminate error from their mental activity and to discover the original intentions of spiritual beings in the phenomena of the world. They kept themselves free of urges and desires of the astral body that turned only toward the world of the senses, and thus they became increasingly free of the astral body's errors. The conditions this brought about in them led them to perceive only with the part of the life body that was separate from the physical body, as described above. Under these conditions, the physical body's perceptive capacity was wiped out, so to speak, and the physical body itself seemed dead. Through their life bodies, these human beings then united completely with the domain of the Spirits of Form, who showed them how they were being led and guided by the exalted being who had assumed leadership during the separation of Sun and Earth and who was later to make human beings receptive to understanding the Christ. These individuals were initiates. However, because human individualities had entered the domain of the Moon beings, as described above, as a rule even these initiates could not be directly touched by the great Sun spirit, who could only be shown to them by the Moon spirits as if in a reflection. They saw only the Sun-being's reflected glory.

These individuals became leaders of the other human beings and were able to communicate to them the mysteries they had beheld. They attracted disciples whom they taught how to attain the state leading to initiation. Their knowledge, previously revealed through the Christ, could be acquired only by people who were "Sun humans" in the sense indicated earlier. They nurtured their mysterious knowledge and the practices that led to it in a special place we'll call the Christ oracle or Sun oracle—that is, "oracle" in the sense of a place where the intentions of spiritual beings are perceived. What is said here about the Christ will be misunderstood unless we consider the fact that supersensible knowledge necessarily sees the appearance of the Christ on Earth as an event that was foretold by those who were already aware of the meaning of the Earth's evolution prior to this event. It would be a mistake to assume that these initiates had a relationship to the Christ that would only be possible later, after His actual appearance on Earth. However, they were able to grasp in a prophetic way and make comprehensible to their disciples that anyone touched by the power of the Sun-being sees the Christ approaching the Earth.

Other oracles were called into being by the Saturn, *[92]* Mars, and Jupiter humans. The vision of the initiates of each group was directed upward only as far as the being who could be discerned as the corresponding higher I in the life bodies of the members of their group. This is how the wisdom of Saturn, Jupiter, and Mars acquired followers.

In addition to these methods of initiation, there were also methods for those who had absorbed too much of the Luciferic principle to allow as large a part of the life body to separate from the physical body as was the case in Sun humans. In these people, the astral body retained more of the life body in the physical body, and they were incapable of being brought to a prophetic revelation of the Christ through the above-mentioned conditions. Because of the Luciferic principle's greater influence on their astral bodies, they had to undergo more difficult preparations before being able, in a less body-free state than the others, to behold the other higher beings, though not the Christ. Among the beings they were able to behold, however, were certain ones who, although they had left the Earth when the Sun separated from it, were not yet at a level that would have permitted them to participate in the Sun's evolution for any length of time. After the Sun's separation from the Earth, these beings pulled Venus out of the Sun in order to make it their dwelling place. The being who became their leader also became the higher I of the group of initiates and their followers described above. Something similar happened with the leading spirit of Mercury with regard to humans of a different type. This is how the Venus and Mercury oracles came about.

Human beings of the particular type who had absorbed the most Luciferic influence were able to reach up only as far as the leader of the beings who had been the first to be expelled from the Sun's evolution. This being did not occupy a particular planet in cosmic space, but lived in the surroundings of the Earth itself, having reunited with it after returning from the Sun. This being manifested as the higher I of human beings who can be called followers of the Vulcan oracle. Their vision was directed more toward earthly phenomena than was the case with the other initiates, and they laid the first foundations for what later became the arts and sciences among human beings. In contrast, the Mercury initiates laid the basis for knowledge of more supersensible things, and the Venus initiates did this to an even greater extent. The fact that the Vulcan, Mercury, and Venus initiates received their knowledge more in the form of their own thoughts and ideas distinguished them from the Saturn, Jupiter, and Mars initiates, who received their mysteries more as a revelation from above and in a more finished state. The Christ initiates occupied the middle ground, receiving the ability to clothe their mysteries in human concepts along with their direct revelations. The Saturn, Jupiter, and Mars initiates had to express themselves in symbols to a greater extent, while the Christ, Venus, Mercury, and Vulcan initiates were more able to communicate through concepts.

What reached Atlantean humanity in this way happened indirectly, by way of the initiates. However, the rest of humankind also received special faculties as a result of the Luciferic principle, because the exalted cosmic beings transformed certain faculties that might otherwise have led to ruin into a blessing. One such faculty was speech. Human beings received it as a result of the densification into the physical, material nature and the separation of part of the life body from the physical body. [93]

During the time following the Moon's separation, human beings at first felt united with their physical ancestors through the "group I." But this common consciousness connecting descendants and ancestors was gradually lost over the course of the generations. Later descendants had an inner memory that no longer reached back to their earlier ancestors, but only to not very distant ones. People's memories of one or the other ancestor appeared only during contact with the spiritual world in their sleep-like states. They were then likely to feel at one with their ancestors. They believed these ancestors had reappeared in themselves. This was an erroneous idea of reincarnation that emerged primarily in the last part of the Atlantean age. The truth about reincarnation could only be experienced in the schools of the initiates. Only the initiates, who saw human souls in the body-free state passing from one incarnation to another, were able to communicate the truth about this to their disciples.

*[94]*    At the point in the distant past that we are talking about here, the human physical figure was still very different from how it is at present. To a great extent, it was still the expression of soul characteristics. Human beings still consisted of matter that was softer and more delicate than what they acquired later. What is solid today was then still soft, supple, and malleable. Human beings with more pronounced soul and spiritual elements were delicate, mobile, and expressive in their bodily structure, while those who were spiritually less developed had body forms that were coarse, immobile, and less malleable. Advancement on a soul level contracted the limbs and kept a person's stature small, while delayed soul development and entanglement in sensuality expressed itself in gigantic size. During their growth period, people's bodies took shape according to what was forming in their souls in a way that seems incredible or even fantastic to our modern way of looking at things. Moral depravity in a person's passions, drives, and instincts resulted in a gigantic increase in material substance.

Our present human physical form came about through contracting, densifying, and solidifying the Atlantean one. Prior to the Atlantean age, human beings were faithful copies of their soul character, but the causes that led to the post-Atlantean human form, which is solid and relatively independent of any soul qualities, were inherent in the processes of Atlantean evolution. (The animal kingdom on Earth became dense in its forms much earlier than human beings.) Under no circumstances can the laws currently governing the shaping of forms in the kingdoms of nature be extended to the distant past.

## The End of Atlantis

Toward the middle of the Atlantean age, a great disaster was gradually building up within humankind. The secrets of the initiates should have been carefully protected from individuals who had not prepared their astral bodies to receive this knowledge by cleansing them of error. When such people did acquire an insight into this hidden knowledge, into the laws through which higher beings guided the forces of nature, they used these laws for purposes that served their aberrant needs and passions. The danger became even greater when these people entered the domain of the inferior spiritual beings who could not participate in Earth's normal evolution and worked against it. These beings were constantly influencing human beings, arousing interests in them that actually worked contrary to human well-being.

At that time, human beings still had the ability to use the natural growth and reproductive forces of animals

[95]

and humans for their own purposes. Not only ordinary people but also some initiates succumbed to the temptations of the inferior spiritual beings and used these supersensible forces in the service of aims that ran counter to humanity's evolution. To carry this out, they chose associates who were not initiates and who used the mysteries of nature's supersensible workings exclusively for baser purposes. The consequence was great depravity among humankind. The evil spread further and further, and since the forces of growth and reproduction, when uprooted and applied out of context, have a mysterious connection to certain forces at work in air and water, these human actions released powerfully destructive natural forces. This led to the gradual destruction of the Atlantean region through catastrophes involving the Earth's air and water.

The Atlanteans—at least those who did not perish in the storms—were forced to emigrate. The storms were changing the entire face of the Earth. Europe, Asia, and Africa on one side and America on the other were gradually acquiring the shapes they have today. Hordes of emigrants headed for these lands. As far as our present situation is concerned, the most important migrations were the ones that moved eastward from Atlantis. Europe, Asia, and Africa were gradually settled by descendants of the Atlanteans. Various peoples differing in their degrees of both development and depravity took up residence there. In their midst marched the initiates, who guarded the mysteries of the oracles and established centers in various regions where the services of Jupiter,

Venus, and so on, were cultivated in both the good sense and the bad.

The betrayal of the Vulcan mysteries had an especially negative effect, because their followers' view was the most focused on earthly circumstances. This betrayal forced human beings to become dependent on spiritual beings whose prior development made them reject everything coming from the spiritual world that had evolved as a result of the Earth's separation from the Sun. As a result of this, these beings worked specifically in the human element that resulted from having sensory perceptions that drew a veil over the spiritual element. From this point onward, these beings acquired a great deal of influence over many of the Earth's human inhabitants. This influence first made itself felt in the fact that human beings were increasingly deprived of the feeling for the spiritual element.

Since the size, form, and flexibility of the human physical body were still determined by soul qualities to a very great extent during this period, the betrayal of the mysteries also came to light in corresponding changes in the human race. Amorphous human figures, grotesque in both size and shape, were created wherever human depravity was especially evident, wherever supersensible forces were placed in the service of baser drives, desires, and passions. Such figures, however, could not persist beyond the actual Atlantean period. They died out. Physically, post-Atlantean humankind developed from Atlantean ancestors whose bodily forms had already solidified in a way that did not allow them to succumb to soul forces that were contrary to nature.

There was a certain period in Atlantean evolution when the laws prevailing in and around the Earth resulted in conditions that forced human forms to solidify. Although the races of humanity that had already solidified before this period were able to continue reproducing for a long time, their bodies gradually grew so restricting for the souls incarnating into them that these races were forced to die out. In actual fact, some of these racial forms persisted into post-Atlantean times, and modified forms of the ones that remained sufficiently flexible continued to exist for a very long time. However, the ones among them that did remain flexible beyond this time tended to embody souls that had experienced the damaging influence of the betrayal of the mysteries to a very great extent. These forms were destined to die out quickly.

[96]     Thus, ever since the middle of the Atlantean age, beings had been present who exerted their influence in human evolution by making human beings live their way into the physical world of the senses in an unspiritual way. This went so far that instead of the true form of this world, people saw phantasmagoric delusions and illusions of all sorts. However, human beings were exposed not only to the Luciferic influence, but also to the influence of those other beings we spoke about earlier, whose leader can be called Ahriman. (This is the name that was given to this being later on during the Persian civilization. Mephistopheles is the same being.) Through this influence, human beings who had died fell into the hands of powers that made them appear like beings exclusively

inclined toward earthly, sensual circumstances. They were increasingly deprived of their free view into the processes of the spiritual world. They had to feel that they were in Ahriman's power and were excluded from the fellowship of the spiritual world to a certain extent.

One especially significant oracle had preserved the ancient service in the purest form amid the general decline. It was one of the Christ oracles, and for that reason was able to preserve not only the mystery of the Christ but also the mysteries of the other oracles, since revealing the most exalted Sun spirit also disclosed the leading spirits of Saturn, Jupiter, and so on. The initiates of this Sun oracle knew the secret of how to generate for this or that human being the types of life bodies that had been possessed by the best initiates of Jupiter, Mercury, and so on. With the means at their disposal, which cannot be discussed further here, they effectively perpetuated reproductions of the best life bodies of ancient initiates and implanted them later in suitable individuals. The Venus, Mercury, and Vulcan initiates made it possible for similar processes to take place with regard to astral bodies. *[97]*

At a certain point in time, the leading Christ initiate was isolated with a few associates who were only capable of receiving the secrets of the cosmos to a very limited extent, because they were naturally predisposed to having physical and life bodies with the least degree of separation between them. At that time, such individuals were the best ones to assure the further progress of humankind. Because they experienced less and less during the sleeping state, the spiritual world was increasingly closed to *[98]* them and they lacked all understanding of what had been revealed in ancient times when human beings occupied only life bodies rather than physical bodies. The individuals in the immediate surroundings of this leader of the Christ oracle were the most advanced with regard to reuniting the physical body with the portion of the life body that was formerly separate from it. This reunification was gradually being accomplished among human beings as a consequence of changes that had taken place in their Atlantean home and on Earth in general. Human physical and life bodies were coinciding to an ever greater extent.

As a result of this, human beings lost their previously boundless faculty of memory, and a life of thought began for them. The part of the life body that was united with the physical body transformed the physical brain into the actual instrument of thinking. Only after this did human beings actually experience the I within the physical body. Self-awareness awakened for the first time. To begin with, this was actually true of only a small percentage of human beings, primarily associates of the leader of the Christ oracle. The masses of human beings scattered over Europe, Asia, and Africa preserved the remnants of older states of consciousness to varying degrees and therefore experienced the supersensible world directly.

### Post-Atlantean Civilizations: Ancient India

The Christ initiate's associates were people of highly developed intellect, but of all the people living at that time, they had the least experience in the supersensible domain.

This initiate moved with them from the west to the east, to an area in central Asia, wanting to protect them as much as possible from contact with human beings of less advanced consciousness. He educated these associates of his, and more especially their descendants, in accordance with the mysteries that were revealed to him. Thus, he trained a whole host of human beings who took to heart impulses that were in harmony with the mysteries of the Christ initiation. From among them, he selected the seven best to receive life bodies and astral bodies that were reproductions of those of the seven greatest Atlantean initiates. In this way he educated one successor for each of the initiates of Christ, Saturn, Jupiter, and so on. These seven new initiates became the teachers and leaders of the human beings who had settled in the southern part of Asia, specifically in ancient India. Since these great teachers were actually endowed with reproductions of the life bodies of their spiritual ancestors, what was present in their astral bodies— namely the knowledge and understanding they had assimilated themselves—did not extend to what was revealed to them through their life bodies. If this revelation was to speak in them, they had to silence their own knowledge and understanding. When they did so, the exalted beings who had spoken to their spiritual ancestors also spoke through them and out of them. Except when such beings were speaking through them, these were simple people gifted with whatever degree of intellectual and emotional education they had acquired on their own.

At that time, India was occupied by human beings who had superbly preserved a living memory of the ancient   *[99]*

Atlantean state of soul that had permitted experience in the spiritual world. A large number of these people also possessed a very strong tendency of heart and mind to want to experience this supersensible world. Thanks to the wise guidance of destiny, the majority of people of this type, who came from the best portions of the Atlantean population, had migrated to southern Asia. In addition to this majority, others had immigrated at different times. The Christ initiate mentioned above appointed his seven greatest disciples to be the teachers of this association of human beings, to give their wisdom and their commandments to this group of people.

For many of these ancient Indians, very little preparation was required to enliven in them the barely extinguished faculties that led to observing the supersensible world, because a longing for this world was actually a fundamental mood of Indian souls. They felt that the original home of human beings was in this supersensible world, that they had been transplanted from this world to the world that can be provided by outer sensory perception and the sense-bound intellect. They felt that the supersensible world was the true one and that the sensory world was *maya*, an illusion of human perception. They strove by all possible means to open a view into the spiritual world. They were unable to develop any interest in the illusory world of the senses, or only to the extent that it proved to be a veil over the supersensible world. The power that the seven great teachers could exert on people like this was tremendous, and what they revealed made its way deep into Indian souls. And because the life bodies and astral bodies that had been passed down to them bestowed sublime powers on these teachers, they were able to have magical effects on their disciples. They did not actually teach, but their personalities acted upon those of others as if through magical powers. The civilization that came about in this way was completely imbued with supersensible wisdom.

What is contained in the Vedas, the books of Indian wisdom, is not the original form of the exalted wisdom fostered by these great teachers in ancient times, but only a feeble echo of it. Only supersensible sight can look back to the original unrecorded wisdom behind what was written. An especially prominent characteristic of this original wisdom is the harmony and accord that existed among the various oracles of Atlantean times. Each of the great teachers could divulge the wisdom of one of the oracles, and these various aspects of wisdom were in complete harmony, because the fundamental wisdom of the initiation that prophesied the coming of the Christ stood behind all of them. However, the teacher who was the spiritual successor of the Christ initiate did not present what this initiate himself, who had remained in the background of evolution, was capable of revealing. Initially, it was not possible for the Atlantean Christ initiate to pass on his high office to any post-Atlantean individual. In contrast to the Atlantean Christ initiate, who was able to completely transmute his perception of the Christ mystery into human concepts, the Indian Christ initiate was only capable of presenting a reflection of this mystery in signs and symbols, because his humanly acquired conceptual abilities could not encompass this mystery.

Nonetheless, the result of the union of the seven teachers was a panorama of wisdom expressing their knowledge of the supersensible world, only parts of which could have been promulgated in the old Atlantean oracle. This panorama revealed the exalted leadership of the cosmic world and quietly alluded to a great Sun spirit, the concealed being who was enthroned above the beings revealed by the seven teachers.

[100]     What the term "ancient Indians" means here is not what is usually understood by it. No outer documents have come down to us from the time we are speaking of here. The nation of people now known as Indians belongs to a historical stage of evolution that came about only much later than this. We must recognize the "Indian" culture described here as the prevailing culture of the first post-Atlantean epoch in Earth's history. After that came a second post-Atlantean epoch, when the "old Persian" civilization described later on in this book was the dominant culture. Still later, the Egypto-Chaldean civilization developed. It too will be described later. While the second and third post-Atlantean cultural epochs were taking shape, the "ancient" Indian culture also underwent its own second and third periods. The third period is what is commonly described as "ancient India." We must not confuse what is described here with the historical ancient India spoken of elsewhere.

[101]     What later led to separating people into castes was another characteristic of the culture of ancient India. The

inhabitants of India were descendants of Atlanteans who had belonged to different human types: the Saturn humans, Jupiter humans, and so on. Through supersensible teaching, they understood that a soul's position in a certain caste was not a matter of coincidence but a matter of self-determination. The fact that many people were able to stir up inner memories of their ancestors, as described earlier, made it easier for them to understand supersensible teachings in this way, but it also easily led to erroneous ideas about reincarnation. During the Atlantean age, the truth about reincarnation could only be acquired through the initiates. Similarly, during the earliest Indian times this truth could only be acquired through direct contact with the great teachers. In fact, the mistaken concept of reincarnation that was described earlier was extremely prevalent among the people who had spread out over Europe, Asia, and Africa after the sinking of Atlantis. And because initiates who had gone astray during the Atlantean evolutionary period had also shared this mystery with people who were not ready to receive it, people increasingly confused the correct idea with the false one. Many of these people still possessed a dusk-like kind of clairvoyance as a legacy of the Atlantean age. While the Atlanteans entered the domain of the spiritual world during sleep, their descendants experienced this spiritual world in abnormal intermediate states between waking and sleeping. In these states, images of an older time to which their ancestors had belonged appeared in them, so they considered themselves reincarnations of people who had lived in those times. Teachings about reincarnation that contradicted the initiates' genuine ideas on the subject spread over the entire Earth.

### Ancient Persian Civilization

[102]     Ongoing migrations from west to east since the beginning of the destruction of Atlantis led to the settlement of the Middle East by a group of people whose descendants went down in history as the Persians and their affiliated tribes. Supersensible cognition, however, must look much further back in time than the recorded history of these ethnic groups. We must first speak about the later Persians' very distant ancestors, who issued in the second great epoch of civilization in post-Atlantean evolution. It came about after the Indian civilization. The people of this second epoch had a different task from the Indians. Their inclinations and longings were not directed only at the supersensible world but were also adapted to the physical world of the senses. They began to love the Earth. They valued what human beings could conquer for themselves on Earth and what they could gain through earthly forces. Their accomplishments as a warrior nation and the methods they invented for extracting the Earth's treasures are related to this characteristic of their nature. There was no danger that their longing for the supersensible would turn them completely away from the "illusion" of the physical, sense-perceptible world. On the contrary, they were more in danger of completely losing their souls' connection to the supersensible world because of their appreciation for the physical world.

The character of the oracles that had been transplanted from Atlantis also reflected the general character of the people. Formerly, human beings had been able to acquire certain powers by experiencing the supersensible world. At this time, it was still possible to control some lower forms of these powers. Of these powers, there were those cultivated in the oracles that guided natural phenomena in ways that served personal human interests. At this time in the past, people still had great ability to control forces in nature that later retreated beyond the reach of human will. The guardians of the oracles, who had inner forces at their command that were related to fire and other elements, can be called "magi" or magicians. The legacy of supersensible knowledge and supersensible forces that they had preserved for themselves, although insignificant in comparison to what human beings had been capable of in the still more distant past, appeared in many different forms, ranging from the noblest arts whose only purpose was the welfare of human beings to the most reprehensible practices. The Luciferic principle prevailed in these people in a very particular way, connecting them with everything that could distract human beings from the intentions of the higher beings who would have been the sole guides of human progress if the Luciferic intervention had not happened. Even the members of this people who were still gifted with remnants of the ancient clairvoyant state, the intermediary state between waking and sleeping that was described earlier, felt very drawn to the inferior beings of the spiritual world. Because these people needed a spiritual impetus that would counteract this character trait in them, they were supplied with leadership by what had also been the source of ancient Indian spiritual life, namely the guardian of the mysteries of the Sun oracle.

[103]     For these people, the guardian of the Sun oracle provided a leader who can be known by the name that has come down to us in history as Zarathustra or Zoroaster, but it must be emphasized that the person we are speaking about here belonged to a much earlier age than the historical bearer of that name. However, we are dealing here with a question of spiritual science rather than one of outer historical research. Anyone who cannot help but think of a later age in connection with the bearer of the name Zarathustra can reconcile this with spiritual science by thinking of the historical Zarathustra as a successor to the first great Zarathustra, as someone who assumed his name and worked in the spirit of his teaching.

The impulse Zarathustra needed to provide for his people consisted in pointing out that the physical world of the senses is more than just the spiritless thing people encounter when they fall exclusively under the influence of the being of Lucifer. Human beings owe their personal independence and their sense of freedom to this being. However, Lucifer is supposed to work in them in harmony with the opposite spiritual principle. It was important for the ancient Persian people to remain alert to the presence of this other spiritual being. Their inclination toward the physical world of the senses threatened to make them merge completely with the Luciferic beings.

Now, the initiation Zarathustra had received through the guardian of the Sun oracle allowed him to receive the revelations of the exalted Sun beings. His training had led him to special states of consciousness in which he was able to behold the Sun beings' leader, who had taken the human ether body under his protection as described earlier. Zarathustra knew that this being was guiding the evolution of humanity but would only be able to descend to Earth from cosmic space at a certain point in the future. For this to happen, this being would have to be able to live in the astral body of a human being in the same way that he had been able to work in the human life body ever since the Luciferic intervention took place. For this to happen, a human being would have to appear who had transformed the astral body back to the stage it would have attained without Lucifer at a certain other point in time (in the middle of the Atlantean period of evolution). Without Lucifer, human beings would have reached this stage earlier, but without personal independence and without the possibility of freedom. From this point onward, however, human beings were to regain this high level in spite of these traits of their character.

In his clairvoyant states, Zarathustra saw that in humankind's future evolution, it would be possible for a specific person to have an astral body of this sort. He also knew that until this time arrived, it was impossible to find the spiritual forces of the Sun on Earth; they could be perceived, however, by means of supersensible sight in the domain of the spiritual portion of the Sun. He was able to behold these forces when he turned his clairvoyant gaze toward the Sun, and he brought his people tidings of the nature of these forces, which at that time could be found only in the spiritual world but would later descend to Earth. In this way he proclaimed the great Spirit of the Sun, the Spirit of Light (the Sun aura, Ahura-Mazdao or Ormuzd). For Zarathustra and his followers, this Spirit of Light became manifest as the spirit who turns his countenance toward human beings from the spiritual world and prepares the future within humankind. This spirit, who points to the Christ before His appearance on Earth, was the spirit Zarathustra proclaimed as the Spirit of Light.

In contrast, Zarathustra depicted Ahriman (*Angra Mainju*) as a power whose influence causes the human soul life to deteriorate when it surrenders to this influence in a one-sided way. This power is none other than the one described earlier as having achieved a particular dominion over the Earth ever since the betrayal of the Vulcan mysteries. Alongside his tidings of the Light God, Zarathustra also proclaimed the doctrine concerning spiritual beings that reveal themselves to the purified consciousness of the seer as the companions of the Spirit of Light. In stark contrast to these beings were the tempters who were appearing to the unpurified remnants of clairvoyance that had been retained from Atlantean times. It had to be made clear to the ancient Persians that the human soul, to the extent that it was inclined toward working and striving in the physical world of the senses, was the battleground in a conflict between the power of the Light God and that of His adversary. Zarathustra showed how human beings had to act so as not to be led into the abyss by this adversary, whose influence might be turned to good through the power of the Spirit of Light.

*Egypto-Chaldean Civilization*

A third post-Atlantean cultural epoch first developed   *[104]*
among the peoples who eventually migrated into the Middle East and North Africa—the Chaldeans, Babylonians, and Assyrians on the one hand and the Egyptians on the other. They developed a still different understanding of the physical, sense-perceptible world than the ancient Persians. In comparison to other ethnic groups, they had acquired much more of a spiritual predisposition for intellectual endowment, for the ability to think that had been developing since the later part of the Atlantean age. As we know, it was the task of post-Atlantean humanity to develop soul faculties that could be acquired through awakened powers of thought and feeling that are not directly stimulated by the spiritual world but come about when human beings observe the world of the senses, find their way into it, and adapt it. Conquering the physical world with these human faculties must be seen as the mission of post-Atlantean humanity.

This conquest proceeded step by step. In ancient India, although people's soul makeup already directed them toward the physical world, they still saw it as an illusion, and their spirits turned toward the supersensible world. In contrast, the people of ancient Persia began an attempt to conquer the physical world of the senses, but to a large extent they still did so with soul forces that were the legacy of a time when human beings could reach directly into the supersensible world. Among the peoples of the third cultural epoch, souls had lost much of their supersensible faculties. They had to investigate the spirit's manifestations in their sense-perceptible environment; their progress came from discovering and inventing the cultural means of advancement that this environment yielded. Humankind's sciences came about through deriving the laws of the spiritual world from the physical sense-world that concealed it; technology and the arts and their tools and methods came about through recognizing and applying the forces of this sensory world. The Chaldeans and Babylonians no longer saw the world of the senses as an illusion. They saw its natural kingdoms, its mountains and seas, its air and water, as manifestations of the spiritual deeds of powers standing behind this world, and they attempted to discover the laws governing these powers. To the Egyptians, the Earth was the setting for their work. In the state in which it was given to them, it was in need of being transformed through their own intellectual forces so that it would reflect the impact of human power.

The oracles that had been transplanted from Atlantis to Egypt originated primarily in the Atlantean Mercury oracle, but there were also others—the Venus oracles, for example. What these oracles cultivated in the Egyptian people became the seed of a new civilization. This seed originated with a great leader who had been trained in the Persian mysteries of Zarathustra and was a reincarnation of one of the disciples of the great Zarathustra himself. If we want to cite a historical name, we can call him Hermes. Through absorbing the Zarathustra mysteries, he was able to find the right way to guide the Egyptian people. In earthly life between birth and death, the Egyptians approached the physical world of the senses with their understanding in a way that allowed them to perceive the spiritual world behind the world of the senses only to a very limited extent; however, they were able to recognize spiritual laws in the sense-perceptible world. Therefore, they could not be taught about this spiritual world as one they would be able to enter during life on Earth, but it was possible to show them how human beings in the body-free state after death would commune with the world of spirits that left impressions in the sense-perceptible, physical domain during an earthly human lifetime. Hermes taught that to the extent human beings on Earth applied their forces to working in accordance with the intentions of spiritual powers, they make it possible for them to unite with these powers after death. In particular, those who had worked most diligently in this direction between birth and death would be united with Osiris, the exalted Sun-being.

The Chaldean-Babylonian aspect of this cultural stream was more emphatic than the Egyptian in directing the human mind toward the physical world of the senses. The laws of this world were investigated and spiritual archetypes were perceived in their sense-perceptible images. However, in many respects this people remained caught in the sense-perceptible element. Instead of a star's spirit, the star was pushed into the foreground, and the same was true of other spiritual beings and their earthly manifestations. Only their leaders acquired really deep knowledge of the laws of the supersensible world and of how these laws worked together with the sense world. The contrast between the knowledge of the initiates and the mistaken beliefs of the people was stronger here than anywhere else.

*Greco-Latin Civilization*

[105]     Conditions were quite different in the areas of southern Europe and Asia Minor where the fourth post-Atlantean cultural epoch blossomed. We can call this the Greco-Latin epoch. The migrants to these countries were the descendants of people from many different parts of the ancient world, and their oracles followed the traditions of many different Atlantean oracles. Some individuals possessed the legacy of ancient clairvoyance as a natural faculty; for others, it was relatively easy to acquire it through training. Particular centers not only preserved what had come down from the ancient initiates but also developed worthy successors, who in turn trained disciples who were capable of rising to high levels of spiritual perception. This meant that these ethnic groups possessed an inner urge to create a place in the sense-perceptible world that would express the spiritual element in its perfect form within the physical element.

This urge resulted in Greek art, among many other things. If we can understand the Greek temple through spiritual sight, we will recognize that in this marvelous work of art, human beings have transformed the sense-perceptible, material element in such a way that every part of it has become an expression of the spiritual element. The Greek temple is the "house of the spirit." In beholding its forms, we perceive what is otherwise seen only by seers. A temple of Zeus (or Jupiter) is fashioned in a way that presents our physical sense of sight with a worthy vessel for what the guardian of the Zeus or Jupiter initiation beheld with spiritual sight. This is true of all Greek art.

In mysterious ways, the wisdom of the initiates flowed into poets, artists, and thinkers. In the constructs of ancient Greek philosophy, the mysteries of the initiates are found in the form of concepts and ideas. The influence of the spiritual life, the mysteries of the Asian and African initiation centers, flowed into these people and their leaders. The great Indian teachers, the associates of Zarathustra, and the followers of Hermes had all trained disciples, and either these disciples or their successors then founded initiation centers in which the ancient wisdom came to life in a new form. These were the mysteries of antiquity, where disciples were prepared to reach states of consciousness that would allow them to attain perception of the spiritual world. (More will be said about these mysteries of antiquity in the final chapters of this book; other details are available in my book *Christianity as Mystical Fact.*[4]) Wisdom flowed out of these initiation centers to those who cultivated the mysteries of the spirit in Asia Minor, Greece, and Italy. (In the Greek-speaking world, the Orphic and Eleusinian mysteries developed into important initiation centers. The great teachings and methods of wisdom from earlier times worked on in the Pythagorean school of wisdom because Pythagoras had been initiated into the secrets of a variety of mysteries during his extensive travels.)

---

4. Steinerbooks, Blauvelt, NY, 1988.

### The Coming of the Christian Era

[106]    During the post-Atlantean period, human life between birth and death also had its effect on the post-death, body-free state. As human beings increasingly turned their interests toward the physical world of the senses, it became ever more possible for Ahriman to work his way into their souls during earthly life and then to retain this power beyond death. This danger had been very slight among the peoples of ancient India, because they experienced the physical world of the senses as an illusion during earthly life, thus extricating themselves from Ahriman's power after death. The danger was greater for the ancient Persians, who took an active interest in the physical world during the time between birth and death. They would have succumbed to Ahriman's enticements to a great extent if Zarathustra's teachings about the Light God had not impressed on them the fact that a world belonging to the Spirits of Light stands behind the physical world of the senses. To the extent that the souls of the people of this culture absorbed the world of ideas stimulated by Zarathustra, they were able to escape from Ahriman's clutches, not only during earthly life but also during life after death when they were preparing for a new earthly life. During life on Earth, Ahriman's power makes us see physical, sense-perceptible existence as the only one and thus blocks our view into the spiritual world. In the spiritual world, this power makes us completely isolated and focuses all our interests on ourselves. Human beings who are in Ahriman's power when they die are reborn as egoists.

At the present time, through spiritual science, we can   *[107]*
describe life between death and a new birth as it is when
the Ahrimanic influence has been overcome to a certain
extent. This is how the author of this book has described
it in other works and in the first chapters of this book, and
this is how it must be depicted in order to illustrate what
people can experience after death if they have acquired a
purely spiritual view of what is actually present. Whether
individuals experience this to a greater or to a lesser
degree depends on the extent of their victory over Ahriman's influence. We are drawing ever closer to being all
that we can be in the spiritual world. However, the fact
that other influences can restrict our possibilities must be
kept clearly in mind as we consider the course of human
evolution.

Among the Egyptian people, Hermes had made sure   *[108]*
that individuals prepared themselves during earthly life
for fellowship with the Spirit of Light. However, because
at that time the pattern of people's interests between birth
and death already permitted very little penetration of the
physical/sensory veil, their souls' spiritual gaze remained
clouded after death, and their perception of the world of
light remained faint. This veiling of the spiritual world
after death reached a peak among souls who entered the
body-free state from incarnations during the Greco-Latin
civilization. They had brought the cultivation of sensory,
physical existence to full flower, thus condemning themselves to a shadow existence after death. It was not empty
talk but a feeling for the truth that made a hero of that
age—inclined as he was toward the life of the senses—

say, "Rather a beggar on Earth than a king in the realm of shades."[5]

All this was still more pronounced among the Asiatic peoples, who instead of turning their gaze to spiritual archetypes had also made sensory representations the focus of their reverence and adoration. A large part of humanity was in this situation during the Greco-Latin cultural period. As we see, post-Atlantean humanity's mission of conquering the physical world of the senses necessarily led to estrangement from the spiritual world. The greatness of this age was therefore inevitably bound up with its decline.

In the mysteries, the human being's connection to the spiritual world was cultivated. In specific soul conditions, their initiates were able to receive revelations of this world. These initiates were the successors of the Atlantean guardians of the oracles, more or less. What had become veiled to others through the impact of Lucifer and Ahriman was disclosed to them. Lucifer veiled that aspect of the spiritual world that had streamed into people's astral bodies without any involvement on their part until the middle of the Atlantean age. If the life body had not been

---

5. The soul of Achilles, conjured up out of Hades by sacrifices to the dead, speaks to Odysseus:

> *Speak not wrongly of death, Lord Odysseus.*
> *I would much rather be a slave and a drudge in the fields,*
> *A pitiable man in search of his miserable food,*
> *Than a king down here in the realm of the dead.*

— Homer, *The Odyssey*, Song XI

partially separated from the physical body, people would have been able to experience this area of the spiritual world as an inner soul revelation. Because of Luciferic intervention, they could do so only during special states of soul; then a spiritual world appeared to them in astral array. In this way, superhuman beings revealed themselves, appearing as figures that consisted only of the higher members of the human makeup. These members bore astrally visible symbols of these beings' particular spiritual forces.

After Ahriman's intervention in the middle of the Atlantean age, another type of initiation was added to this one. Ahriman concealed all of that aspect of the spiritual world that would have appeared behind physical sense perceptions if this intervention had not taken place. Initiates owed the disclosure of this aspect to the fact that their souls had practiced all the faculties that human beings had acquired since that time, but to a far greater extent than was required to gain impressions of physical, sense-perceptible existence. Through this, the spiritual powers lying behind the forces of nature were revealed to these initiates, who were then able to speak about the spiritual beings behind the natural world. The creative powers of the forces at work in nature below the human level were disclosed to them. What had continued to work since the time of the Saturn, Sun, and old Moon phases of evolution, shaping the human physical, etheric, and astral bodies as well as the mineral, plant, and animal kingdoms, formed the content of one type of mystery. These were the mysteries Ahriman tried to conceal. What had led to the sentient, mind, and consciousness souls was revealed in mysteries of a second type.

However, there was one thing that the mysteries could only prophesy—namely, that in the course of time an individual would appear with an astral body in which consciousness of the Sun Spirit's world of light could come about through the life body, in spite of Lucifer and without any special states of soul. This individual's physical body would have to make it possible for Him to receive the revelations of the aspect of the spiritual world that Ahriman can conceal until the time of physical death. Physical death would be able to change nothing in this individual's life; that is, it would have no power over Him. In such an individual, the I would manifest in such a way that His complete spiritual life would be present simultaneously in physical life. This being is the bearer of the Spirit of Light to whom initiates lifted themselves up in one of two ways, by being led during special soul states either to the spirit of the superhuman element or to the essence of the powers of nature. Since the initiates of the mysteries predicted that such a human being would appear in the course of time, they were the prophets of the Christ.

[109]     An exceptional prophet, in this sense, arose among the Israelites, a people who had acquired Near Eastern ethnic characteristics through natural heredity and Egyptian teachings through education. This prophet was Moses. His soul had been so thoroughly influenced by initiation that in exceptional states of consciousness it received the revelation of the being who had formerly assumed the role of shaping human consciousness from the Moon in

the normal course of Earth's evolution. In thunder and lightning, Moses saw not only physical phenomena but also the manifestations of this spirit. However, his soul had also been worked on by mysteries of the other sort, so he had astral visions of the superhuman element becoming human through the I. Thus the being who was to come was disclosed to Moses from two directions as the highest form of the I.

With the appearance of the Christ, the great prototype *[110]* prepared for humanity by the exalted Sun-being appeared in human form. In certain respects, all mystery wisdom had to take on a new form at this point. Previously, this wisdom had existed only in order to make people capable of entering a state of soul in which they could perceive the domain of the Sun spirit *outside* of earthly evolution. From this point onward, mystery wisdom was given the task of making people able to recognize the Christ who had become human and to understand the natural and spiritual worlds out of this center of all wisdom.

At that moment in the life of Christ Jesus when His *[111]* astral body first contained everything that Lucifer's intervention can conceal, He began to appear as the teacher of humanity, and human evolution on Earth began to be implanted with the potential to take up the wisdom that will allow the gradual attainment of Earth's physical goal. And at the moment when the event of Golgotha took place, the other possibility, which can allow Ahriman's influence to be turned toward the good, was implanted in humanity. From this point onward, human beings can take with them into death that which frees them from isolation in the spiritual world. This event in Palestine stands in the center, not only of humankind's physical evolution, but also of that of the other worlds to which human beings belong. When the Mystery of Golgotha was accomplished, when the Christ had undergone death on the cross, He appeared in the world where souls lingered after death and set limits on Ahriman's power, illuminating the regions that the Greeks had called "the kingdom of shades" with a spiritual bolt of lightning that showed its inhabitants that light was meant to enter it again. What was accomplished on behalf of the physical world through the Mystery of Golgotha cast its light into the spiritual world.

Until this event, humankind's post-Atlantean evolution had been a time of ascent for the physical world of the senses, but also a time of decline for the spiritual world. Everything that flowed into the sensory world had its origins in what had already been present in the spiritual world since primeval times. But ever since the Christ event, people who lift themselves up to the Christ mystery are able to take what they have struggled to achieve in the sensory world with them into the spiritual world. From the spiritual world it then flows back into the earthly world of the senses through reincarnating human beings who bring with them what the Christ impulse has become for them in the spiritual world between death and a new birth.

[112]    What flowed into humanity's evolution through the appearance of the Christ worked within it like a seed that could only ripen gradually. Until now, only the very

smallest part of this profound new wisdom has flowed into physical existence, which is only at the very beginning of its Christian evolution. During the ages that have elapsed since the Christ's appearance, Christian evolution has always been able to disclose only as much of its inner essence as individuals and peoples were able to receive and absorb through their capacity for thought. This knowledge was first cast in a form that could be called a comprehensive ideal for life. As such, it opposed the forms of life that post-Atlantean humanity had developed.

Earlier in this book, the conditions prevailing in humanity's evolution since the repopulating of the Earth in Lemurian times were described. We saw that with regard to their souls, human beings may be traced back to various beings who came from other heavenly bodies and incarnated into the bodily descendants of the ancient Lemurians. The different races of human beings result from this fact. As a result of their karma, these reincarnated souls had widely diverging interests in life. As long as all of this was still in effect, the ideal of "universal humanity" could not exist. Humanity had its origins in a unity, but up to this point all of Earth's evolution led only to separation. The Christ concept supplied an ideal that counteracts all separation, because the forces of the exalted Sun-being who is the origin of each human I also lived in the human being who bore the name of Christ. The Israelites still experienced themselves first and foremost as an ethnic group; the individual was a member of that group. To begin with, the fact that the ideal human being dwells in Christ Jesus and is untouched by divisive circumstances was grasped only as a thought, and Christianity became the ideal of all-embracing fellowship. Above and beyond all special interests and relationships, the feeling arose that each person's inner I has the same origin. Alongside all of our earthly ancestors, the common father of all human beings appears: "I and the Father are one" [John 10:30].

*[113]*    In Europe, the fourth, fifth, and sixth centuries A.D. paved the way in Europe for a cultural epoch that began in the fifteenth century and is still going on today. This fifth post-Atlantean epoch was to gradually replace the fourth or Greco-Latin epoch. The ethnic groups who became the vehicle for this age after undergoing various migrations and destinies were descended from the Atlanteans who had been least touched by everything that had taken place in the four preceding cultural epochs. They had not moved into areas where these cultures took root, but had reproduced the cultures of Atlantis in their own way. There were many individuals among them who had retained the legacy of ancient dusklike clairvoyance—the condition we described as being halfway between waking and sleeping—to a great extent. These people knew the spiritual world as a matter of personal experience and were able to communicate what was going on in that world to their fellows. A whole world of tales about spiritual beings and spiritual events was built up. Our ethnic treasure troves of fairy tales and legends originally developed out of spiritual experiences of this sort, since the dusklike clairvoyance that many people

possessed persisted right down into the recent past. Others had lost their clairvoyance, but they developed their acquired abilities, which related to the physical world of the senses, according to feelings and sensations that were in harmony with these clairvoyant experiences.

Here, too, the Atlantean oracles had successors in the mystery centers that were everywhere. However, the secrets of initiation that developed in these mysteries were primarily ones leading to revelation of the spiritual world that Ahriman had blocked; that is, they disclosed the spiritual powers behind the forces of nature. The various European mythologies contain the remnants of what the initiates of these mysteries could disclose to people. However, these mythologies also include the other secret, although in a less perfect form than the southern and eastern mysteries. Superhuman beings were also known in Europe, but people saw them as constantly doing battle with Lucifer's companions. They did in fact proclaim the God of Light, but in such a form that it was impossible to tell whether he would succeed in overcoming Lucifer. However, the figure of the Christ who was to come also illuminated these mysteries. It was prophesied that His kingdom would succeed that of the other god of light. (All the legends about the twilight of the gods and the like have their origin in this European mystery-knowledge.)

These influences led to a split within the human soul during the fifth cultural epoch. This split still exists today and is evident in many different phenomena of life. Human souls did not retain enough of an inclination toward the spirit from ancient times to be able to preserve the connection between the spiritual and sense-perceptible worlds. This connection was retained only as a matter of feeling and sensation, but not as a direct perception of the spiritual world. In contrast, human beings were paying more and more attention to perceiving and controlling the sense-perceptible world. The intellectual forces that awakened in the last Atlantean period—all those forces in the human being that use the physical brain as their instrument—were developed in the context of knowing and controlling the sense world. Two worlds developed within the human breast, so to speak. One of them is turned toward physical, sense-perceptible existence, while the other is receptive to the revelation of the spiritual element in order to penetrate it by means of feeling and sensation but without direct perception.

This split in the soul was already prefigured when the teaching of the Christ flowed into these areas of Europe. People took this message of the spirit to heart, imbuing their sensation and feeling with it, but were not able to build a bridge between it and what their sense-oriented intellect was exploring in physical, sense-perceptible existence. The divergence we recognize today between outer science and inner spiritual knowledge is simply a consequence of this state of affairs. The Christian mysticism of Eckhart, Tauler, and others was the result of imbuing feeling and sensation with Christianity,[6] while the exclusively sense-oriented natural sciences and their

---

6. Master Eckhart (1260–1327), and Johannes Tauler (1300–1361), Dominican monks and mystics.

effects on our life are the results of the soul's other predisposition. We owe all our accomplishments in the domain of outer material culture entirely to this separation of our capacities. Through our one-sided turning toward physical life, the faculties that use the brain as their instrument were enhanced to the point where modern science, technology, and so on, became possible. This material culture could originate only among the peoples of Europe, because they were the Atlantean descendants who developed their inclination toward the physical, sense-perceptible world into specific faculties only once that inclination had already achieved a certain maturity. They had previously allowed it to remain dormant, subsisting on their legacy of Atlantean clairvoyance and on the communications of their initiates. Whereas outwardly the spiritual culture was devoted wholly to these influences, their sense for controlling the material world was gradually maturing.

At present, however, the sixth post-Atlantean cultural   *[114]* epoch is already dawning, for whenever something is meant to come about at some future point in humanity's evolution, it gradually matures during the preceding age. It is already possible now to begin to discover the thread that will bind the two sides of the human breast—material culture and life in the spiritual world—together again. On the one hand, this requires that we understand the results of spiritual perception; on the other, that we recognize the manifestations of the spirit in our observations of and experiences in the world of the senses. The sixth cultural epoch will fully develop the harmony between these two things.

This brings our narrative to the point where we can shift from looking at the past to looking at the future. However, we will do better to consider the process of initiation and knowledge of the higher world first, and then follow this up by briefly presenting a view of the future, to the extent that this is possible within the scope of this book.

# CHAPTER 5

# KNOWLEDGE OF HIGHER WORLDS —INITIATION

Between birth and death, human beings at our present  *[1]*
stage of evolution experience three states of consciousness during ordinary life: waking, sleeping, and the state
between them, dreaming. Dreaming will be considered
briefly later on in this book, but here let's look at life in
its two main alternating states, waking and sleeping.

We achieve knowledge of higher worlds by acquiring a
third state in addition to sleeping and waking. When we
are awake, our souls are devoted to sensory impressions
and the mental images they stimulate. When we sleep,
these sensory impressions are silenced, but our souls also
lose consciousness; the experiences of the day sink down
into a sea of unconsciousness. Now let's imagine that the
sleeping soul is capable of becoming conscious in spite of
the fact that all sensory perceptions are excluded, as is
otherwise the case in deep sleep, and that not even a memory of the day's experiences is present. In that case, would
the soul find itself in a state of nothingness? Would it be
unable to have any experiences at all?

It is only possible to answer these questions if we can actually induce a state of consciousness similar to this, if the soul is actually able to experience something even in the total absence of current and remembered sensory impressions. In this case, although the soul would seem asleep with regard to the ordinary outer world, it would not be asleep but would confront a real world just as it does in the waking state. Now, this state of consciousness can be induced if we bring about the soul experiences made possible by spiritual science. Everything spiritual science tells us about the worlds lying beyond the world of the senses—including the information given in preceding chapters of this book—has been investigated by means of this state of consciousness. This chapter will discuss, to the extent possible in this book, the methods used to create the state of consciousness needed for this research.

*[2]*    This state of consciousness is similar to sleep in only one respect, namely that it puts an end to all outer sense impressions and eliminates all the thoughts stimulated by these impressions. But although during sleep the soul does not have the strength to experience anything consciously, this other state of consciousness provides this strength, awakening a perceptive ability that only sensory impressions can arouse during our ordinary life. The soul's awakening to this higher state of consciousness can be called *initiation*.

*[3]*    Initiation methods lead us out of our usual state of waking consciousness into a soul activity that makes use of spiritual instruments of observation. These instruments are already present in the soul in a seminal state, but they

need to be developed. Now it's possible for people to discover at a certain point in the course of their lives that these higher instruments have developed spontaneously, without any special preparation, and that a certain involuntary self-awakening has taken place. As a result, these people find that their essential nature is totally transformed and that their soul experiences are infinitely enriched. They also find that no knowledge of the sensory world can possibly provide the bliss, soul satisfaction, and inner warmth that they now experience as a result of what is being disclosed to understanding that is not accessible to the physical eye. Strength and certainty will flow into their will from a spiritual world.

Such instances of self-initiation do occur, but they should not tempt us to believe that the only right thing to do is to wait for this to happen and do nothing to bring initiation about through appropriate training. Since self-initiation can come about without observing rules of any sort, it is not necessary to talk about it here, but what will be described is how training can develop the seminal organs of perception lying dormant in the soul. People who feel no particular urge to do something for the sake of their own development may easily say that human life stands under the guidance of spiritual powers and that instead of intervening in this guidance, we should patiently await the moment when these powers find it right to disclose another world to our souls. These people may well feel that there is a certain presumptuousness or unjustified desire in wanting to interfere with wise spiritual guidance. People who think like this will change their minds only when one particular thought makes a strong enough impression on them. This thought is: "This wise guidance has given me certain faculties, not so that they will remain unused, but so that I can put them to use. The wisdom in this guidance lies in the fact that it has planted the seeds of a higher state of consciousness in me. I understand this guidance only if I feel that human beings have an obligation to reveal everything their own spiritual powers can possibly reveal." If this thought has made a strong enough impression on the soul, then the above-mentioned doubts about training for a higher state of consciousness will disappear.

[4]     However, another doubt can still arise about this training. We might say, "Developing inner soul faculties constitutes an intervention in an individual's hidden holiest of holies and involves a certain transformation of that person's entire nature. It is inherently impossible for us to independently conceive of the means for bringing about such a transformation, because only those who have personally experienced reaching a higher world can know how to do it. But if we turn to a person like this, we permit that person to have an influence on our own soul's hidden holiest of holies." Even having methods for bringing about a higher state of consciousness presented in book form would not be particularly reassuring to people who think like this, because the point is not whether we receive this information as an oral communication or learn about these methods from someone who knows about them and presents them in a book.

There are indeed people who are knowledgeable about the rules for developing spiritual organs of perception but subscribe to the view that these rules should not be entrusted to a book. In general, these people also consider it impermissible to communicate certain truths having to do with the spiritual world. Given the present stage of humankind's evolution, however, this view must be considered outdated in a certain way. It is true that we can go only so far in communicating the rules in question, but the information that can be provided leads far enough so that those who apply it to their own souls will reach a point in the development of their knowledge where they will then be able to discover the rest of the way. Only personal previous experience on the path to spiritual knowledge can give us the right idea about how this path then leads on.

All these facts can give rise to doubts about the path to spiritual knowledge, but these doubts disappear when we consider the nature of the course of development indicated by the training that is appropriate to our times. This is the path that will be discussed here. Other methods of training will be mentioned only briefly.

The training that will be discussed here will provide   *[5]* those who have the will to develop their higher faculties with the means for beginning to transform their souls. There is no question of dubious intervention in the student's inner nature unless the teacher attempts to bring about this transformation through methods that elude the student's consciousness, and no instruction in spiritual development that is appropriate for our times makes use of methods like that. Appropriate instruction does not make the student into an unconscious instrument; it supplies rules of conduct which the student then implements.

When the occasion arises, the reason for laying down some particular rule will not be withheld. People searching for spiritual development do not need to receive and apply these rules as a matter of blind faith. In fact, blind faith is totally out of place in this area.

If we have not yet begun spiritual training ourselves but have considered the nature of the human soul simply as it reveals itself to our ordinary self-observation, we can ask ourselves after receiving the recommended rules of spiritual training: How can these rules affect our soul life? Even without any training, we can answer this question adequately by applying our healthy common sense in an unbiased way. We can get the right idea of how these rules work even before we subject ourselves to them, although only training itself allows us to actually experience how they work. Even then, our experience will always be accompanied by understanding only if sound judgment accompanies each step we take. In this day and age, any true science of the spirit will provide only rules that can stand up to the scrutiny of sound judgment. If we are ready and willing to undertake only this kind of training and do not permit any bias to drive us into blind faith, all our doubts will disappear. We will not be disturbed by any objections that can be raised about an appropriate training in attaining a higher state of consciousness.

[6]     This training is not superfluous even for those whose inner maturity can eventually lead to self-awakening of their spiritual organs of perception. On the contrary, it is especially suitable for them, because people like this almost invariably have to make many roundabout, useless

detours before self-initiation takes place. Training spares them these detours and leads them forward on a straight path. Self-initiation is a result of having achieved the appropriate degree of maturity during preceding lifetimes. It can very easily happen that a soul rejects training out of a certain dim sense of its own maturity, since this feeling can create a certain arrogance that prevents the person from having confidence in a true spiritual training. It is also possible for a certain level of soul development to remain concealed and appear only at a certain age. In such cases, training can be exactly the right way to make it appear, but if the person in question remains closed to the possibility of training, it may well be that his or her ability will remain concealed during the present lifetime and will appear again only during some subsequent life.

It is important to avoid certain obvious misunderstandings with regard to the training in supersensible knowledge that is intended here. One such misunderstanding can arise from thinking that this training intends to make its students into different beings with regard to how they lead their entire lives. But this is not a question of giving people general instructions on how to conduct their lives, it's a question of telling them about soul practices they can carry out in order to learn to observe the supersensible element. These practices have no direct influence on the parts of their lives that lie outside of supersensible observation. People acquire the gift of supersensible observation *in addition to* these other parts of their lives. This perceptive activity is just as separate from life's ordinary functions as the waking state is from sleep. One state cannot interfere

*[7]*

with the other in the least. Wanting to have impressions of the supersensible interspersed in the course of life's ordinary events would be like dealing with constant, unhealthy interruptions to your sleep when you are ill. The student must be able to induce the state of observing supersensible reality through an act of free will.

Indirectly, however, supersensible training is related to certain standards of conduct inasmuch as insight into the supersensible is either impossible or harmful without a certain ethical attitude toward life. For this reason, much of what leads to supersensible observation is also a means of ennobling how we lead our lives. On the other hand, insight into the supersensible world allows us to recognize higher moral impulses that also apply to the physical world of the senses. Certain moral necessities can only be recognized from the supersensible world.

A second misunderstanding consists in believing that soul practices leading to supersensible cognition might involve changes in the physical body's structure or functioning. On the contrary, these practices have nothing at all to do with anything that is any business of physiology's, or of any other branch of natural science, for that matter. They are purely spiritual soul-processes that are as far removed from anything physical as healthy thinking and perception are. What happens in the soul as a result of such practices is no different in character from what happens during healthy thinking or conclusion-forming. The processes involved in a real training in supersensible knowledge have just as much or little to do with the body as healthy thinking does, and anything that relates to the human being in any other way is a distortion of true spiritual training rather than the real thing. The presentation that follows is to be taken in the spirit of what has been said here. If supersensible training seems to require things that would make a person into something else, this is simply because supersensible cognition proceeds from a person's entire soul. In actual fact, it is simply a question of instruction in practices that make it possible for the soul to bring about moments in its life when it can observe the supersensible.

. . . . . . . .

It is only possible to rise to a state of supersensible con-   *[8]*
sciousness from ordinary waking consciousness, the state the soul lives in prior to its ascent. Training provides the soul with methods that will lead it out of the ordinary waking state. Among the first methods provided by the training we are discussing here are some that can still be described as functions of ordinary waking consciousness. The most important of these consist of silent activities of the soul. The soul is meant to devote itself to certain specific mental images that have the intrinsic power to awaken certain hidden faculties in the human soul. Such mental images are different from those of our daily waking life, whose purpose is to depict outer things—the more truly they do this, the truer they themselves are, and it is part of their essential nature to be "true" in this sense. This is not the purpose of the mental images the soul concentrates on when its goal is spiritual training. These images are not structured so as to reproduce anything

external, but to have an awakening effect on the soul. The best thought pictures for this purpose are *symbolic* ones, but others can be used also. The content of these mental images is not the point; the point is that the soul devotes all its energies to having nothing in its consciousness other than the mental image in question.

In our everyday soul life, the soul's energies are divided among many different things and our mental images shift rapidly. In spiritual training, however, the point is to concentrate the soul's entire activity on a single mental image that is freely chosen as a focus for consciousness. For this reason, symbolic images are better than ones that represent outer objects or processes and have a point of contact with the outer world, since these do not force the soul to rely on itself to the same extent as it does with symbols that it creates out of its own energy. It's not important *what* is imagined, but only that the process of visualizing the image frees the soul from dependence on anything physical.

*[9]*    By calling to mind the concept of *memory*, we can begin to grasp what it means to immerse ourselves in a visualized image. For example, if we look at a tree and then turn away from it so that we can no longer see it, we can reawaken the mental image of the tree out of our memory. The mental image we have of a tree when it is not actually present before our eyes is the *memory* of the tree. Now let's imagine that we retain this memory in our soul; we allow the soul to rest on this memory image and attempt to exclude all other images. Then the soul is *immersed in* the memory image of the tree. But although

the soul is immersed in a mental image, this image is a copy of something perceived by our senses. However, if we attempt the same thing with an image that we insert into our consciousness through an act of free will, we will gradually be able to achieve the necessary effect.

We will illustrate this with a single example of con-   *[10]* templating or meditating on a symbolic mental image. First, this mental image must be built up in the soul. I can do this as follows: I imagine a plant taking root in the ground, sprouting one leaf after another, and continuing to develop up to the point of flowering. Then I imagine a human being alongside this plant. In my soul, I bring to life the thought that this human being has qualities and abilities that can be called more perfect than those of the plant. I think about how human beings are able to move around in response to their feelings and intentions, while plants are attached to the ground. But then I also notice that although human beings are certainly more perfect than plants, they also have characteristics that we cannot perceive in plants, characteristics whose absence can actually make plants seem more perfect than humans. Human beings are filled with desires and passions which their actions obey, and certain errors result from these drives and passions. In contrast, I see how plants obey the pure laws of growth as they develop one leaf after another and open their flowers without passion to the chaste rays of the Sun. I can say that human beings have an advantage over plants with regard to a certain type of perfection, but that the price they have paid for this per-fection is to allow urges, desires, and passions to enter their nature alongside the forces of the plants that seem so pure to me.

Next I visualize the green sap flowing through the plant and imagine this as an expression of the pure, passionless laws of growth. Then I visualize the red blood flowing through human arteries and imagine it as an expression of urges, desires, and passions. I allow all this to arise in my soul as a vivid thought. Then I think about how human beings are capable of development, how they can use the higher soul faculties to cleanse and purify their urges and passions. I think about how this destroys a baser element in these urges and passions, which are then reborn on a higher level. The blood may then be imagined as the expression of these cleansed and purified urges and passions. For example, in the spirit I see a rose and say: In the red sap of the rose blossom I see the color of the plant's green sap transformed into red, and the red rose, like the green leaf, obeys the pure, passionless laws of growth. Let the red of the rose symbolize the blood that is an expression of purified urges and passions. They have been stripped of their baser element and are now similar in purity to the forces that are active in the red rose.

I now try not only to assimilate these thoughts with my intellect, but also to bring them to life in my feeling. I can have a blissful sensation when I imagine the growing plant's purity and absence of passion; I can generate a feeling in myself for the price human beings must pay for greater perfection by acquiring urges and desires. This can transform my earlier bliss into a serious feeling. Next, a feeling of liberating happiness can stir in me as I devote myself to the thought of the red blood that can become the vehicle of inwardly pure experiences, just like the red sap of the rose blossom.

It is important not to unfeelingly confront the thoughts [11] that serve to build up a symbolic mental image such as this. After having basked in these thoughts and feelings, we transform them into this symbolic image: We imagine a black cross. Let this be the symbol of the baser element that has been eliminated from our urges and passions. We imagine seven radiant red roses arranged in a circle where the two beams of the cross intersect. Let these be the symbol of the blood that is an expression of cleansed, purified passions and urges.[1] This symbolic image must now be called up before our mind's eye in the way described earlier with regard to a memory image. A symbolic mental image such as this has the power to awaken our souls when we inwardly immerse ourselves in it and devote ourselves to it. We must try to exclude all other mental images while we are immersed in this one. We must allow only this symbol to linger before our mind's eye in the spirit, and it must be as vivid as possible.

---

1. The point here is not the extent to which any particular natural scientific view can or cannot find these thoughts justifiable. The point is to develop thoughts about plants and human beings that can be acquired by means of simple, direct observation without any theory whatsoever. These thoughts do have a value alongside other, more theoretical ideas (which are no less valuable in other respects) about things in the outer world. In this case, the purpose of these thoughts is not to present facts in a scientific way, but to build up a symbol that proves effective on a soul level, regardless of whatever objections may occur to one or the other individual as it is being built up.—R. STEINER.

It is not without significance that this symbol was not immediately proffered as a soul-awakening image but was first built up by means of specific ideas about plants and human beings, because the effectiveness of a symbol like this depends on its being put together in this way before it is used for meditation. If we imagine it without first having gone through this buildup in our own souls, the symbol remains cold and is much less effective than if it has received its soul-illuminating power through this preparation. During meditation, however, we should not summon up all of these preparatory thoughts but should only allow the image to linger vividly before us in the spirit while permitting the *feeling* we had as a result of these preparatory thoughts to resonate. In this way, the symbol becomes a token of this experience of feeling, and its effectiveness is due to the fact that the soul dwells on this experience. The longer we can dwell on it without a different and disruptive image intervening, the more effective the whole process will be. However, outside of the time we set aside for actual meditation, it is a good idea to frequently repeat the process of building up the image through thoughts and feelings of the type described above, so that the feeling doesn't fade away. The more patience we have in renewing it, the more significant the image becomes for our souls. (Additional examples of methods of meditation are explained in my book *How to Know Higher Worlds*.[2] Described there are

---

2. *How to Know Higher Worlds: A Modern Path of Initiation,* Anthroposophic Press, Hudson, NY, 1994.

meditations on becoming and dying in plants, the creative forces lying dormant in seeds, the forms of crystals, and so on, which are especially effective. The intent here was to use a single example to demonstrate the nature of meditation.)

A symbol such as the one described here is not a copy of any outer thing or being that nature has produced, but this very fact gives it the power to awaken certain faculties that are strictly soul-like in character. However, an objection could be raised to this. Someone might say, "It's true that the symbol as a whole is not present in nature, but all its details have been borrowed from nature: the black color, the roses, and so on. All these things are perceived by the senses." Anyone who is bothered by this objection should consider the fact that the process of reproducing the sense perceptions is not what leads to awakening our higher soul faculties, but that this is brought about solely through how these details are combined, and the combination itself does not depict anything that is present in the world of the senses.

This symbol was intended to illustrate the process of *[12]* effective meditation. In spiritual training, any number of images of this sort could be used, and they could be built up in many different ways. Certain sentences, phrases, or single words may also be assigned as subjects for meditation. The goal of all of these methods of meditation, however, is to tear the soul away from sensory perception and to rouse it to activity in which physical sense impressions are meaningless and the development of dormant inner soul faculties becomes the essential thing.

It is also possible to meditate only on feelings, sensations, and so on, and such meditations prove to be especially effective. Let's take the feeling of joy, for example. In the normal course of our lives, our souls may experience joy when an outer stimulus for it is present. A soul with healthy feelings who sees a person doing something out of the goodness of his or her heart will experience satisfaction and joy. But this soul can then proceed to think about an action of this sort, saying "When something is done out of the goodness of someone's heart, the person in question is acting not in his or her own interest but in the interest of fellow human beings. Such an action may be called morally good." The meditating soul, however, can free itself completely from its mental image of the individual case in the outer world that has given it joy or satisfaction, and it can then form a comprehensive idea of goodheartedness. Perhaps it thinks of how goodheartedness comes about when one soul absorbs another's interest and makes it its own. The meditating soul can then feel joy in this moral idea of goodheartedness. This joy is not due to any process in the sensory world; it is joy in an *idea* as such. If we attempt to keep such joy alive in the soul for a certain length of time, we are meditating on a feeling, a sensation. What then becomes effective in arousing our inner soul faculties is not the idea itself, but rather the ongoing influence of a feeling within the soul that has not been stimulated by a mere individual outer impression.

Since supersensible knowledge is able to delve more deeply into the essence of things than our ordinary thinking, meditating on feelings derived from supersensible experience is much more effective in developing soul faculties. As necessary as this may be for higher levels of training, we must be aware that we can go quite far simply through energetic meditation on feelings and sensations of the sort typified by the meditation on goodheartedness.

Since people differ in their essential character, different training methods will be effective for different individuals. With regard to how long meditation should last, we must keep in mind that the calmer and more deliberate this meditation can become, the stronger its effect will be. However, any excesses in this direction should be avoided. The exercises themselves teach us a certain inner discretion and can show us the limits to observe in this regard.

As a rule, such meditation exercises will have to be carried out for a long time before the person doing them is able to perceive their results. Patience and persistence are absolute prerequisites of spiritual training. People who do not summon up both of these attitudes, who do not calmly continue to do their exercises with patience and persistence forming a constant underlying mood in their souls, will not accomplish much. [13]

It should have become evident by now that meditation is a means of acquiring knowledge about higher worlds. However, it should also be evident that not just any arbitrary thought content will lead to this knowledge, but only one that has been organized as described. [14]

The path that is pointed out here leads first to what can be called *imaginative* cognition, which is the first stage of higher knowledge. Cognition based on sensory perceptions and their assimilation by the sense-bound intellect [15] can be called "object cognition" in the sense of spiritual science. Beyond this lie higher levels of cognition, the first of which is imaginative cognition. The term *imaginative* may cause doubts on the part of those who think of imagination only in terms of illusory ideas that don't correspond to anything real. In spiritual science, however, "imaginative" cognition must be understood as cognition that comes about through a supersensible state of consciousness in the soul. Our senses have no access to the spiritual realities and beings that are perceived in this state. Because this state of consciousness is awakened in the soul by meditating on symbols, or imaginations, the world belonging to this higher state of consciousness can be called the *imaginative world* and the cognition that applies to it can be called *imaginative cognition*. Therefore, *imaginative* means something that is "real" in a different sense than the realities and beings of sensory, physical perception. The *content* of the mental images that fill our imaginative experience is not important at all; what is important is the soul faculty this experience develops.

*[16]*   One very natural objection to using the symbolic images described here is that they are shaped by dreamlike thinking and arbitrary imagination and can therefore only have dubious results. Doubts of this sort are unjustified with regard to the particular symbols that form the basis of genuine spiritual training, because these symbols are chosen in such a way that it is entirely possible to disregard their connection to any outer sensory reality and to seek their value only in the force they exert on the soul when it withdraws all of its attention from the outer world, suppresses

all sensory impressions, and excludes all thoughts it might entertain as a result of external stimulation.

The meditative state is best illustrated by comparing it to the sleeping state. These two states are similar in one respect and totally opposite in another. Meditation is sleep that constitutes a higher form of wakefulness in comparison to our ordinary consciousness during the day. The important point is that concentrating on the idea or image in question forces the soul to summon up much stronger forces from its own depths than it does in ordinary life or ordinary cognition. This increases its inner liveliness. It frees itself from the body just as it does during sleep, but without falling into a state of unconsciousness. Instead, it experiences a world it did not experience before. Although this soul state is similar to sleep in that the soul is released from the body, in comparison to ordinary day consciousness it can be described as a state of heightened wakefulness. This allows the soul to experience itself in its true inner independent nature. In contrast, because the soul's own forces do not develop to the same extent in the ordinary daily waking state, it can only become conscious of itself there with the help of the body. As a result, it does not experience itself but only becomes aware of itself in the reflection-like image that the body (or actually the body's processes) presents to it.

By their very nature, symbols built up in the way *[17]* described above do not yet relate to anything real in the spiritual world. They serve to free the human soul from sensory perception and from the brain, the instrument to which our intellect is initially bound. This cannot happen before we feel that we are imagining something by means of forces that do not use the brain and the senses as their tools. The first thing we experience on this path is this process of being freed from our physical organs. We can then say that our consciousness is not extinguished when we disregard sensory perceptions and ordinary intellectual thinking; we are able to rise above them and experience ourselves as individual beings *alongside* what we were previously. This is the first purely spiritual experience—observing an "I"-being of soul and spirit, a new self that has risen up out of the self that is bound only to the physical senses and the physical intellect.

If we freed ourselves from the world of the senses and the intellect without meditation, we would sink down into the "nothingness" of unconsciousness. Of course, we each have a being of soul and spirit prior to meditation, but at that point it has no tools for observing the spiritual world. It is something similar to a physical body without eyes for seeing or ears for hearing. The energy applied during meditation first creates organs of soul and spirit in a previously unorganized soul-spiritual being. What is created in this way is also the first thing we perceive, so in a certain sense our first experience is a self-perception. It belongs to the very nature of spiritual training that at this point in its development, the soul practicing self-education is fully conscious of the fact that it first perceives *itself* in the world of images (imaginations) that appears as a result of the exercises that have been described. Although these images appear to be living in a new world, the soul must recognize that to begin with they are nothing more than a reflection of its own being, strengthened by these exercises. Not only must the soul recognize this and assess the situation correctly, it must also have developed its will sufficiently to be able to remove or extinguish these images from consciousness at any time. Within these images, the soul must be able to act freely and completely deliberately. This belongs to a genuine spiritual training at this point. If the soul were not able to do this, its situation in the domain of spiritual experience would be similar to that of a soul in the physical world if its eyes were fixated on objects and unable to look away.

There is only one exception to the rule that it must be possible to extinguish images, and that is a group of inner pictorial experiences that must *not* be extinguished at this stage of spiritual training. They correspond to the core of the soul's own being. In these images, each student of the spirit recognizes his or her fundamental being, the aspect of the self that moves through repeated Earth lives. At this point, sensing repeated Earth lives becomes a real experience. In all other instances, however, the above-mentioned independence with regard to spiritual experiences must prevail. Only after having acquired the ability to extinguish our experiences do we approach the real spiritual world outside of ourselves. In place of what we have extinguished, something else appears, and we recognize its spiritual reality. We feel that our souls are outgrowing something undefined and becoming something defined. We must then move on from self-perception to observing an outer world of soul and spirit. This happens when we structure our inner experience along the lines of what will be described next.

[18]     To begin with, the souls of spiritual students are weak with regard to everything that is perceptible in the world of soul and spirit. During meditation, they will have to expend a great deal of inner energy to hold onto the symbols or mental images that they have built up out of the sense world's stimuli. But if they also want to achieve real observation in a higher world, they must be able to do more than merely hold onto these visualizations. Having done this, they must also be able to spend a certain amount of time in a state that not only permits no stimuli from the outer world of the senses to affect the soul, but also eliminates the earlier visualizations from consciousness. Only after this has been done can what has taken shape through meditation appear in consciousness. The point is that from now on the soul must have enough inner strength so that what has taken shape in this way is really perceived spiritually and does not escape attention, which is all too possible when the soul's inner energy is still only weakly developed. The organism of soul and spirit which begins to develop, and which the student is meant to grasp in self-perception, is delicate and fleeting. The disturbances from the sense-perceptible outer world and from its aftereffects in memory are great, no matter how hard we try to keep them at bay. It is not just a question of the disturbances we notice, but even more of those we are completely unaware of in ordinary life.

However, in this context the very nature of the human being makes a transitional state possible. It is possible for the soul to accomplish in the sleeping state what is initially impossible for it in the waking state because of disturbances from the physical world. If we devote ourselves to inner contemplation and are then properly attentive to what happens during sleep, we will notice that we are not "fast asleep," that our souls have times when they are still active in a certain way in spite of being asleep. During these states, natural processes keep the influences of the outer world at bay even though the waking soul is not yet strong enough to ward them off under its own power. But if the meditation exercises have already taken effect, the soul frees itself from unconsciousness during sleep and senses the world of spirit and soul.

This can happen in two different ways. Either we are able to realize during sleep that we are now in another world, or we are able on waking to recall having been there. The first instance requires greater inner energy than the second, which is therefore more prevalent among beginners in spiritual training. Students can gradually get to the point where they realize after they wake up that the whole time they were sleeping was spent in another world, and that they emerged from this world when they woke up. Their memories of the beings and realities of this other world will become ever more definite. In one sense or another, what can be called "continuity of consciousness"—that is, the continuation of consciousness during sleep—has set in. This does not mean, however, that these people are *always* conscious during sleep. It is already a big step toward continuity of consciousness if people who otherwise sleep just like anyone else have certain times during sleep when they can look, as though consciously, into a world of spirit and soul, or if they can look back in memory on these brief conscious states when they are awake.

We must not forget, however, that what is described here is only meant to be a transitional state. If our purpose is to train ourselves, it's good to go through this transitional state, but we should not believe that we should derive a conclusive view of the world of spirit and soul from it. In this state, the soul is uncertain and not yet able to trust its perceptions. Through such experiences, however, it gathers more and more strength in order eventually to be able to keep the disturbing influences of the physical outer and inner worlds at bay when it is awake— and thus to observe the world of spirit and soul without being distracted by any impressions coming from the senses, by the intellect that is bound to the physical brain, or even by the mental images of meditation, which were merely a preparation for spiritual sight and have now been removed from consciousness.

Anything spiritual science makes public in any form should never originate in any other kind of soul-spirit observation than the one that occurs in the fully waking state.

[19]     Two soul experiences are important as our spiritual training continues. One is what makes us able to say, "From now on, when I disregard all the impressions the physical outer world can give me and look into my inner self, I will not be looking at a being whose activity is totally extinguished but at a being who is aware of itself

in a world I knew nothing about as long I allowed myself to be stimulated only by impressions from my senses and from my ordinary intellect." At this moment, the soul has the feeling of having given birth to a new being within itself, to the essential core of its own being, as described above. This new being has characteristics that are totally different from those previously present in the soul.

The other experience is that of having the old being standing like a second being alongside the new. What we formerly experienced as containing us now turns into something we confront from outside in a certain respect. At times we experience ourselves outside of what we each otherwise regarded as our own essential being, as the individual I. It is as if we were now fully conscious of living in two I's. One of them we have known all along; the other stands above it like a newborn being. We feel how the first acquires a certain independence with regard to the second, somewhat similar to how the human body has a certain independence with regard to the first I. This experience is very significant, because it makes us realize what it means to live in the world we are trying to reach through our training.

The second, newborn I can now be guided into perception in the spiritual world. Within it, something can develop that has the same significance for this spiritual world as the sense organs have for the physical world of the senses. Once this development has advanced to the necessary level, we will not only sense ourselves as newborn I's but will begin to perceive spiritual realities and spiritual beings in the surroundings, just as we perceive [20] the physical world through our physical senses. This is a third important experience.

To really cope at this level of spiritual training, we must count on the fact that self-love and egotism will accompany the strengthening of our soul forces, appearing to a degree that we never experience in our ordinary soul life. It would be a mistake to believe that mere ordinary self-love is what we are talking about at this point. At this level of development, this powerful egotism is intensified to the point where it seems like a force of nature within our own souls, and a rigorous will-training is required in order to overcome it. This egotism is not produced by spiritual training; it is always present but becomes conscious only when we experience the spirit. It is absolutely necessary for will-training to go hand in hand with our other spiritual training. We have a strong urge to feel blissfully happy in the world we have just created for ourselves; as described above, we must be able to extinguish, so to speak, what we have just worked so hard to bring about. Having reached the imaginative world, we must extinguish *our selves*, but egotism's strongest urges agitate against this.

It is easy to believe that the exercises of spiritual training are something external and disregard the soul's moral development. In response, it must be said that the moral strength that is needed to overcome egotism, as has been described, cannot be acquired without elevating the soul's moral state to the corresponding level. Progress in spiritual training is unthinkable unless it is accompanied by moral progress. Without moral strength, it would be impossible to defeat egotism. All talk of genuine spiritual training's not being a moral training at the same time is inaccurate. Only those who have not experienced this personally can doubt our ability to know that we are dealing with realities in what we believe to be spiritual perceptions and not with mere self-deceptions (visions, hallucinations, and the like.)

The real fact of the matter, however, is that if we have reached this level through a genuine training, we will be able to distinguish mental images of our own creation from spiritual realities in the same way that any individuals of sound common sense can distinguish their own mental images of a hot piece of iron from the actual existence of a piece they are touching. Healthy experience, and nothing else, reveals the difference. Even in the spiritual world, life itself is the touchstone. Just as we know in the sense-perceptible world that an imagined piece of iron will not burn our fingers no matter how hot we imagine it to be, trained students of the spirit know whether they are experiencing a spiritual fact only in their imagination or whether *real* facts or beings are making an impression on their awakened spiritual organs of perception. The general rules we have to observe during spiritual training so as not to fall victim to deceptions in this regard will be described later on.

At this point, it is extremely important for students of [21] the spirit to have acquired a very specific state of soul when they first became conscious of the newborn I, since it is through the I that we become able to guide our sensations, mental images, and feelings; our urges, desires, and passions. Perceptions and mental images cannot be left to their own devices in the soul. They must be controlled through thoughtful deliberation. The I is what implements the laws of thinking and uses them to bring order into our life of thoughts and mental images. Something similar is true of our desires, urges, inclinations, and passions. Our ethical principles become the guides for these soul forces. Through moral judgment, the I becomes the soul's guide in this area. If an individual then extracts a higher I from the ordinary one, the original I becomes independent in a certain respect, and it loses as much vital strength as is given to the higher I.

Let's suppose, however, that an individual who has not yet developed sufficient ability and stability with regard to laws of thinking and powers of judgment chooses to give birth to the higher I on this level. This person will only be able to leave behind as much thinking ability for his or her lower I as was developed previously. If the amount of orderly thinking is insufficient, a disorderly, confused, fantastical type of thinking and judging will appear in this person's newly independent ordinary I. Because the newborn I in such a person can also only be weak, the confused lower I will dominate supersensible perception and the person in question will not demonstrate balance in judging his or her observations of the supersensible. If this person had developed the faculty of logical thinking sufficiently, it would have been quite safe to allow the lower I to be independent.

This is also true in the domain of ethics. If we have not achieved firmness in our moral judgments, if we have not sufficiently mastered our inclinations, urges, and passions, we will allow the ordinary I to become independent under circumstances in which these soul forces are still active. As a result, we may not apply the same high standards of truthfulness to our experiences of supersensible cognition as we do to what we raise to the level of consciousness in the outer physical world. With this slackened sense of truth, we could take all kinds of fantastic imaginings for spiritual reality. Firmness in ethical judgments, steadiness of character, and thoroughness of conscience must work into our sense for truth, having first been developed in the I that is left behind before the higher I becomes active for purposes of supersensible cognition. This is not meant to scare people away from spiritual training, but it does have to be taken very seriously.

If we have the strength of will to do everything neces- [22] sary to make the first I inwardly secure in carrying out its functions, we have no reason to be afraid of freeing the second I through spiritual training to pursue supersensible cognition. However, we must be aware of how powerful self-deception is when it comes to feeling "mature" enough to undertake something. Students in the spiritual training that is described here develop their thought life to the extent that they will never be in danger of going astray, although this is often assumed to be inevitable. This thought development makes all the necessary inner experiences appear and be played out in the soul as they should be, without being accompanied by harmful aberrations of fantasy. Without appropriate thought development, these experiences can cause profound uncertainty in the soul. Through the method emphasized here, these experiences appear in such a way that it is possible to become completely familiar with them, just as we become familiar with perceptions of the physical world if we are in a sound state of mind. By developing our thought life, we become more able to observe what we are experiencing in ourselves; if we do not develop it, we will not be able to face this experience in a calm and collected manner.

*[23]*    An appropriate training lists certain qualities that those who want to find the way into the higher world should acquire through practice. These are, above all, the soul's mastery over its train of thought, its will, and its feelings. The method for bringing this mastery about through practice has two goals. On the one hand, this practice is meant to imbue the soul with stability, certainty, and equilibrium to the extent that it retains these qualities even when a second I is born out of it. On the other hand, it is meant to give this second I strength and support for its journey.

*[24]*    Objectivity is what our thinking needs most of all for spiritual training. In the physical world of the senses, life is the great teacher of the human I as far as objectivity is concerned. If the soul chose to allow its thoughts to wander aimlessly, it would have to be immediately corrected by life so as not to come into conflict with it. The soul's thinking must correspond to the actual course of life's realities. When we turn our attention away from the physical world of the senses, we are no longer subject to its automatic correction, so our thinking will go astray if it is not able to self-correct. This is why students of the spirit

must train their thinking so that it can set its own direction and goals. Their thinking must teach itself inner stability and the ability to stick strictly to one subject. For this reason, the appropriate "thought exercises" we undertake should not deal with unfamiliar and complicated objects, but with ones that are simple and familiar.

Over a matter of months, if we can overcome ourselves to the point of being able to focus our thoughts for at least five minutes a day on some ordinary object (for example, a pin, a pencil, or the like), and if, during this time, we exclude all thoughts unrelated to this object, we will have made a big step in the right direction. (We can consider a new object each day or stay with the same one for several days.) Even those who consider themselves thinkers because of their scientific education should not scorn this means of preparing themselves for spiritual training, because if we fix our thoughts on something very familiar for a certain period of time, we can be certain that we are thinking objectively. If we ask: What is a pencil made of? How are these materials prepared? How are they put together to make pencils? When were pencils invented? and so on, our thoughts correspond to reality much more closely than they do if we think about the origin of human beings or the nature of life. Simple thought exercises are better for developing objective thinking about the Saturn, Sun, and Moon phases of evolution than any complicated scholarly ideas, because what we think about is not the point, at least initially. The point is to think objectively, using our own inner strength. Once we have taught ourselves objectivity by practicing on sense-perceptible physical processes that are easily surveyed, our thinking becomes accustomed to striving for objectivity even when it does not feel constrained by the physical world of the senses and its laws. We break ourselves of the habit of allowing our thoughts to wander without regard for the facts.

[25]     The soul must become a ruler in the domain of the will just as it is in the world of thoughts. Here again, life itself appears as the controlling element in the physical world of the senses. It makes us need certain things, and our will feels roused to satisfy these needs. For the sake of higher training, we must get used to strictly obeying our own commands. If we do this, we will become less and less inclined to desire nonessentials. Dissatisfaction and instability in our life of will, however, are based on desiring things without having any clear concept of realizing these desires. This dissatisfaction can disrupt our entire mental life when a higher I is trying to emerge from the soul.

A good exercise is to tell ourselves to do something daily at a specific time, over a number of months: Today at this particular time I will do *this*. We then gradually become able to determine what to do and when to do it in a way that makes it possible to carry out the action in question with great precision. In this way, we rise above damaging thoughts, such as: "I'd like this, I want to do that," which disregard totally the feasibility of what we want. A very great man put these words into the mouth of a seer: "I love whomever longs for the impossible."[3] This

---

3. Goethe, *Faust*, Part Two, Act 2.

great man himself said, "Living in ideas means treating the impossible as if it were possible."[4] These statements, however, should not be used as objections to what has been presented here, because what Goethe and his seeress Manto ask can only be accomplished by those who have trained themselves in desiring what is possible in order to then be able to apply their strong will to "impossibilities" in a way that transforms them into possibilities.

For the sake of spiritual training, the soul should also *[26]* acquire a certain degree of composure with regard to the domain of feeling. For this to happen, the soul must master its expressions of joy and sorrow, pleasure and pain. There are many prejudices that become evident with regard to acquiring this particular quality. We might imagine that we would become dull and unreceptive to the world around us if we are not meant to empathize with rejoicing or pain. However, that is not the point. The soul should indeed rejoice when there is reason to rejoice, and it should feel pain when something sad happens. It is only meant to master its *expressions* of joy and sorrow, of pleasure and displeasure. With this as our goal, we will soon notice that rather than becoming dulled to pleasurable and painful events in our surroundings, the opposite is true. We are becoming more receptive to these things than we were previously. Admittedly, acquiring this character trait requires strict self-observation over a long period of time. We must make sure that we are able to empathize fully with joy and sorrow without losing ourselves and

---

4. Goethe, *Verses in Prose.*

expressing our feelings involuntarily. What we are meant to suppress is not our justified pain, but involuntary weeping; not our abhorrence of a misdeed, but blind rage; not alertness to danger, but fruitless fear, and so on.

Exercises like this are the only way for students of the spirit to acquire the mental tranquillity that is needed to prevent the soul from leading a second, unhealthy life, like a shadowy double, alongside the higher I when this I is born and especially when it begins to be active. Especially with regard to these things, it is important not to succumb to self-deception. It can easily seem to people that they already possess a certain equilibrium in ordinary life and that they therefore do not need this exercise, but in fact it is doubly necessary for people like this. It's quite possible to be calm and composed in confronting things in ordinary life and yet have our suppressed lack of equilibrium assert itself all the more when we ascend into a higher world. It is essential to realize that for purposes of spiritual training, what we seem to possess already is much less important than systematically practicing what we need to acquire. This sentence is quite correct, regardless of how contradictory it may seem. No matter what life may have taught us, *what we teach ourselves* is what serves the purposes of spiritual training. If life has taught us excitability we need to break that habit, but if it has taught us complacency we need to shake ourselves up through self-education so that our souls' reactions correspond to the impressions they receive. People who cannot laugh at anything have as little control over their lives as people who are constantly provoked to uncontrollable laughter.

An additional way of training our thinking and feeling [27] is by acquiring a quality we can call "positivity." There is a beautiful legend that tells of Christ Jesus and several other people walking past a dead dog.[5] The others all turned away from the ugly sight, but Christ Jesus spoke admiringly of the animal's beautiful teeth. We can practice maintaining the soul-attitude toward the world that this legend exemplifies. The erroneous, the bad, and the ugly must not prevent the soul from finding the true, the good, and the beautiful wherever they are present. We must not confuse this positivity with being artificially uncritical or arbitrarily closing our eyes to things that are bad, false, or inferior. It is possible to admire a dead animal's "beautiful teeth" and still see the decaying corpse; the corpse does not prevent us from seeing the beautiful teeth. We cannot consider bad things good and false things true, but we can reach the point where the bad does not prevent us from seeing the good and errors do not keep us from seeing the truth.

Our thinking undergoes a certain maturing process in [28] connection with the will when we attempt never to allow anything we have experienced to deprive us of our unbiased receptivity to new experiences. For students of the spirit, the thought: "I've never heard of that; I don't believe it," should totally lose its meaning. During specific

---

5. A story attributed to the Persian poet Nizami (1141–1203), and adapted by Goethe for inclusion in his *West-östlicher Divan*. It is translated into English as "Agraphon" in *Selected Poems*, Angelos Sikelianos, Princeton University Press, Princeton, 1979, pp. 137–139.

periods of time, we should be intent on using every opportunity to learn something new concerning every thing and
every being. If we are ready and willing to take previously
unaccustomed points of view, we can learn from every
current of air, every leaf, every babbling baby. Admittedly, it is easy to go too far with regard to this ability. At
any given stage in life, we should not disregard all our previous experiences. We should indeed judge what we are
experiencing in the present on the basis of past experiences. This belongs on one side of the scales; on the other,
however, students of the spirit must place their inclination
to constantly experience new things and especially their
faith in the possibility that new experiences will contradict
old ones.

[29]     We have now listed five soul qualities that students in
a genuine spiritual training need to acquire: control of
one's train of thought, control of one's will impulses,
composure in the face of joy and sorrow, positivity in
judging the world, and receptivity in one's attitude
toward life. Having spent certain periods of time practicing these qualities consecutively, we will then need to
bring them into harmony with each other in our souls. We
will need to practice them in pairs, or in combinations of
three and one at the same time, and so on, in order to bring
about this harmony.

[30]     Methods of spiritual training recommend these exercises because if conscientiously carried out, they not only
have the above-mentioned direct effects on students but
also affect them in many indirect ways that they need on
their path to the spiritual worlds. If we do these exercises

enough, we will encounter many shortcomings and errors in our soul life and will discover the necessary means of strengthening and safeguarding the activity of our intellect, our feelings, and our character. Depending on our abilities, temperament, and character, we will certainly need many other exercises, but these will follow quite naturally from ample practice of the ones described above. In fact, we will notice that these exercises indirectly and gradually supply things that did not initially seem inherent in them. For example, after a certain time, people with too little self-confidence will notice that doing these exercises develops the self-confidence they need. The same is true of other soul qualities. (Specific and more detailed exercises can be found in my book *How to Know Higher Worlds*.)

It is significant that students of the spirit are able to advance to ever higher levels of the faculties indicated. They must develop their control of thoughts and feelings to the point where their souls have the power to establish times of complete inner tranquillity. During these times, students must keep their hearts and minds free of everything outer daily life brings with it in the way of joy and sorrow, satisfactions and concerns, and even tasks and demands. The only things that are allowed to enter the soul in this state of meditation are what the soul itself chooses to admit. It is easy for a certain prejudice to become apparent with regard to this. People might think that we would estrange ourselves from daily life and its tasks if we withdrew our heart and mind from them for certain periods during the day. In reality, however, this is not the case at all. If we give ourselves up to periods of inner stillness and peace, this engenders many powerful forces that are applicable even to our duties in daily life. As a result, we will not only not be worse at fulfilling our daily obligations but will certainly be better at it than we were before.

It is extremely valuable when people are able to detach themselves completely during these periods from thoughts about their personal concerns and rise to concerns that are shared by all. If they are able to fill their souls with communications from the higher spiritual worlds, and if this information is able to capture their interest to the same extent as their personal cares or concerns, this will prove especially fruitful for their souls.

If we make an effort to intercede in our soul life and regulate it in this way, we will also find it possible to observe ourselves and our own concerns with the same composure we apply to the concerns of others. Being able to look at our own experiences, joys, and sorrows as if they belonged to someone else is a good preparation for spiritual training. We can gradually acquire this ability to the necessary extent by taking time after our day's work is done to allow our experiences of the day to pass in front of us in the spirit. We should see ourselves in the images of these experiences; that is, we must look in on ourselves in our daily lives as if from outside. We acquire a certain facility in self-observation of this sort by beginning with visualizations of small isolated portions of our daily life. With practice, we become increasingly skillful in doing this retrospective view, so that after considerable practice we are able to form a complete picture in a short time. Looking at our experiences in reverse order is especially valuable for spiritual training because it forces us to free our visualizations from our normal habit of merely tracing the course of sense-perceptible events with our thinking. In this reversed thinking, we visualize things correctly but are not bound by their sense-perceptible sequence. This is something we need in order to find our way into the spiritual world. It makes our visualizing stronger in a healthy way. That's why it is also good, in addition to visualizing our daily life in reverse, to do the same with other things such as the sequence of a drama, a narrative, a melody, and so on.

For students of the spirit, the ideal increasingly becomes to relate to the events they encounter in life with inner certainty and tranquillity of soul and to judge them according to their own inherent significance and value rather than on the basis of a personal state of mind. With this ideal in view, students are able to create a foundation in their own souls for devoting effort to the above-mentioned meditation exercises on symbolic ideas or other thoughts and feelings.

The prerequisites described here must be met, because   *[31]* we build up our supersensible experience on the basis of our standing in ordinary soul life before entering the spiritual world. In two different ways, everything we experience supersensibly is dependent on the soul's point of departure for entering this world. If we are not concerned from the very beginning with making a healthy faculty of judgment the basis of our spiritual training, we will develop supersensible faculties that perceive the spiritual world inexactly and incorrectly. Our spiritual organs of perception will not develop properly, so to speak. Just as we cannot see properly in the world of the senses if our eyes are defective or diseased, we also cannot perceive properly with spiritual organs that have not been developed on the basis of a healthy faculty of judgment.

And if we take an immoral attitude as our point of departure, the way we ascend into the spiritual worlds will make our spiritual view seem clouded or dazed. We will confront supersensible worlds like someone observing the sensory world in a daze. Although in the sensory world, such a person will surely not be capable of saying anything significant about that world, even dazed spiritual observers are more awake than people in a normal state of consciousness, so their statements become errors with regard to the spiritual world.

. . . . . . . .

[32]     Inner soundness of the imaginative stage of cognition is achieved when the habit of what we might call "sense-free thinking" supports the soul meditations described here. If we form a thought on the basis of observing something in the physical world of the senses, this thought is not sense-free. However, such thoughts are not the only ones human beings are capable of having. Our thinking does not necessarily have to become empty and without content simply because we do not allow it to be filled with sensory observations. The safest and most obvious way for students of the spirit to learn sense-free thinking is by studying the

facts that spiritual science communicates about the higher world and by taking possession of them with their own thinking. Although these facts cannot be observed by our physical senses, we will find that we are able to comprehend them if we have enough patience and persistence. We cannot do research in the higher world or make observations of our own without higher training, but even without it we can understand everything researchers communicate about this world.

There is no reason for anyone to say: How am I supposed to accept on faith what spiritual researchers say, since I can't see it for myself? Simply by thinking about it, we can come to the conviction that this information is true. If we can't do this, it's not because it is impossible to believe in something we do not see, but simply because how we have applied our thinking has not yet been sufficiently unbiased, comprehensive, and thorough. To come to clarity on this point, we must realize that human thinking, if it gets a strong inner grip on itself, can comprehend much more than we usually imagine it can. There is an inner entity inherent in thought itself that already has connections to the supersensible world. The soul is usually not aware of these connections because it is in the habit of developing its thinking abilities only by applying them to the sensory world. As a result, the soul finds information about the supersensible world incomprehensible. However, this information actually is understandable not only to a spiritually trained way of thinking, but to any thinking that is aware of its full power and is willing to make use of it.

By constantly making the statements of spiritual research our own, we become accustomed to thinking in a way that does not draw on sensory observations. We learn to recognize how thoughts interweave within the soul, how one thought seeks out another even when the connections between them are not brought about by the power of sensory observation. Here, the essential thing is that we become aware of the inner life of the thought world. We become aware that if we are truly thinking, we are already in the domain of a living supersensible world. We realize that something within us is building up a thought-organism, and that we ourselves are one with this "something." When we give ourselves up to sense-free thinking, we experience that something being-like is flowing into our inner life, just as the characteristics of sense-perceptible things flow into us through our physical organs when we observe by means of our senses. Observers of the sense-perceptible world say to themselves: There is a rose in the space out there, and it is not strange to me because it makes itself known through its color and its smell. When sense-free thinking is at work in us, we only need to be sufficiently unbiased to have the corresponding thought: Something being-like that links one thought to another within me, forming a thought-organism, is making itself known to me.

However, there is a difference between the sensations we have of things we observe in the outer sensory world and our sensations of the inherent reality that makes itself known in sense-free thinking. People observing a rose feel that they are observing it from outside, while people devoting themselves to sense-free thinking feel that the inherent reality that is making itself known to them is present within them; they feel one with it. Of course those who can only bring themselves—either consciously or subconsciously—to acknowledge the existence of things that confront them in the way that external objects do will not be able to have the feeling that something being-like in character can make itself known through the fact that they feel one with it. In order to see correctly in this connection, we must be able to have this inner experience: We must learn to distinguish the connections between thoughts that we create freely and arbitrarily from the ones we experience within ourselves when we silence our personal arbitrary will. In the case of the latter, we may then acknowledge that while we ourselves are quite still and are not creating any connections between thoughts, we are giving ourselves up to what "thinks in us." We are then as fully justified in saying that something being-like in character is working in us as we are in saying that the rose is working on us when we perceive a certain red color or a particular scent.

This is not contradicted by the fact that the contents of these particular thoughts of ours have been communicated to us by spiritual researchers. Although these thoughts are already present when we give ourselves up to them, it would be impossible for us to think them without recreating them anew in our souls in each single instance. In any case, the important point here is that when spiritual researchers awaken thoughts in their listeners and readers, these people must first draw these thoughts up out of themselves. In contrast, researchers who describe sense-perceptible realities point to things that their listeners and readers can observe in the world of the senses.

*[33]*     (The path that leads us to sense-free thinking by means of information conveyed by spiritual science is absolutely reliable. However, there is another one that is even more reliable and, above all, more exact. It is presented in my books *Goethe's World View* and *Intuitive Thinking as a Spiritual Path*.[6] These books present the knowledge human thinking can gain when it does not devote itself to the impressions of the external physical world of the senses, but only to itself. What is then at work is not the thinking that indulges only in memories of sense-perceptible things. It is pure thinking, which acts like a living entity within the human being. Although these books include none of the information conveyed by spiritual science, they demonstrate that pure thinking, working only within itself, is capable of unlocking the secrets of the universe, life, and the human being. These works constitute an important intermediate level between knowing the world of the senses and knowing the spiritual world. They present what thinking can gain by rising above sensory observation while not yet becoming involved in spiritual research. If we allow these books to work on our entire souls, we are already in the spiritual

6. *Goethe's World View*, Mercury Press, Spring Valley, NY, 1985; *Intuitive Thinking as a Spiritual Path: A Philosophy of Freedom*, Anthroposophic Press, Hudson, NY, 1995.

world, but it makes itself known to us as the world of thoughts. People who feel that they are in a position to allow an intermediate stage such as this to work on them are traveling a safe path. It will give them a feeling for the higher world that will bear the most beautiful fruit in all times to come.)

. . . . . . . .

To put it precisely, the goal of meditating on the symbolic mental images and feelings characterized above is to develop higher organs of perception within the human astral body. Initially, these organs are created out of the substance of the astral body. They inform us about a new world where we get to know ourselves as new I's. These new perceptual organs are already different from those of the physical world of the senses in that they are *active* organs. Eyes and ears passively allow light and sound to work on them, but our perceptual organs of spirit and soul can be said to be constantly active during perception and grasp objects and facts in full consciousness, so to speak. As a result, we experience soul-spiritual cognition as a process of uniting with the facts in question and "dwelling in them."

*[34]*

Metaphorically speaking, these developing individual organs of soul and spirit can be called "lotus flowers," because this corresponds to the imaginative picture supersensible consciousness has to make of them. (Of course, we must realize that this term has nothing more to do with the actual thing in question than the term *chamber* does when we speak of the "chambers" of the heart.) Through very specific types of meditation, we work on the astral body in such a way that one or the other soul-spiritual organ, or lotus flower, takes shape.

After everything that has been described in this book, it should be superfluous to mention that we must not imagine such an organ as something whose reality is reflected by our sensory mental image of it. These "organs" are supersensible and consist of soul activity that is shaped in a particular way. They exist only inasmuch and as long as this soul-activity is being exercised. There is nothing sense-perceptible about these organs, just as no "vapor" is present around a human being who is thinking. We fall into misunderstandings if we insist on imagining the supersensible as sense-perceptible in any way. Although this remark is quite superfluous, it is inserted here because we repeatedly encounter people who are convinced of the existence of the supersensible but try to imagine it only as something sense-perceptible. We also repeatedly encounter opponents of supersensible cognition who believe that spiritual researchers are speaking of "lotus flowers" as if they were talking about delicate sense-perceptible formations.

Any genuine meditation that is done with regard to imaginative cognition has an effect on one or the other of these organs. (Details on methods of meditation and exercises that influence specific organs may be found in my book *How to Know Higher Worlds*.) In any genuine training, the student's individual exercises are set up and arranged in a sequence so that the organs can develop accordingly—either in conjunction with one another or one after the other. This training requires a great deal of patience and persistence on the student's part. The usual amount of patience people acquire as a result of their situation in life is not sufficient, because it often takes a long, long time before these organs have developed enough to be used for perception in the higher world. When this finally happens, it can be called "enlightenment," in contrast to the period of preparation, or *purification*, that consists of exercises to develop the organs. (The word *purification* is used here because these exercises purify a certain part of the student's inner life, eliminating everything that comes exclusively from the world of sensory observation.)

It's certainly possible for people who have not yet experienced actual enlightenment to receive repeated "flashes of light" from a higher world. Even such "flashes" allow them to bear witness to spiritual worlds and should be accepted with gratitude. But students should not waver if these flashes do not appear during the preparation period, which may seem unduly long. People who are still capable of becoming impatient because they "don't see anything yet" have not yet acquired the right relationship to the higher world, a relationship understood only by those who are capable of seeing the training exercises as almost an end in themselves. In actual fact, these exercises are working on our soul-spiritual nature; that is, on the astral body. Even if we cannot "see," we can feel that we are doing soul-spiritual work. The only possible reason for not being able to feel this is having a preconceived idea of what we are actually trying to "see." In that case, we will think nothing of something that is actually immensely significant. However, we must be subtly attentive to all of our experiences while practicing, because they are so very different from all of our experiences in the world of the senses. We will then notice that we are not simply making impressions on the astral body as if it were some indifferent substance. There is a whole world in there that is different from the life our senses tell us about. Higher beings work on the astral body in the same way the outer physical world of the senses works on the physical body. We "bump into" the higher life in our own astral body if we do not close ourselves off to it, but if we repeatedly say to ourselves: "I don't perceive anything," it's usually because we have preconceived ideas of how this perception is supposed to look. Because we are not seeing what we have convinced ourselves we ought to see, we say that we don't see anything.

*[35]*     However, once we have the right attitude about doing these training exercises, we will increasingly find something in them that we can love for its own sake. We will realize that the very act of practicing places us in the midst of a world of spirit and soul, and we will wait patiently and humbly for what may follow. This attitude can best become conscious in us in these words: I will do all the exercises that are suitable for me, knowing that at the right time, as much will come to me as is important for me to have. I do not demand this impatiently, but I am constantly preparing to receive it.

It is not legitimate to object that students of the spirit have to grope around in the dark indefinitely because success alone can show them that they are on the right path. It's not true that this is the only way to know that we are doing the right exercises. If we take the right approach to our exercises, the satisfaction we gain will make it clear that we are doing the right thing. We do not have to wait for success to have this certainty. Appropriate practice in the field of spiritual training goes hand in hand with a satisfaction that is more than just satisfaction. It is also knowledge, the knowledge of being able to see that what we are doing is leading us in the right direction. We can have this knowledge at any time if we pay attention to the subtleties of what we are experiencing. If we do not, this experience escapes us and we pass it by like hikers lost in thought who fail to see the trees on either side of the trail, although they would be able to see them if they simply paid attention to them.

Success invariably does come if we continue to practice, and it is not at all desirable to force results to appear more quickly. If we did, the result might be only a small part of what actually should have appeared. With regard to spiritual development, partial success is often the reason for a great delay in achieving complete success. Moving among the forms of spiritual life that constitute partial success dulls us to the influences of forces that can lead to higher levels of development. We only appear to have gained something by having "seen into the spiritual world," because seeing it in this way gives us deceptive images instead of the truth.

. . . . . . . .

[36]     As the soul-spiritual organs, or lotus flowers, take shape, they appear to supersensible consciousness to be located close to certain organs in the physical body of the person undergoing training. Of these soul organs, we may mention the following: the so-called two-petalled lotus flower that we feel as if between the eyebrows, the sixteen-petalled lotus flower in the area of the larynx, the twelve-petalled lotus flower in the area of the heart, and a fourth that is located near the solar plexus. Other such organs appear in the vicinity of other parts of the physical body. (The names *two-petalled* or *sixteen-petalled* can be used because the organs in question can be compared to flowers with a corresponding number of petals.)

[37]     We become conscious of the lotus flowers through the astral body. As soon as we have developed one or the other of these organs, we are also aware that we have it. We feel that we are able to make use of it and that in doing so we are actually entering a higher world. In many respects, our impressions of this world are still similar to impressions of the physical world of the senses. People with imaginative cognition will be able to speak of this new higher world in terms of sensations of warmth or cold, perceptions of sounds and words, and impressions of light or color, because that is how they experience it. However, they are aware that these perceptions express something different in the imaginative world than they do in the world of sense-perceptible reality. They realize that the causes underlying them are soul-spiritual rather than physical-material ones. If they receive something like an impression of warmth, they do

not attribute it to a piece of hot iron, for example, but think of it as emanating from a soul process similar to the ones they had, until now, been familiar with only in their own soul life. They know that soul-spiritual things and processes stand behind these imaginative perceptions just as material, physical beings and realities stand behind physical perceptions.

Alongside the similarity between the imaginative and physical worlds, however, there is also a significant difference. One thing that is present in the physical world appears quite differently in the imaginative world. In the physical world, we can observe things constantly coming into existence and disappearing again; there is a constant alternation between birth and death. In the imaginative world, this phenomenon is replaced by the constant *transformation* of one thing into another. For example, in the physical world we see a plant die and decompose. In the imaginative world another configuration that is physically imperceptible comes about as the plant withers away. The decaying plant is gradually transformed into this other configuration. Once the plant has completely disappeared, this figure has developed fully and taken its place. Birth and death are ideas that lose their significance in the imaginative world. They are replaced by the concept of one thing being transformed into another.

Because of this, certain truths about our human makeup become accessible to imaginative cognition. These truths are the ones presented in chapter 2 of this book. As far as physical, sensory perception is concerned, only the processes of the physical body are perceptible. These are played out in the "domain of birth and death." The other members of our human makeup—the life body, the sentient body, and the I—are subject to the laws of transformation and are perceptible to imaginative cognition. Anyone who has advanced to this stage perceives how something that goes on living after death in another state of existence releases itself, so to speak, from the physical body at death.

[38]     However, inner development does not stop at the level of the imaginative world. If we chose to stop here, we would perceive beings who are undergoing processes of transformation, but we would not be able to interpret these processes, nor would we be able to orient ourselves in this newly won world. The imaginative world is a restless region, full of movement and transformation; there are no resting places in it. We reach such resting places only by developing beyond the level of imaginative cognition to what can be called *cognition through inspiration*.

It is not necessary for those seeking knowledge about the supersensible world to acquire the faculty of imaginative cognition to its fullest extent before moving on to inspiration. Their exercises may be arranged so that what leads to imagination develops parallel to what leads to inspiration. After the appropriate amount of time, these students will enter a higher world where, in addition to being able to perceive, they will also be able to orient themselves and interpret what they see. Typically, however, they first perceive some of the phenomena of the imaginative world and only later feel that they are gaining the ability to orient themselves.

Compared to the world of mere imagination, however, the world of inspiration is something totally new. Through imagination, we perceive the transformation of one process into another, but through inspiration we become familiar with the inner qualities of the *beings* who are undergoing transformation. Through imagination, we recognize the soul expression of these beings, but through inspiration we penetrate their inner spiritual nature. Above all, we recognize a multitude of spiritual beings and the relationships between them. In the physical world of the senses, we are also dealing with a multitude of different beings, but the multitude in the world of inspiration is different in character. There, each being's very specific relationships to others are determined by its inner makeup rather than by external influences as is the case in the physical world. When we perceive a being in the world of inspiration, we do not perceive any outer effect it might have on another—that is, any effect comparable to how physical beings affect each other. Instead, the relationship between beings comes about through how they are each inwardly constituted.

In the physical world, this relationship can be compared to the relationship between individual sounds or letters in a word. Let's take the word *human*. It is brought about by the combined sounding of the speech sounds *h-u-m-a-n*. Although there is no impetus or other external influence connecting the *h* to the *u*, the two sounds work together within the totality because of how they are inwardly constituted. For this reason, observing the world of inspiration can only be compared to reading, and beings in this world are like letters of the alphabet in how they affect observers. We must become familiar with these letters and decipher their interrelationships like supersensible writing. This is why spiritual science also calls cognition through inspiration "reading the hidden script." How this hidden script is read and how what has been read can be communicated will now be made clear using previous chapters of this book as examples.

[39]     The first thing described was how the makeup of the human being consists of different components. Next, it was shown how the cosmic body on which human beings evolve has passed through various conditions during the Saturn, Sun, Moon, and Earth phases of evolution. The perceptions that allow us to recognize the members of our human makeup on the one hand, and the Earth's successive stages and earlier metamorphoses on the other, are perceptible to imaginative cognition.

However, it is also necessary to recognize the connections that exist between the Saturn state and the physical human body, the Sun state and the ether body, and so on. It must be possible to demonstrate that the seminal nucleus of the physical human body came about already during the Saturn state, and that it then continued to evolve during the Sun, Moon, and Earth states until it reached its present form. For example, it was necessary to show what changes took place in the human being as a result of the separation of the Sun from the Earth, and that something similar happened in relation to the Moon. It was also necessary to describe the interactions that were needed for the transformations in humanity that occurred during the Atlantean age and the successive periods of the Indian, Persian, and Egyptian cultures, and so on.

Depicting these connections does not result from imaginative perception, but from cognition through inspiration, from reading the "hidden script" in which imaginative perceptions are like letters or sounds. This sort of reading, however, is needed for other things in addition to explaining what has been described above. We would not be able to understand the whole course of a human life if we were able to look at it only through imaginative cognition. If we were not able to orient ourselves within our imaginative perceptions, we would perceive how the soul-spiritual members are released from what remains behind in the physical world at death, but we would not understand the connections between what happens after a person's death and the states that precede and follow. Without cognition through inspiration, the imaginative world would remain like writing that we stare at without being able to read.

When we advance from imagination to inspiration as [40] students of the spirit, it becomes evident very quickly how wrong it would be to renounce understanding the great phenomena of the cosmos and to attempt to restrict ourselves only to facts that touch upon immediate human interests, so to speak. Those who are not initiated into these things might well say, "It seems to me that the only important thing is to find out what the fate of the human soul is after death. If someone tells me about that, that's enough. Why does spiritual science tell me about distant things like the Saturn and Sun states and the separation of the Sun and Moon from the Earth?" However, if we have been introduced to these things in the right way, we realize that we can never really know what we want to know if we do not also know about these other things that seem so unnecessary. Any description of the human condition after death will remain completely incomprehensible and worthless if we cannot link it to concepts derived from those distant things. Even the simplest supersensible observation makes it necessary to know about such things.

For example, when a plant passes from the flowering stage to the fruiting stage, supersensible observers see a transformation taking place in an astral entity that covers and surrounds the flowering plant like a cloud coming from above. If fertilization did not take place, this astral entity would metamorphose into a form quite different from the one it assumes as a result of fertilization. We can understand this whole process as supersensible observation perceives it if we have learned to understand its nature from the great cosmic process undergone by the Earth and all its inhabitants at the time when the Sun separated from the Earth. Before fertilization, the plant's situation is like that of the whole Earth prior to the Sun's detachment. After fertilization, the plant's flower resembles the Earth when the Moon forces were still active in it after the Sun had detached itself. If we have personally acquired the ideas that can be gained from studying the Sun's detachment, we will then objectively perceive the meaning of the process of fertilization in the plant. We will say that the plant is in a sun state before fertilization and in a moon state afterward. Even the very smallest processes in the world can only be understood if we see them as copies of great cosmic processes. Otherwise their nature remains just as incomprehensible as Raphael's Madonna would be to someone who saw only a little speck of blue because the rest of the picture was covered up.

Everything that is now happening in the human being is a copy of all the great cosmic processes that have to do with our existence. If we want to understand what supersensible consciousness observes about phenomena taking place between birth and death and those taking place between death and a new birth, we will be able to do so if we have acquired the ability to decipher imaginative observations by means of concepts acquired from the study of macrocosmic processes. This study provides us with a key for understanding human life. This is why, in the sense of spiritual science, we are also observing the human being when we observe the Saturn, Sun, and Moon states.

Through inspiration, we acquire the ability to recognize *[41]* the relationships between beings in the higher world. The next higher stage of cognition makes it possible to recognize the actual inner nature of these beings. This level of cognition can be called "intuitive cognition." (The word *intuition* is misused in everyday life to mean an indefinite, uncertain insight into something; although it may coincide at times with the truth, we cannot prove that this sudden insight is justifiable. What is meant here, of course, has nothing to do with an "intuition" of that sort. Here, the term *intuition* is used to designate a cognitive process of the highest degree of light-filled clarity. If we have it, we are fully conscious of its justification.)

To have knowledge of a sense-perceptible being means to stand outside it and assess it according to external impressions. To have knowledge of a spiritual being through intuition means having become completely at one with it, having united with its inner nature. Students of the spirit rise to this level of knowledge step by step. Imagination brings us to the point where we no longer feel that perceptions are external qualities of beings; instead, we recognize in them the emanations of something that is soul-spiritual in character. Inspiration leads us still further into the inner nature of beings and teaches us to understand what these beings are for each other. In intuition, we penetrate into the beings themselves.

Here too we can use the accounts in this book to demonstrate the significance of intuition. The preceding chapter not only told how development proceeded through the Saturn, Sun, and Moon phases of evolution, and so on, it also informed us that beings were involved in this development in a great variety of ways. The thrones, or Spirits of Will, the Spirits of Wisdom, the Spirits of Movement, and others were all introduced. In the Earth phase of evolution, the Luciferic and Ahrimanic spirits were mentioned. The structure of the cosmos was traced back to the beings involved in it. We can learn about these beings through intuitive cognition, something we already need if we want to understand even the course of a human life. In the time after death, what has freed itself from the physical, bodily aspect of the human being passes through various states. Imaginative cognition would still be more or less able to describe the states immediately following death. However, what happens when a human being advances further into the period between death and a new birth would remain totally incomprehensible to imagination if inspiration were not added to it. Only inspiration is able to discover what can be said about human life after purification in the "land of spirits." However, inspiration is no longer adequate for the next stage; it loses the thread of understanding at this point, so to speak. There is a period in human development between death and a new birth when the human being is accessible only to intuition.

However, this part of the human being is always within us, and if we want to understand it in its true inner nature, we must also use intuition to seek it out in the time between birth and death. If we attempted to understand the human being exclusively by means of imagination and inspiration, the processes that belong to this innermost being and play from one incarnation into the next would elude us. Therefore, only intuitive cognition makes it possible for us to objectively investigate repeated earthly lives and karma. All the truths that can be communicated about these processes must result from research that makes use of intuitive cognition. Knowledge of the inner being within us can also come only from intuition. Through intuition, we perceive the aspect of ourselves that progresses from one earthly life to another.

. . . . . . . .

*[42]*    Exercises for the soul and spirit are the only way we can achieve the knowledge that comes from inspiration and intuition. These exercises are similar to the contemplations or meditations described for acquiring imagination. However, while these exercises that lead to imagination are linked to impressions of the physical world of the senses, this link must increasingly disappear in exercises that lead to inspiration. To clarify what has to happen, let's think again about the symbol of the rose cross. By immersing ourselves in it, we have an image before us whose components are taken from impressions of the sensory world—the black color of the cross, the roses, and so on. However, the way these components are combined into the rose cross is not derived from the physical world of the senses. If we attempt to eliminate the black cross and red roses from our consciousness as images of sensory realities and retain in our souls only the spiritual activity that combined them, then we have a means of meditation that will gradually lead to inspiration.

Within our souls, we should ask: What have I done inwardly in order to combine the cross and roses into this symbol? I want to hold fast to what I have done, to the personal soul process I have undergone, but to allow the image itself to disappear from my consciousness. I will feel everything within me that my soul did in order to bring the image about, but I will not picture the image itself. From this point onward, I will dwell quite inwardly in the activity of mine that created the image. Instead of meditating on an image, I will become absorbed in my own image-creating soul activity.

Such absorption, if carried out repeatedly with regard to many symbols, will lead to cognition through inspiration. Here is another example: We meditate on the mental image of a plant that first grows and then decays. We allow an image to come about in our souls of a gradually developing plant as it emerges from the seed, as one leaf after another unfolds, as flowers and fruit develop. Then we picture how the plant begins to wilt; we follow this process to the point of complete dissolution. As we meditate on this image, we gradually arrive at a feeling of becoming and decaying for which the plant is only an image. When we persevere at this exercise, this feeling develops into an imagination of the process of transformation that underlies physical becoming and decay. However, if we want to achieve the corresponding inspiration, we must do the exercise differently. We must reflect on the actual soul activity that derived the idea of becoming and decay from the image of the plant. We must allow the plant to disappear completely from our consciousness and meditate only on our own inner activity. Only exercises of this sort make it possible to rise to the level of inspiration.

Initially, it will not be easy to get a thorough grasp of how to approach such an exercise, because if we are in the habit of allowing our inner life to be determined by outer impressions, we immediately become uncertain and start to vacillate when we have to develop another soul life that has cast off all its connections to these outer impressions. To an even greater degree than in acquiring imaginations, it must be clear to us that we should only undertake exercises that lead to inspiration if we are willing to accompany them with all the precautionary measures that will safeguard and solidify our power of judgment, our feeling life, and our character. Taking these precautions has two results. First, our personalities will not become unbalanced during supersensible perception; second, we will acquire the ability to really carry out what these exercises demand of us. We will find these exercises difficult only as long as we have not acquired a certain very specific soul makeup, very specific feelings and sensations. If we patiently and persistently cultivate inner faculties in our souls that favor the growth of supersensible cognition, we will soon acquire not only an understanding of these exercises but also the ability to actually do them.

We will gain much by acquiring a habit of often withdrawing into ourselves in a way that is less concerned with brooding about ourselves than with quietly organizing and digesting our experiences in life. We will find that our ideas and feelings are enriched by bringing one experience into relationship with another. We will become aware to what a great extent we experience new things not only by having new impressions and encounters but also by allowing the old ones to work in us. If we begin to allow the experiences and even the opinions we have acquired to interact as if we ourselves with all our sympathies and antipathies and personal interests and feelings were not even present, we will prepare the ground well for the forces of supersensible cognition. We will truly develop what we can call a rich inner life. However, the most important thing in this regard is the stability and balance of our soul qualities. In devoting ourselves to a certain soul activity, we tend to fall into onesidedness all too easily. As a result, if we once become aware of the advantages of inner reflection and dwelling in our own world of ideas, we may develop such an inclination toward this that we increasingly shut ourselves off from the impressions of the outer world. This, however, makes our inner life dry and desolate.

We will go the farthest if, alongside the ability to retreat into ourselves, we preserve our open receptivity to all impressions of the outer world. This does not apply only to life's so-called important impressions. Any individual in any situation, even in the most miserable surroundings, can experience enough simply by remaining open and receptive. We do not need to go looking for experiences; they are everywhere.

It is also especially important how we transform these experiences in our souls. For example, we might make the discovery that someone we or others greatly admire has a certain character trait we would have to consider a shortcoming. This experience can lead our thinking in one of two directions. We could simply say: Now that I've realized this, I can no longer respect this person the way I used to." Or we could ask ourselves: "How is it possible for this respected person to be afflicted with this particular fault? What must I do to imagine this fault not only as a shortcoming, but as something caused by this person's life or perhaps even by his or her great qualities?" If we were to ask ourselves these questions, we might come to the conclusion that our respect is in no way diminished by having observed this shortcoming. Every time we come to such a conclusion, we learn something and increase our understanding of life.

Now it would certainly be a bad thing if the merits of this way of looking at life were to mislead us into excusing everything possible in people or things that have our sympathy, or if we were to acquire a habit of disregarding everything that deserves criticism on the grounds that doing so is advantageous for our inner development. This is *not* the case when the impulse not only to censure but also to understand the faults comes from our own motivations; however, it is advantageous if the instance at hand elicits this attitude regardless of whether we who judge stand to gain or lose by it. It is absolutely correct that we *cannot learn* by condemning a fault, but only by understanding it. However, if we want to exclude disapproval entirely for the sake of understanding, we will not get far either. Once again, the important thing is stability and balance in our soul forces, not onesidedness in one direction or another.

This is particularly true of one soul quality that is exceptionally significant for individual development, namely the feeling we call reverence or devotion. This feeling, whether we develop it in ourselves or already possess it as a fortunate gift of nature, forms an excellent basis for supersensible powers of cognition. Being able to look up to certain people in our childhood and youth with devoted admiration in the same way that we would look up to high ideals means that supersensible cognition will find fertile ground in our souls where it can thrive. Later on in life, when our judgment has matured, if we look up at the starry heavens and sense the revelation of higher powers with complete devotion and admiration, we are preparing ourselves for knowledge of supersensible worlds, and this is also true when we are able to appreciate the forces that prevail in human life. It is of no little significance if as adults we are still able to have the highest degree of reverence for other people whose worth we surmise or believe to recognize. Only when such reverence is present can a view into the higher worlds open up. If we are not capable of reverence, we will never advance very far in our knowledge. If we do not want to acknowledge the worth of anything in the world, the essence of things will remain closed to us.

In contrast, however, if our feelings of reverence and devotion tempt us to totally kill off our healthy self-awareness and self-confidence, we sin against the law of soul stability and balance. Students of the spirit will work on themselves continually to make themselves ever more mature, but when they do so, they are also permitted to be confident in their individual personalities and in their continuing growth. If we achieve the right feelings along these lines, we will say to ourselves: There are latent forces within me, and I am capable of bringing them up out of my inner being. Therefore, wherever I see something I must honor because it is superior to me, not only must I honor it, but I may also trust myself to develop everything within me that will make me similar to it.

The greater our ability to be attentive to certain processes in life that are not immediately familiar to our personal judgment, the greater the possibility of laying the [43] foundations for leading our development into the spiritual worlds. An example may illustrate this: Individuals may find themselves in a situation in life where they can either do something or leave it undone. Their judgment says: Do it; but there is still a certain inexplicable something in their feelings that keeps them from doing whatever it is. They can choose to pay no attention to this inexplicable something and simply do whatever their powers of judgment suggest. However, they can also give in to the urging of the inexplicable and refrain from going through with the action in question. If they then follow up the matter further, it may become evident that the results would have been disastrous if they had followed their judgment, and that it was a blessing that they refrained from that particular action. An experience like this can guide our thinking in a very specific direction, allowing us to recognize that there is something in us that guides us better than the degree of judgment we possess at present. We need to be open-minded about this "something" within us, which we are not mature enough to reach through our faculty of judgment.

It is of the greatest possible benefit for the soul to pay attention to such instances in life, because they provide a healthy premonition that there is more in us than we can survey with our power of judgment at any given time. Such attentiveness works to expand our soul life. Once again, however, it is also possible for serious onesidedness to result. If we got into the habit of always disregarding our judgment because of "premonitions" impelling us to do this or that, we might become the playthings of all sorts of undefined urges. It is a short step from a habit of this sort to lack of judgment and superstition.

For students of the spirit, superstition of any sort is disastrous. It becomes possible for us to truly make our way into the domains of spiritual life only if we carefully guard ourselves against superstition, fantastic ideas, and daydreaming. We do not enter the spiritual world in the right way if we rejoice at every opportunity to experience something "that cannot be grasped by the human mind." A preference for the inexplicable certainly does not make anyone a student of the spirit. We must break ourselves of the biased habit of thinking that mystics are those who "assume the existence of the inexplicable and the unfathomable" wherever they please. For students of the spirit, the appropriate attitude is to acknowledge the presence of hidden forces and beings everywhere, but also to assume that the unfathomable can be successfully investigated if the necessary forces are available.

A certain soul disposition is important to students of the *[44]* spirit at every level of development. It consists not in expressing their desire for knowledge in a one-sided way, constantly asking how one question or another may be answered, but by asking how they can develop certain faculties. Once these faculties have developed through patient inner work, the answers to these questions appear by themselves. Students of the spirit will always cultivate this soul disposition in themselves. This leads them to constantly work on themselves, to make themselves ever more mature, and to relinquish the desire to force answers to certain questions. They will wait until such answers come to them.

Once again, if we become one-sided in this respect, we will not make much progress. At certain times, students of the spirit can also have the feeling that they themselves are able to answer the most exalted questions with the forces currently at their disposal. Here, too, steadiness and balance in our soul disposition play an important role.

[45]     It is helpful to cultivate and develop many more soul qualities if we are attempting to achieve inspiration through doing such exercises. Each of these qualities could be described individually, but in each case it would have to be emphasized that steadiness and balance are the all-important soul qualities. They prepare us to understand and to be able to carry out the exercises that have been described as necessary for achieving inspiration.

[46]     The exercises for achieving intuition require students of the spirit to extinguish from consciousness not only the images to which they devoted themselves in attaining imagination, but also the life of their own soul activity, which they contemplated in acquiring inspiration. Literally nothing must remain in their souls from any previously known outer or inner experiences. However, if there were nothing in their consciousness after discarding these experiences—that is, if their consciousness disappeared and they sank into unconsciousness—they would realize that they had not yet matured enough to be able to undertake exercises to develop intuition, and they would have to continue the exercises for imagination and inspiration. Eventually, however, there comes a time when our consciousness is not empty when the soul casts off its inner and outer experiences, but something remains as an

effect. It then becomes possible for us to give ourselves up to this effect, just as we previously gave ourselves up to something that owed its existence to outer or inner impressions. This residual effect is nevertheless very specific in character. In comparison to all our previous experiences, it is something really new. When we experience it, we know that this is something we were not familiar with before. It is a perception, just as an actual sound is a perception when our ears hear it. This new perception, however, is something that can only enter our consciousness through intuition, just as sound can only enter our consciousness through our ears. Intuition strips our impressions of their last sensory, physical remnants, and the spiritual world begins to be apparent to our cognition in a form that no longer has anything in common with the characteristics of the physical world of the senses.

. . . . . . . .

Imaginative cognition is achieved when the lotus flowers *[47]* develop out of the astral body. Through the exercises we undertake in order to reach inspiration and intuition, specific movements, configurations, and currents that were not there before appear in our ether body or life body. These are the organs that allow us to acquire the ability to read the "hidden script" and what lies beyond it. The changes in the ether body of a person who has achieved inspiration and intuition present themselves to supersensible cognition as follows: A new center in the ether body, located approximately in the area of the physical heart, becomes conscious and develops into an etheric organ. A great variety of movements and currents run from it to the various parts of the human body. The most important of these currents go to the lotus flowers, permeating them and their individual petals, and then pour out like rays into external space. The more highly developed the person in question, the larger the surrounding area where these currents are perceptible.

In a genuine training, however, this center in the area of the heart does not develop immediately. First, the way is prepared for it. A temporary center appears in the head, which then slips down to the vicinity of the larynx and then moves into the area of the physical heart. In an abnormal development, the organ in question might form immediately in the vicinity of the heart. In this case, instead of achieving supersensible perception calmly and objectively, the person in question would be in danger of becoming a visionary and a fanatic.

As students of the spirit develop further, they learn how to take the currents and differentiations that have developed in the ether body, make them independent of the physical body, and use them independently. In this process, the lotus flowers are used as tools for moving the ether body. Before this can happen, however, certain currents and rays must have formed all around the ether body, closing it off as if in a delicate network and making it a self-contained entity. Once this has happened, nothing hinders the movements and currents taking place in the ether body from coming into contact with the external world of soul and spirit, so that outer soul-spiritual events and inner ones taking place in the human ether body intermingle. At this point, such a person consciously perceives the world of inspiration. Cognition of this sort does not appear in the same way as the cognition that applies to the physical world of the senses. In the sensory world, we receive perceptions through our senses and then form mental images and concepts about them. This is not the case when we know about something through inspiration. What we know there is immediately present in a single action; there is no such thing as thinking about a perception after it occurs. In inspiration, what we acquire in the form of a concept after the fact in sensory, physical cognition is presented simultaneously with the perception. This is why we would flow into and merge with the surrounding world of soul and spirit and be unable to distinguish ourselves from it if we had not developed the network in the ether body that has just been described.

When we do the exercises that lead to intuition, they not only affect the ether body but also work into the supersensible forces of the physical body. We must not imagine, however, that the effects within the physical body are accessible to our ordinary sense perception. They can only be assessed by means of supersensible cognition and have nothing to do with external cognition. They are a result of consciousness maturing to the point where it is able to have intuitive experiences even after having excluded all previous outer and inner experiences.

*[48]*

Intuitive experiences, however, are tender, subtle, and delicate. At its present stage of evolution, the physical human body is coarse in comparison to them and presents a major obstacle to the success of intuition exercises. But if these exercises are carried out with energy, persistence, and the necessary inner tranquillity, they eventually over-come the mighty obstacles presented by the physical body. Students of the spirit notice that this has happened when they gain control over certain expressions of the physical body that formerly occurred completely uncon-sciously. They may notice it also because they feel the need to regulate their breathing, for example, for short periods of time so that it harmonizes with what their souls are doing in these exercises or other meditations. In inner development, the ideal is to not perform any exercises, including breathing exercises of this sort, by means of the physical body itself. Instead, everything that needs to happen with regard to the physical body should come about only as a consequence of pure intuition exercises.

. . . . . . . .

[49]   At a certain level in their ascent along the path to worlds of higher cognition, students of the spirit notice that the forces of their personalities are being held together differ-ently than they are in the physical world of the senses. In the physical world, the I makes the soul forces of think-ing, feeling, and willing work together in a unified way; under the ordinary circumstances of our lives, these three soul forces always relate to each other in specific ways. For example, we see something in the outer world, and our souls like it or dislike it—that is, the mental image of the thing is necessarily followed by a feeling of liking or disliking. We may desire the thing in question or have an impulse to change it in one way or another. This means

that our will and our ability to desire something are associated with an idea and a feeling. This happens because the I unites visualizing (thinking), feeling, and willing, thus bringing order into the forces of the personality. This healthy order would be disrupted if the I were to prove powerless in this respect—if our desires wanted to take a different direction from our feeling or thinking, for example. Thinking that a certain thing is right while wanting to do something that we do not think is right, or wanting what we dislike instead of what we like, would not indicate a healthy state of mind.

On the path toward higher cognition, however, we actually notice that thinking, feeling, and willing separate and acquire a certain independence from each other—for example, that certain thoughts no longer seem to automatically impel us toward a specific way of feeling and willing. At this point, although in thinking we can perceive something correctly, we again require an independent impulse coming from ourselves in order to come to any feeling or willed decision about it. During supersensible observation, thinking, feeling, and willing do not remain three forces radiating from their common center in the I of the person in question. They become independent beings—three separate personalities, so to speak. The individual I must become that much stronger, because rather than simply having to impose order on three forces, it must now guide and direct three beings. This separation, however, should persist only as long as supersensible observation continues. Here again it becomes apparent how important it is for exercises leading to higher training to be accompanied by ones that provide stability and firmness for our capacity for judgment and our life of feeling and will. If we do not bring these qualities with us into the higher world, we will soon see that the I proves too weak to act as an appropriate guide for thinking, feeling, and willing. In this case, the soul is torn apart in different directions by three personalities, so to speak, and its inner unity comes to an end. But if a student's development proceeds in the right way, the transformation of these forces signifies true progress, and the I retains its mastery over the independent beings that now make up the soul.

In the further course of personal development, this evolution continues. Thinking, having become independent, stimulates the appearance of a fourth specific soul-spiritual being that can be described as a direct influx of thought-like currents into the human being. The entire cosmos then appears as a thought structure that confronts us just as the world of plants or animals confronts us in the physical domain of the senses. Similarly, our newly independent feeling and willing stimulate two forces in the soul that also act like independent beings within it. Still a seventh force and being appears, which is similar to our own I.

[50]     This whole experience is linked to another one. Before entering the supersensible world, we know our thinking, feeling, and willing only as inner soul experiences. As soon as we enter this world, we perceive things that express the element of soul and spirit rather than the physical, sensory element. There are now beings of soul

and spirit standing behind the perceived qualities of this new world and presenting themselves to us as an outer world in the same way that stones, plants, and animals present themselves to our senses in the physical domain. Students of the spirit can perceive a significant difference between the world that is now disclosing itself to them and the one they were accustomed to perceiving with their senses. A plant in the world of the senses remains the same regardless of what the human soul feels or thinks about it. Initially, this is not the case with the images of the world of soul and spirit. They change according to what we feel or think. We imprint a certain character on them in accordance with our own essence.

Let's imagine that a certain image appears in the imaginative world in front of us. It shows itself in one form if our souls remain indifferent to it, but as soon as we experience liking or disliking with regard to this image, it changes its form. To begin with, therefore, these images not only express something independent of and external to us but also reflect what we are. They are thoroughly permeated with our own human essence, which is drawn over the beings in question like a veil. Even when we are confronted by a real being, we see something of our own creation instead of the being itself. We can actually have something totally true in front of us and still see something false. And this is not only the case with regard to the aspects of our essential nature that we actually notice in ourselves, but everything else in us also influences this world in the same way. For example, we may have hidden tendencies that do not become evident in our life because of our education and character, but they do influence the world of spirit and soul, which assumes a particular coloration as a result of the total being of each one of us, regardless of how much we ourselves know or do not know about this essential being.

To advance beyond this level of development, we must learn to distinguish between ourselves and the spiritual outer world. We must learn to exclude all the effects of the individual self on the world of soul and spirit around us. The only way we can do this is by knowing about what we ourselves bring into this new world. The important thing, therefore, is that we must first have a true and thorough knowledge of ourselves so that we can perceive the surrounding world of soul and spirit in a pure way. It is inherent in certain facts of human inner development that knowing ourselves in this way takes place quite naturally and as a matter of necessity when we enter the higher world.

As we know, we each develop our I, our self-awareness, in the ordinary physical world of the senses. This I now acts as a center of attraction for everything that belongs to the human individual. All our inclinations, sympathies, antipathies, passions, opinions, and so on gather around this I, as it were, which is also the point of attraction for everything we call an individual's karma. If we were to see this I exposed, we would recognize its need to encounter specific forms of destiny in this and subsequent incarnations, according to how it lived in earlier incarnations and what it acquired there. With all of this clinging to it, the I is necessarily the first image that appears to the human soul ascending into the world of soul and spirit. According to a law of the spiritual world, this double of ours must be the very first impression we receive there. This underlying law becomes easily understandable if we consider the following: In our physical, sensory life we perceive ourselves only to the extent that we have inner experiences of ourselves in our thinking, feeling, and willing. However, these perceptions are inner ones that do not present themselves to us in the same way that stones, plants, and animals present themselves. In addition, we also become only partially familiar with ourselves through inner perception because something within us prevents deeper self-knowledge. What prevents this is an impulse to immediately transform any character trait if self-knowledge forces us to acknowledge it and we do not want to succumb to self-deception.

If we do not give in to this impulse, if we simply divert    *[51]* our attention from this aspect of ourselves and remain the way we are, we deprive ourselves of the possibility of getting to know ourselves on this particular point. But if we delve into ourselves and hold up certain character traits for inspection without deceiving ourselves, either we will be in a position to correct them or we will be unable to do so in our present situation. In this latter instance, a feeling that we must describe as "shame" creeps into our souls. This is how healthy human nature actually works—it experiences many different types of shame in the process of self-knowledge. Now, this feeling already has a very specific effect even in our ordinary life. People with sound thinking will make sure that the aspects of themselves that give them this feeling have no outer effects, that they are not played out in outer actions. Shame, therefore, is a force that impels us to conceal something within us and not allow it to become outwardly perceptible.

If we give this due consideration, we will understand why spiritual research ascribes much more wide-ranging effects to an inner soul experience that is very closely related to the feeling of shame. This research reveals a type of hidden shame in the hidden depths of the soul, a shame that we do not become conscious of in our physical, sensory life. However, this hidden feeling works in a way that is similar to how the ordinary feeling of shame works in everyday life—it prevents a person's innermost being from appearing to that person as a perceptible image. If this feeling were not there, we would confront a perception of what we are in truth. We would not only have inner experiences of our ideas, feelings, and will; we would also perceive them just as we perceive stones, animals, and plants. This feeling conceals us from ourselves, and at the same time it conceals the entire world of soul and spirit, because the fact that our own inner being is concealed from us means that we are also unable to perceive the means of developing tools for recognizing the world of soul and spirit. We are unable to transform our own being to receive the organs of spiritual perception.

However, if we work toward acquiring these organs through genuine training, the first impression that appears to us is an impression of what we ourselves are. We each perceive our own double. This self-perception cannot be separated from perceiving the rest of the world of soul and spirit. In ordinary life in the physical, sensory world, the effect of the feeling described above is that it constantly closes the door of the soul-spiritual world in our faces. If we want to take even a single step toward entering this world, this subconscious feeling of shame immediately appears and conceals the part of the world of soul and spirit that wants to become evident. The exercises that were described earlier, however, open this world to us. And in fact, this concealed feeling acts like a great benefactor of human beings, because any powers of judgment, feeling life, or character we acquire without spiritual scientific training do not make us capable of standing up to the perception of our own nature in its true form without further preparation. Perceiving this would deprive us of all of our self-esteem, self-confidence, and self-awareness. We need to take precautionary measures in cultivating our sound judgment, feeling life, and character in addition to doing the exercises for higher knowledge in order to ensure that this does not happen. Through proper training, we learn, as if unintentionally, enough spiritual science and the necessary means of self-knowledge and self-observation to have sufficient strength to encounter our double.

For students of the spirit, it is then like seeing what they have already learned in the physical world in another form, as a picture of the imaginative world. If we have already acquired a rational grasp of the law of karma in the physical world, we will not be unduly shaken by seeing the seeds of our destiny imprinted on the image of our double. If we have used our powers of judgment to become familiar with the evolution of the cosmos and of humankind, and if we know that at a certain point in this evolution the forces of Lucifer invaded the human soul, it will not be difficult for us to bear it when we become aware that Luciferic beings and all their influences are contained in this image of our own essential nature.

We see from this how necessary it is that we not demand to enter the spiritual world ourselves before we have understood certain truths about this world through the ordinary powers of judgment that we develop in the physical world of the senses. Before wanting to actually enter the supersensible worlds, students of the spirit should make their own the information in this book that precedes the discussion of knowing higher worlds. In the course of a legitimate self-development process, they should do this on the basis of their ordinary powers of judgment.

[52]     In a training that does not pay attention to safeguarding and solidifying the power of judgment, their life of feeling and their character, it could happen that the higher world would approach the students before they had the necessary inner faculties. If this happened, encountering their doubles would depress them and lead them into errors. If, however, human beings avoided this encounter entirely and were nevertheless led into the supersensible world—which would also be possible—they would be equally incapable of recognizing this world in its true form. It would be totally impossible for them to distinguish between what they themselves were projecting onto things and what these things really were. It is only

possible to make this distinction if we perceive our own essence as an image in itself. If we do so, everything flowing from our own inner nature detaches itself from what surrounds it.

In our life in the physical world of the senses, the double immediately makes itself invisible by means of the sense of shame described above when we approach the world of soul and spirit. Simultaneously, however, the double also conceals this entire world. It stands like a guardian in front of that world, refusing entry to anyone not yet suitable for entering. The double can therefore be called "the guardian of the threshold to the world of soul and spirit." We encounter this guardian of the threshold not only when we enter the supersensible world in the way described but also when we enter it through physical death. The guardian reveals itself gradually in the course of our soul-spiritual development between death and a new birth. In this case, however, we are not oppressed by this encounter because we know about worlds we did not know about during life between birth and death.

If we were to enter the world of soul and spirit without *[53]* encountering the guardian of the threshold, we would succumb to one deception after another, because we would never be able to distinguish between what we ourselves were bringing into this world and what really belongs to it. Genuine training, however, is only permitted to lead students of the spirit into the domain of truth and not into the domain of illusion. It is inherent in this training that the encounter with the guardian must take place at some point, since it is an indispensable precautionary measure against the deception and illusory fantasy that are possible when we are observing supersensible worlds.

One of the most indispensable precautions all students of the spirit must take as individuals is to work carefully on themselves to avoid becoming delusional visionaries who may succumb to deception and autosuggestion. Whenever instructions for spiritual training are followed correctly, the potential sources of deception are destroyed. Of course this is not the place to go into all the numerous details that have to be considered with regard to these precautions; only the most important points can be indicated here. The deceptions that come into consideration here come from two sources. Some of them come from the fact that we color reality with our own soul nature. In ordinary life in the physical world of the senses, this source of deception poses relatively little danger, because there the outer world always forces itself upon our observations in its actual form, regardless of how we might attempt to color it with our desires and interests. But as soon as we enter the imaginative world, the images we perceive change because of these desires and interests of ours, and we confront a seeming reality that we have shaped ourselves, or have at least contributed to shaping. Through encountering the guardian of the threshold, students of the spirit become familiar with everything that is within them that they might carry into the world of soul and spirit. This eliminates the first source of deception. The preparation that students undergo before entering the world of soul and spirit accustoms them to disregarding themselves even when observing the physical world of the senses, allowing only the essence of things and events to speak to them. If we have prepared thoroughly enough, we can wait calmly to encounter the guardian of the threshold. This encounter will be the ultimate test of whether we are really also in a position to exclude our own being when we face the world of soul and spirit.

In addition to this, still another source of deceptions    *[54]* appears when we misinterpret an impression we receive. A simple example of this type of deception in our physical, sensory life is what happens when we sit in a train and think that the trees are moving in the opposite direction, while we ourselves are actually moving with the train. Although in many cases such deceptions in the physical world of the senses are more difficult to correct than this simple one, it is easy to see that in this world we find the means to do away with such deceptions if our sound judgment takes everything into account that can contribute to an appropriate explanation. The situation is different, of course, as soon as we make our way into supersensible domains. In the world of the senses, facts do not change when human beings are deceived, so it is possible for unbiased observation to use the facts to correct the deception. In the supersensible world, however, the matter is not that simple. If we apply false judgments in approaching a supersensible process we are trying to observe, we insert these false judgments into the process itself, where they become so entangled with actual fact that it is not immediately possible to distinguish them from the fact. In this case, the error is not inside us and the correct fact outside; our error has become a component of the external fact and can therefore not be corrected simply by observing the fact in an unbiased way. With this, we have pointed to a superabundant source of possible deceptions and illusory fantasies for those who approach the supersensible world without the right preparation.

Just as students of the spirit acquire the ability to exclude deceptions that come about because of how their own nature colors supersensible phenomena, they must also acquire the gift of inactivating this second source of deception. They become able to exclude what comes from themselves once they have recognized the image of their own double, and they will be able to exclude this second source of deception once they have acquired the ability to recognize from the makeup of a supersensible fact whether it is the truth or a deception. If deceptions looked exactly the same as facts, it would be impossible to distinguish between them, but this is not the case. In the supersensible worlds, deceptions have inherent qualities that distinguish them from realities. It is essential for students of the spirit to know which qualities distinguish the realities.

It seems self-evident that someone unacquainted with spiritual training might ask, "How is there any possibility of protecting ourselves against deception, since there are so many sources of it? And are students of the spirit ever certain that all their so-called higher knowledge is not based only on deception and autosuggestion?" Anyone who talks like this is not taking into account the fact that the very way a true spiritual training takes place blocks deceptions at the source. In the first place, through their preparation true students of the spirit will have acquired enough knowledge about the causes of deception and autosuggestion to be able to protect themselves. In this respect, they have more opportunities than any others to become sufficiently matter-of-fact and competent to judge what they encounter in life. Everything they experience makes them distrust indefinite premonitions and questionable flashes of so-called inspiration. Their training makes them as careful as possible. In addition, any true training first guides its students to thoughts about great cosmic events—that is, to things that force them to exert their powers of judgment, refining and sharpening them in the process. The only way we could miss out on this sharpening of our healthy powers of judgment, which give us certainty in distinguishing between deception and reality, would be by refusing to enter such distant realms and insisting on restricting ourselves to "revelations" closer at hand.

However, all of this is not the most important thing. What is most important is inherent in the very exercises that are used in genuine spiritual training. They have to be arranged in such a way that the student's consciousness has a complete and exact overview of what is going on in the soul during meditation. First of all, a symbol is developed to bring about imagination. There are still images taken from outer perceptions in this symbol; we are not solely responsible for its content. And since we do not create it ourselves, it is possible for us to delude ourselves about how it comes about. We may misinterpret its origin. However, students of the spirit remove this content from their consciousness when they move up to the exercises for inspiration, where they contemplate only their own souls' activity that shaped the symbol. Here too error is possible. We have acquired the character of our soul activity through our upbringing, education, and so on. We cannot know everything about the origin of this activity. However, students of the spirit also remove this activity of theirs from their consciousness, so if something still remains, there is no remnant of anything that cannot be surveyed. Anything that can possibly mingle with this can be assessed with regard to its entire content.

In their intuition, students of the spirit thus possess something that shows them the makeup of anything that is a totally clear reality in the world of soul and spirit. If they then apply the signs they have recognized as being characteristic of soul-spiritual reality to everything that presents itself to their observation, they will be able to distinguish semblances from realities. And they can be certain that applying this law will protect them from deception in the supersensible world just as certainly as they will not mistake an imagined piece of hot iron for a real one that actually burns them in the physical world of the senses. It goes without saying that we will only apply these criteria to knowledge we regard as our own experience in the supersensible worlds, and not to what we receive as communications from others and understand with our physical intellect and our healthy feeling for the truth. Spiritual students will attempt to draw a precise boundary between what they have acquired in these two different ways. They will willingly receive information about the higher worlds and attempt to understand it with their powers of judgment, but when they categorize something as personal experience or direct observation, they will have tested whether it presents the very same characteristics that infallible intuition has taught them to perceive.

. . . . . . . .

Once students of the spirit have the encounter with the guardian of the threshold behind them, they face further experiences as they ascend into supersensible worlds. First of all, they notice a certain inner relationship between this guardian and the seventh soul force that was described above as forming itself into an independent entity. In a certain respect, this seventh being is none other than the double, the actual guardian of the threshold. It poses a specific task to students of the spirit. They must use their newborn selves to guide what they are in their ordinary selves, which appear to them in images. This results in a sort of struggle against the double, who will constantly try to gain the upper hand. Achieving the right relationship with the double, not allowing it to do anything that does not happen under the influence of the newborn I, strengthens and consolidates the forces of the human being.

*[55]*

In the higher world, self-knowledge is different in some respects than it is in the physical world of the senses, where self-knowledge appears only as an inner experience. In contrast, the newborn self immediately presents itself as an external soul phenomenon. We each see our own newborn self as a separate being in front of us, but we are not able to perceive it fully. Regardless of what level we have reached on the path to supersensible worlds, there are always still higher levels where we will perceive ever more of the higher self, which can therefore reveal itself only partially at any given level. However, when we first become aware of some aspect of the higher self, we are overcome by an extremely great temptation to look at it from the standpoint we acquired in the physical world of the senses, so to speak. This temptation is actually a good thing, and it must happen if our inner development is to proceed properly. We must each observe our double, the guardian of the threshold, and place it in front of the higher self in order to notice the discrepancy between what we are and what we are meant to become. When we do this, however, the guardian of the threshold begins to assume a completely different form. It presents itself as an image of all the obstacles confronting the development of the higher self. We perceive what a burden we are each dragging around with us in the form of the ordinary self. If our preparations have not made us strong enough to say: "I am not going to stop here; I will strive unceasingly to develop toward my higher self," we will falter and shrink back from what is ahead of us. In this case, we have plunged into the world of soul and spirit but quit working our way forward. We become prisoners of the form that now stands before our souls as the guardian of the threshold.

The significant thing about this experience is that we don't have the feeling of being prisoners. We are much more likely to believe that we are experiencing something completely different. The figure summoned up by the guardian of the threshold can create the impression in our souls that the images appearing to us at this stage of our development already encompass all possible worlds, that we have arrived at the pinnacle of knowledge and no longer need to exert ourselves. Instead of feeling like prisoners, it's possible for us to feel that we possess all the immeasurably rich secrets of the cosmos. We will not be surprised by this experience, which is the exact opposite of the true state of affairs, if we consider that we are already in the world of soul and spirit when we have this experience and that one of this world's idiosyncrasies is that experiences can appear in reverse. This fact was already pointed out earlier in this book when life after death was described.

The figure that we perceive at this stage of our development shows us something different from what first appeared to us as the guardian of the threshold. In the double as we first perceived it, we saw all the character traits that the ordinary self possesses as a result of the influence of Luciferic forces. However, in the course of human evolution another power has also been able to move into the human soul because of Lucifer's influence. This is what was described as the power of Ahriman in earlier chapters of this book. It is the power that prevents us from perceiving the soul-spiritual beings of the outer world lying behind the surface of sense-perceptible things. What the human soul has become under the influence of this power is shown in image form in the figure that appears during the experience that has just been described.

*[56]*

If we approach this experience with the right preparation, we will interpret it correctly, and then another figure will soon appear. In contrast to the lesser guardian described earlier, we can call this figure the "greater guardian of the threshold." The greater guardian tells us that we must not remain at this stage but must continue to work energetically. The greater guardian awakens in us the awareness that the world we have conquered will only become a truth and not metamorphose into illusion if we continue to work in the appropriate way.

However, if we approach this experience without having been prepared for it by a proper spiritual training, when we encounter the greater guardian something that can only be compared to a feeling of immeasurable horror or boundless fear will fill our souls.

[57]     Just as the encounter with the lesser guardian makes it possible for us to test whether we are protected against the deceptions that can arise when we insert our own being into the supersensible world, the experiences that ultimately lead us to the greater guardian allow us to test whether we are capable of overcoming the deceptions that can be traced back to the second source described above. If we are able to resist the immense illusion that leads us to believe that the world of images we have reached is a rich possession while in reality we are mere prisoners, we will also be protected against mistaking semblance for reality in the further course of our development.

[58]     To a certain extent, the guardian of the threshold will assume an individually different form for each human being. The encounter with the guardian corresponds to

the experience that overcomes the personal character of our supersensible observations and makes it possible for us to enter an area of experience that is free of personal coloring and valid for every human being.

. . . . . . . .

Students of the spirit who have had the experiences   *[59]*
described above are then able to distinguish what they themselves are from what is outside of them in their soul-spiritual surroundings. They will then realize that we need to understand the cosmic process described in this book in order to understand human beings themselves and their lives. We understand the physical body only if we recognize how it has been built up through the Saturn, Sun, Moon, and Earth phases of evolution; we understand the ether body only if we trace its development through the Sun, Moon, and Earth phases, and so on. However, we also understand what is presently involved in the Earth's evolution if we recognize how all this has unfolded gradually. Spiritual training puts us in a position to recognize that everything in the human being is related to corresponding facts and beings in the world outside of us. It is a fact that every part and organ of the human being is related to all the rest of the world. In this book, it has only been possible to present a sketchy outline of the facts. However, we must keep in mind that the physical human body, for example, was present only in seminal form during the Saturn phase of evolution. Later, during the Sun, Moon, and Earth phases, its organs—heart, lungs, brain—evolved from this seminal endowment. Thus our

heart, lungs, and so on are related to the Sun, Moon, and Earth phases of evolution. Something similar is true of the organs of the ether body, sentient body, sentient soul, and so on. Human beings took shape out of the entire world immediately surrounding them, and every detail of our human makeup corresponds to a process or being in the outer world.

At the appropriate level of inner development, students of the spirit begin to recognize this relationship between their own individual beings and the greater world. This level of cognition can be described as becoming aware of the correspondence between the microcosm, or smaller world, that is the human being and the macrocosm, or greater world. Having broken through to this stage of knowledge, students of the spirit can then begin to have a new experience. In spite of being aware of themselves in their full independence, they begin to feel as if they have grown together with the entire structure of the cosmos. They have a feeling of merging with the entire cosmos and becoming one with it, yet without losing their essential nature. We can describe this level of development as "becoming one with the macrocosm." It is important not to think of this as a cessation of an individual consciousness, as if the essence of a human individual were flowing out into the universe. To think of it in this way would only reflect the opinion of an untrained faculty of judgment.

In the sense of the initiation process described here, the individual stages of higher cognition can be listed as follows:

1. Studying spiritual science by initially making use    *[60]*
   of the power of judgment, which we have acquired
   in the physical world of the senses.
2. Acquiring imaginative cognition.
3. Reading the hidden script (this corresponds to
   *inspiration*).
4. Living one's way into the spiritual surroundings
   (this corresponds to *intuition*).
5. Recognizing the relationship between the microcosm and the macrocosm.
6. Becoming one with the macrocosm.
7. Experiencing all of these previous experiences as a
   totality, as a fundamental mood of soul.

We do not necessarily need to think of these stages as hap-    *[61]*
pening one after the other. On the contrary, depending on
the individual student, training may proceed so that one
level has been only partially completed before the student
begins with exercises that correspond to the next level. For
example, it may be very good for a certain student to do
exercises leading to personal experiences in inspiration,
intuition, or recognizing the connection between microcosm and macrocosm even though he or she has only
acquired a few imaginations with any degree of certainty.

. . . . . . . .

Once students of the spirit have experienced intuition, in    *[62]*
addition to being able to recognize the images of the world
of soul and spirit and read their interrelationships in the
"hidden script," they also acquire direct knowledge of the

actual beings who work together to bring about the world to which we human beings belong. Through this, they also get to know themselves in the forms they possess as spiritual beings in the world of soul and spirit. They have worked hard to be able to perceive the higher I and have realized how they need to continue working in order to control the double, the guardian of the threshold. But they have also encountered the "greater guardian" who constantly urges them on to greater effort. This greater guardian becomes the example they want to emulate, and once this has happened it becomes possible for them to recognize *who* it is standing in front of them in the form of the greater guardian. In the students' perception, the greater guardian is now transformed into the figure of the Christ. The essence of this being and His intervention in Earth's evolution has been made clear in earlier chapters of this book. In this way, students of the spirit are initiated into that same exalted mystery that is linked with the name of Christ. The Christ discloses Himself to them as the great example for human beings on Earth.

To those who have recognized the Christ in the spiritual world as a result of their initiation, historical events on Earth in the fourth post-Atlantean evolutionary period (the Greco-Latin age) also become comprehensible. For students of the spirit, the intervention of the exalted Sun being, the Christ-being, in Earth's evolution at that time and His ongoing work within this evolution become a matter of direct experience and personal knowledge. Through intuition, therefore, the purpose and significance of Earth's evolution are revealed to students of the spirit.

The path that is described here as leading to knowledge [63] of the supersensible worlds is one that every human being can follow, regardless of his or her present situation in life. In talking about such a path, we must keep in mind that although the goal of knowledge and truth is the same in all ages of Earth's evolution, the starting points have been different at different times. People wanting to set out on the path to the spiritual world at present cannot start from the same point as ancient Egyptian candidates for initiation, for example. That's why present-day individuals cannot simply take up the exercises assigned to students of the spirit in ancient Egypt. Since that time, human souls have progressed through various incarnations, and this progress is not without meaning and significance. The abilities and characteristics of human souls change from incarnation to incarnation. Even if we observe human history only superficially, we can see that all of life's circumstances were different after the twelfth or thirteenth century than they were before: opinions, feelings, and even human abilities changed. The path to higher cognition that is described here is one that is suitable for souls incarnating in the immediate present. It takes its point of departure for spiritual development from where people stand at present, whatever the circumstances of their individual lives may be. Just as the forms of outer life change, evolution from one period to the next leads humankind to ever different forms with regard to the paths to higher cognition. At any given time, outer life and initiation must be in perfect harmony.

# CHAPTER 6

# COSMIC AND HUMAN EVOLUTION NOW AND IN THE FUTURE

[1]  Unless we understand past evolution, it is impossible to know anything about the present and future states of human and cosmic evolution in the sense of spiritual science, because everything spiritual researchers are able to know about the present and the future is simultaneously present in what presents itself to their perception as they observe the hidden facts of the past. This book has dealt with the Saturn, Sun, Moon, and Earth phases of evolution. Without observing the facts of previous evolutionary phases, we cannot understand the Earth phase of evolution in the sense of spiritual science, because in a certain respect the realities of the Moon, Sun, and Saturn phases are present in what confronts us now in the earthly world. The beings and things that were involved in the Moon phase continued to evolve, and everything that belongs to our present Earth came from them.

However, not everything that came from the Moon and has now become the Earth is perceptible to consciousness in the physical world of the senses. Part of what passed from the Moon to the Earth in the course of evolution only becomes evident at a certain level of supersensible consciousness. Having reached this level of cognition, we can perceive that our earthly world is connected to a supersensible world which contains the part of Moon existence that did not condense enough to be physically perceived by our senses. The supersensible world contains this aspect of the Moon as it is at present, not as it was during the ancient Moon phase of evolution. However, it is possible for supersensible consciousness to get a picture of conditions at that time.

When this supersensible consciousness concentrates on the perception that is possible at present, it becomes evident that this perception is gradually separating into two images all by itself. One image represents the form the Earth had during its Moon phase of evolution. But as the other image presents itself, we can recognize that it contains a form that is still in a seminal stage; only in the future will it become a reality in the way that the Earth is a reality now. On further observation, it becomes apparent that in a certain sense the results of what happens on Earth are constantly flowing into this future form, which therefore represents what our Earth is meant to become. The effects of earthly existence will unite with what happens in this other world, giving rise to the new cosmic being into which the Earth will eventually be transformed, just as the Moon was transformed into the Earth. We can call this future form the Jupiter stage.

If this Jupiter stage is observed by means of supersensible perception, it becomes evident that in the future certain processes will have to take place because certain beings and things are present in the supersensible part of the earthly world that came from the Moon. These beings and things will assume certain forms after various events have taken place within the physical, sense-perceptible Earth realm. This means that the Jupiter stage will contain something that has already been predetermined by the Moon phase of evolution, and it will also contain something new that is entering evolution as a whole only because of processes taking place on the Earth. This is why it is possible for supersensible consciousness to experience something of what will happen during the Jupiter stage.

The beings and facts that can be perceived within this field of consciousness do not have the character of sensory images; they do not even appear as delicate airy structures that might give rise to effects reminiscent of sense impressions. The impressions we receive from them are purely spiritual impressions of sound, light, and warmth that are not expressed through material embodiments of any sort. They can only be grasped by means of supersensible consciousness. It is possible to say that such beings have "bodies," but these bodies become apparent within the soul element, their present essential nature, like a sum of condensed memories that these beings carry in their soul-nature. Within such beings, we can distinguish between what they are *now* experiencing and what they have already experienced and now remember. The latter is contained in them like a bodily element, which is experienced in the same way that earthly human beings experience their bodies.

At a higher level of supersensible cognition than that just described as necessary for perceiving the Moon and Jupiter, it is possible to perceive supersensible things and beings that are further evolved forms of what was already present during the Sun stage. At present, these figures have achieved such high levels of existence that they are not perceptible at all to consciousness that has only reached the level of being able to perceive Moon forms. This world's image also splits into two when we contemplate it inwardly. One image leads to knowledge of the past Sun stage, while the other presents a future form of the Earth. The Earth will assume this form when the effects of the Earth and Jupiter processes have flowed into the forms of this world. Spiritual science calls this the Venus stage. Similarly, a future stage of evolution that can be called the Vulcan stage, which has the same relationship to the Saturn stage as Venus to the Sun and Jupiter to the Moon, becomes evident to a still more highly developed supersensible consciousness. Therefore, in considering the past, present, and future of the Earth, we can speak of the Saturn, Sun, Moon, Earth, Jupiter, Venus, and Vulcan phases of evolution.

Several chapters in this book have described how the [*] human world and human beings themselves move through the stages that have been given the names Saturn, Sun, Moon, Earth, Jupiter, Venus, and Vulcan. The relationship of human evolution to certain celestial bodies, which coexist with the Earth and have been given the names Saturn, Jupiter, Mars, and so on, was also indicated. Of course, these heavenly bodies are also undergoing evolutions of their own. At the present time, they have reached the stage where their physical aspects present themselves to our perception as the entities that physical astronomy knows as Saturn, Jupiter, Mars, and so on. In the sense of spiritual science, present-day Saturn is a reincarnation of ancient Saturn, so to speak, and came about because of the presence of certain beings prior to the Sun's separation from the Earth. These particular beings were unable to participate in this separation, because they had incorporated so many characteristics suited to Saturn existence that they were out of place on a cosmic body that concentrated primarily on developing Sun characteristics.

[*]     Present-day Jupiter, however, came about because of the presence of beings with characteristics that will only be able to develop during the future Jupiter stage of general evolution. A dwelling place was made where they could foreshadow this future evolution. Mars is a celestial body inhabited by beings who went through the Moon phase of evolution in a such way that they no longer had anything to gain from staying on Earth. Mars is a reincarnation of old Moon on a higher level. Present-day Mercury is the dwelling of beings who are ahead of the Earth's evolution, because they have developed certain earthly characteristics in a higher form than is possible on Earth. In a similar way, present-day Venus prophetically anticipates the Venus stage of the future.

[*]     Because of all this, we are quite justified in giving the stages before and after the Earth-phase the names of their present representatives in the cosmos. It goes without saying that when people want to use intellects trained in

the outer observation of nature to judge the parallel drawn here between the supersensibly perceived states of Saturn, Sun, and so on and their namesakes among the physical heavenly bodies, they will raise many objections to what has been presented here. But just as it is possible to use mathematical concepts to visualize the solar system as an image of happenings in time and space, it is also possible for supersensible cognition to imbue this mathematical image with a soul content so that it takes on a form that permits drawing this parallel. Imbuing the image with soul content in this way, however, is also fully consistent with the further application of a strict natural-scientific method of observation. At the moment, this natural-scientific method still restricts itself to trying to express the interrelationship between the solar system and the Earth in purely mathematical, mechanical concepts, while the natural science of the future will, of itself, be driven to expand these mechanical concepts to include ones imbued with soul.

It would certainly be possible to show that these modern [*] natural-scientific ideas already provide sufficient grounds for expanding these concepts, but this undertaking would require a whole book in itself. All that can done here is to point to this matter, although doing so exposes it to many misunderstandings as a result. The disagreements between spiritual science and natural science are often only apparent ones. They result simply from the refusal of natural science to formulate ideas that are demanded not only by supersensible cognition but also—if the truth be told—by cognition that restricts itself to sense-perceptible things.

Everywhere in the results of modern natural-scientific observations, unbiased observers can find indications of other fields of purely sensory, physical observation that will have to be investigated in a purely natural-scientific manner in the future. Such investigations will show that a full observation of nature confirms what supersensible perception reveals about any supersensible cosmic events with corresponding sense-perceptible manifestations.

*[\*]*    In addition to the comprehensive circumstances of Earth's evolution, observations of the nearer future also present themselves to our consciousness. Every image of the past corresponds to one of the future. However, in discussing these things, we must emphasize something that urgently needs to be taken into account. If we want to know about things like this, we must totally relinquish the view that philosophical contemplation educated merely by sense-perceptible reality is capable of discovering anything about them. These things cannot and should not ever be researched by thinking about them in this way. If we were to believe that because spiritual science has already supplied us with information about the Moon phase of evolution, we will now be able to discover what things will look like on Jupiter by comparing the circumstances of Earth and Moon and applying this kind of thinking, we will succumb to enormous deceptions. These circumstances should only be researched through supersensible consciousness that rises to the level necessary to observe them. Only when the results of this research have been communicated is it also possible to understand them without supersensible consciousness.

Spiritual researchers are in a different position with   [2]
regard to communications about the future than they are
with regard to those about the past. We are not initially
able to confront future events as impartially as we confront the past. What will happen in the future stirs up our
feeling and willing, but we tolerate the past quite differently. Anyone who observes life will know that this is true
even of our ordinary existence, but only those who are
aware of certain things in the supersensible worlds can
know what forms this tendency assumes and to what an
enormous extent it increases with regard to life's hidden
facts. This is the reason why knowledge of these things is
kept within very specific limits.

Just as the greater cosmic evolution can be presented as a   [3]
succession of states from Saturn through the Vulcan phase,
it is also possible to present shorter spans of time such as
those that make up the Earth phase of evolution. The enormous upheaval that brought an end to life on Atlantis was
followed by the stages in human evolution that have been
described in this book as the ancient Indian, ancient Persian,
Egypto-Chaldean, and Greco-Latin cultural periods. The
fifth period is where we stand now—the present. This
period began gradually around the twelfth, thirteenth, and
fourteenth centuries A.D., after having been prepared ever
since the fourth and fifth centuries. It has been clearly evident ever since the fifteenth century. The Greco-Latin
period that preceded it began around the eighth century B.C.,
and at the end of its first third the Christ event took place.

The disposition and faculties of the human soul
changed during the transition from the Egypto-Chaldean

period to the Greco-Latin. During the Egypto-Chaldean period, what we now know as logical thinking or grasping the world through reason did not yet exist. At that time, the knowledge we now make our own through our intellect was acquired in a way that was appropriate then—directly, through an inner knowledge that was supersensible in a certain respect. While people perceived things, the necessary concept or image of those things simply appeared in their souls. When the faculty of cognition is like this, not only do images of the physical world of the senses appear, but a certain knowledge of non-sensory realities and beings also rises out of the soul's depths. This was a remnant of the ancient, dusk-like supersensible consciousness that all of humankind had formerly possessed.

In the Greco-Latin age, there were more and more people who lacked this faculty. In its place, the capacity for intellectual reflection appeared. People became more and more removed from direct dreamlike perception of the world of soul and spirit and ever more dependent on their intellect and feelings to provide an image of that world. In some respects, this state of affairs continued throughout the fourth post-Atlantean period. Only those individuals who had retained the legacy of the former soul disposition, so to speak, were able to admit the spiritual world into their consciousness directly. These people, however, were holdovers from an earlier age. Their type of cognition was no longer suited to the new age, because as a result of the laws of evolution, an old soul capacity loses its full significance when new faculties appear. Human life adapts to these new faculties and no longer knows what to do with the old ones.

There were also individuals, however, who quite consciously began to develop other, higher powers in addition to the powers of intellect and feeling they had acquired. These powers made it possible for them to break through into the world of soul and spirit again. The way they had to begin to do this was quite different from how it had happened among the students of the ancient initiates, who had not had to consider the soul faculties that developed only during the fourth post-Atlantean period. This fourth period saw the first beginnings of the type of modern spiritual training that has been described in this book. However, at that time it was only in its beginning stages; it could only be fully developed in the fifth post-Atlantean period beginning with the twelfth and thirteenth centuries, and especially since the fifteenth century. People who attempted to ascend into supersensible worlds in this way were able to experience something about higher realms of existence through their own imagination, inspiration, and intuition. To those who were content with the faculties of intellect and feeling that had developed, what ancient clairvoyance had known was accessible only through oral or written traditions that were passed down from generation to generation.

For people born after the Christ event who did not  [4] make their way up into supersensible worlds, such traditions were also their only means of knowing anything about the essential nature of this event. However, there were certain initiates who still possessed the old natural ability to perceive the supersensible world and whose development allowed them to enter a higher world in spite of the fact that they disregarded humankind's new intellectual and emotional powers. They created a transition from the old form of initiation to the new one. People like this were also present in subsequent periods. However, the essential characteristic of the fourth post-Atlantean period was that human powers of intellect and feeling were strengthened by being cut off from direct interaction with the world of soul and spirit. The souls who incarnated then and greatly developed these powers then carried the results of their development over into their incarnation during the fifth period. As compensation for having been cut off from the spiritual world, the mighty traditions of ancient wisdom were available, especially those having to do with the Christ event. Through the very power of their content, these traditions provided human souls with a confident knowledge of the higher world.

There were also always human souls, however, who developed their powers of higher cognition in addition to their faculties of intellect and feeling. It was incumbent upon them to experience the realities of the higher world and especially the mystery of the Christ event by means of direct supersensible knowledge. They always allowed as much of this to flow into other human souls as was comprehensible to them and good for them.

In harmony with the purpose of Earth's evolution, the first expansion of Christianity was meant to take place at a time when most of humankind had not developed faculties of supersensible cognition. This is why the force of tradition was so powerful at that time. An extremely powerful force was needed to make people confident in the supersensible world if they themselves were not able to behold this world. With the exception of a brief time during the thirteenth century, there were almost always individuals who were capable of lifting themselves up into the higher worlds through imagination, inspiration, and intuition. In the Christian era, these people were the successors of the initiates of antiquity who had been leaders and members of the centers of mystery wisdom. The task of these new initiates was to recognize once again, through their own faculties, what had once been comprehended through ancient mystery wisdom and to add to this a knowledge of the essential nature of the Christ event.

Thus the knowledge arising among the new initiates *[5]* encompassed all the subject matter of ancient initiation, but from its center radiated the higher knowledge of the mysteries of the Christ event. As long as the human souls of the fourth post-Atlantean period were meant to be consolidating their faculties of intellect and feeling, this knowledge was only able to flow into general life to a limited extent, so during that time it was really quite hidden. Then the new age of the fifth cultural period dawned. Its main feature was the further development of intellectual abilities, which blossomed exuberantly then and will continue to unfold in the present and future. A gradual buildup to this period began in the twelfth and thirteenth centuries, and its progress accelerated from the sixteenth century onward into the present.

Under these influences, cultivating the forces of reason became the chief concern of evolution in the fifth cultural period. In contrast, traditional knowledge of and confidence in a supersensible world lost more and more of its power over human souls. However, it was replaced by what we may call an increasingly strong influx into human souls of knowledge derived from modern supersensible consciousness. "Hidden" knowledge was now flowing, although imperceptibly to begin with, into people's ways of thinking. It is self-evident that intellectual forces have continued to reject this knowledge right into the present. But what must happen will happen in spite of any temporary rejection. Symbolically, this hidden knowledge, which is taking hold of humanity from the other side and will do so increasingly in the future, can be called "the knowledge of the Grail." If we learn to understand the deeper meaning of this symbol as it is presented in stories and legends, we will discover a significant image of what has been described above as the new initiation knowledge with the Christ mystery at its center. Therefore, modern initiates can also be known as "Grail initiates."

The path to supersensible worlds whose first stages have been described in this book leads to "the science of the Grail." A unique feature of this knowledge is that its facts can only be investigated by those who acquire the means of doing so that are described in this book. Once these facts have been discovered, however, they can then be understood by means of the soul forces that have been developing during the fifth cultural period. In fact, it will become increasingly evident that these forces will find their satisfaction in this knowledge to an ever greater extent. At present, we are living in a time when more of this knowledge ought to enter common consciousness than was formerly the case. This book hopes to convey the information it contains from this point of view. To the extent that human evolution will absorb Grail knowledge, the impulse supplied by the Christ event can become ever more significant. Increasingly, an inner aspect will be added to the external aspect of Christian evolution. What we can recognize through imagination, inspiration, and intuition about the higher worlds in conjunction with the Christ Mystery will increasingly permeate our life of ideas, feeling, and will. "Hidden" Grail knowledge will become evident; as an inner force, it will increasingly permeate the manifestations of human life.

For the duration of the fifth cultural period, knowledge [6] of supersensible worlds will continue to flow into human consciousness; when the sixth period begins, humanity will have been able to reacquire the non-sensory perception it possessed in a dusklike way in earlier times—but now on a higher level and in a form that is quite different from the old perception. In ancient times, what our souls knew about the higher worlds was not imbued with our own forces of reason and feeling; it was received as inspiration from above. In the future, our souls will not only receive these flashes of inspiration, but will also comprehend them and experience them as the essence of human soul-nature. In future, when a soul receives knowledge about a certain being or thing, the very nature of the intellect will find this justified. If knowledge of a different sort asserts itself—knowledge of a moral commandment or a human behavior—the soul will tell itself: My feelings will only be justified if I act in accordance with this knowledge. A sufficiently large number of human beings are meant to develop this state of mind during the sixth post-Atlantean cultural period.

In a certain way, what the third or Egypto-Chaldean period contributed to humanity's evolution is being repeated in the fifth. At that time, the human soul still perceived certain realities of the supersensible world, although this perception was waning as intellectual faculties prepared to emerge. These faculties were to temporarily exclude human beings from the higher world. In the fifth cultural period, the supersensible realities that had been perceived in a dusk-like state of consciousness are becoming evident again but are now being imbued with our personal forces of intellect and feeling and with what human souls can gain through knowledge of the Christ Mystery. This is why they are assuming different forms than they did previously. In ancient times, impressions from the supersensible worlds were experienced as forces that urged human beings on but emanated from an outer spiritual world that did not include them. In contrast, more recent evolution allows us to perceive these impressions as coming from a world we human beings are growing into and are increasingly a part of. No one ought to believe that the Egypto-Chaldean cultural period will be repeated in such a way that our souls will simply be able to take up what was then present and has come down to us from those times. If understood correctly, the effect of the Christ impulse is to make the human souls that receive it feel, recognize, and conduct themselves as members of a spiritual world, whereas formerly they were outsiders.

While the third cultural period is revived in the fifth in order to be imbued with the totally new element in human souls provided by the fourth period, something similar happens in the sixth cultural period with regard to the second and in the seventh with regard to the first or ancient Indian cultural period. All the wonderful wisdom that the great teachers of ancient India could proclaim will be able to reappear as life truths in human souls in the seventh cultural period.

Now, any transformations in things in the earthly world   *[7]* outside of human beings also have a certain relationship to humankind's own evolution. When the seventh cultural period has run its course, the Earth will be struck by an upheaval comparable to the one that took place between the Atlantean and post-Atlantean ages. After this, evolution will continue under transformed earthly circumstances through seven more time periods. On a higher level, the human souls incarnating then will experience the same fellowship with a higher world that the Atlanteans experienced on a lower level.

However, only human beings embodying souls that have become all that they could under the influence of the Greco-Latin cultural period and the subsequent fifth, sixth, and seventh periods of post-Atlantean evolution will be able to cope with these reconfigured earthly circumstances. The inner nature of these souls will correspond to what the Earth has then become. Other souls will have to remain behind at this stage, although earlier they could still have chosen to create the prerequisites for participation in it. The souls mature enough to face the conditions that will exist after the next great upheaval will be the ones who succeeded in imbuing supersensible knowledge with their own forces of intellect and feeling at the transition from the fifth to the sixth post-Atlantean period. The fifth and sixth periods are the decisive ones, so to speak. In the seventh period, although the souls who have achieved the goal of the sixth will continue to develop accordingly, the changed circumstances in their surroundings will provide little opportunity for the others to make up for lost time. The next opportunity will present itself only in the distant future.

This is how evolution is proceeding from one age to the next. Supersensible cognition observes not only future changes involving the Earth alone, but also ones that occur in interaction with the neighboring heavenly bodies. There will come a time when both the Earth and humanity have made such progress in evolution that the forces and beings that had to separate from the Earth during Lemurian times to enable earthly beings to continue to progress will be able to reunite with the Earth. At that time, the Moon will reconnect with the Earth. This will happen because sufficient numbers of human souls possess enough inner strength to make these Moon forces fruitful for further evolution. This will take place at a time when another development that has turned toward evil will be taking place alongside the high level of development reached by the appropriate number of human souls. Souls whose development has been delayed will have accumulated so much error, ugliness, and evil in their karma that they temporarily form a distinct union of evil and aberrant human beings who vehemently oppose the community of good human beings.

In the course of its development, the good portion of humankind will learn to use the Moon forces to transform the evil part so that it can participate in further evolution as a distinct earthly kingdom. Through the work of the good part of humanity, the Earth, then reunited with the Moon, will become able to reunite with the Sun after a certain period of evolution, and also with the other planets. After an interim stage that resembles a sojourn in a higher world, the Earth will transform itself into the Jupiter state.   *[8]*

During the Jupiter stage, what is now called the mineral kingdom will not exist; mineral forces will have been transformed into plant forces. The lowest kingdom appearing during the Jupiter stage will be the plant kingdom, which will have a form entirely different from what it has now. Above that will be the animal kingdom which will have undergone a comparable transformation, followed by a human kingdom consisting of the descendants of the evil union that came about on Earth. Above these, there will be a higher human kingdom consisting of the descendants of the community of good human beings on Earth. A great deal of the work of this second human kingdom will consist of ennobling the fallen souls in the evil union so that they will still be able to find their way back into the actual human kingdom.

At the Venus stage, the plant kingdom will also have disappeared, and the lowest kingdom will be the animal kingdom, transformed once more. Above that there will be three human kingdoms of different degrees of perfection. During the Venus stage, the Earth will remain united with the Sun; in contrast, as evolution proceeds on Jupiter, the Sun will once again break away from Jupiter and influence it from outside. Then a reunification of the Sun and Jupiter will take place, and the transformation into the Venus stage will gradually continue. During the Venus stage, a distinct cosmic body will break away, containing all the beings who have resisted evolution and constituting an "unredeemable moon," so to speak. It will move toward an evolution that is so different in character from anything we can experience on Earth that there are no words that can possibly express it. The part of humanity that has continued to evolve, however, will move on to the Vulcan phase of evolution in a fully spiritualized form of existence. Describing this state falls outside the scope of this book.

[9]     We see that the highest imaginable ideal of human evolution results from Grail knowledge—that is, the spiritualization that we achieve through our own work. Ultimately, this spiritualization will appear as the result of the harmony that human beings were able to bring about in the fifth and sixth cultural periods between their forces of intellect and feeling and their knowledge of supersensible worlds. What they produced there in their inmost souls will ultimately become the outer world. The human spirit raises itself up to the mighty impressions of

its outer world, first divining and later recognizing the spiritual beings behind these impressions, while the human heart senses the infinite loftiness of this spiritual element. However, human beings can also recognize their own inner experiences of intellect, feeling, and morality as the seeds of a future spiritual world.

If we believe that human freedom is incompatible with foreknowledge and with predestination of the shape of things to come, we should think of it like this: Our free action in the future will depend as little on what predestined things will be like then as it does on our intention to be living a year from now in a house we design today. To the extent that our inner nature permits, we will be free in the house we have built for ourselves, and we will also be free in the circumstances that come about on Venus and Jupiter to the extent that our own inner nature permits. Our freedom will not depend on what is predestined by prior circumstances, but on what our souls have made of themselves.   [10]

The Earth stage contains what evolved during the preceding Saturn, Sun, and Moon phases of evolution. Earthly human beings find *wisdom* in the events taking place around them; it is there as the result of what happened previously. The Earth is the descendant of the old Moon, which shaped itself and everything belonging to it into the cosmos of wisdom. The Earth, which is the beginning of an evolution that will inject new force into this wisdom, brings human beings to the point where they experience themselves as independent members of a spiritual world. This is due to the fact that the human I was   [11]

fashioned by the Spirits of Form during the Earth phase
of evolution, just as the physical body was shaped by the
Spirits of Will on Saturn, the life body by the Spirits of
Wisdom on the Sun, and the astral body by the Spirits of
Motion on the Moon. What manifests as wisdom does so
through the interaction of the Spirits of Will, Wisdom,
and Motion. In wisdom, earthly beings and processes can
exist in harmony with the other beings of their world
through the work of these three orders of spiritual beings.

In the future, the independent human I, which was
received through the Spirits of Form, will exist in harmony with the beings of Earth, Jupiter, Venus, and Vulcan, because of the power that the Earth stage injects into
wisdom. This is the power of *love*, which must begin in
human beings on Earth. The "cosmos of wisdom" is
developing into a "cosmos of love." Everything that the I
can develop within itself must turn into love. The exalted
Sun being we were able to characterize in describing
Christ's evolution manifests as the all-encompassing
example of love, planting the seed of love in the innermost core of the human being. From there, it is meant to
flow out into all of evolution. Just as wisdom, which
formed earlier, discloses itself in the forces of the sense-
perceptible earthly world, in present-day forces of nature,
love itself will appear as a new natural force in all phenomena in the future. This is the mystery of all future
evolution: that our knowledge and everything we do out
of a true understanding of evolution sow seeds that must
ripen into love. The greater the power of the love that
comes into being, the more we will be able to accomplish

creatively on behalf of the future. The strongest forces working toward the end result of spiritualization lie in what will come from love. The more spiritual knowledge flows into the evolution of humanity and the Earth, the greater the number of viable seeds will there be for the future. Through its very nature, spiritual knowledge transforms itself into love.

The whole process that has been described, beginning with the Greco-Latin cultural period and extending throughout the present time, shows how this transformation is to proceed. It also shows us the purpose of this future evolution that is now in its beginning stages. The wisdom for which the groundwork was laid on Saturn, Sun, and Moon works in the human physical, etheric, and astral bodies, presenting itself as cosmic wisdom. In the I, however, it becomes inner wisdom. Beginning with the Earth phase of evolution, the wisdom of the outer cosmos becomes inner wisdom in the human being. Internalized in this way, it becomes the seed of love. Wisdom is the prerequisite for love; love is the result of wisdom that has been reborn in the I.

If anyone is misled into believing that evolution as it has [12] been explained above bears a fatalistic stamp, this is a result of having misunderstood the explanations. If we were to believe that evolution condemns a certain number of people to become members of the kingdom of "evil humanity," we would have failed to see how the interrelationship between the sense-perceptible and the soul-spiritual takes shape in the course of this evolution. Within certain limits, these worlds, both the sense-perceptible and the soul-spiritual, each constitute a separate evolutionary current. Through forces inherent in the sense-perceptible current, the forms of "evil human beings" come about. However, it will only be necessary for any given human soul to incarnate in such a body if it has created the necessary preconditions itself. It might also happen that the forms arising out of the forces of the sense-perceptible world find no reincarnating human souls to embody, because these souls have all become too good for such bodies. In that case, the cosmos would have to ensoul these forms with something other than formerly human souls. Such forms will be occupied by human souls only when these same souls have prepared themselves for such an incarnation. In this field, supersensible cognition is bound to report what it sees—for instance, that at a particular point in the future there will be two human kingdoms, one good and one evil. However, this does not mean that the present state of human souls forces supersensible cognition to the rational conclusion that this future state will be the natural and inevitable result. Supersensible cognition's ways of investigating the evolution of human forms and the evolution of the destinies of souls are and must be completely separate, and to confuse the two in our worldview would be a remnant of a materialistic attitude that would seriously impinge on the science of the supersensible.

# CHAPTER 7

# DETAILS FROM THE FIELD
# OF SPIRITUAL SCIENCE

## *The Human Ether Body*

When we perceive the higher members of our human    [1]
makeup through supersensible observation, this perception is never completely similar to a perception we have
through our outer senses. When we touch an outer object
and have a perception of warmth, we must distinguish
between what comes from the object—what streams out of
it, so to speak—and what we experience in our souls. Our
inner soul experience of the perception of warmth is something different from the warmth that flows out of the
object. Now let's imagine this soul experience all by itself,
without the outer object. Let's imagine the experience of a
perception of warmth in the soul with no physical outer
object to cause it. If this experience were simply present
without cause, it would be imaginary. However, students
of the spirit do experience inner perceptions such as this
that have no physical cause. Above all, they are not caused
by the students' physical bodies. But at a certain level of
inner development, these perceptions present themselves

in such a way that the students can tell that the inner perception is not imaginary but has been brought about by a being of soul and spirit in a supersensible outer world, just as an ordinary perception of warmth, for example, is brought about by an external physical, sense-perceptible object. (It was shown earlier how the experience itself lets us know that it is not imaginary.)

This is also true if we speak about perceptions of color. In that case, we have to distinguish between the color of the outer object and the inner sensation of color in the soul. Let's recall the inner sensation the soul has when it perceives a red object in the physical, sense-perceptible outer world; let's imagine that we vividly recollect the impression while averting our eyes from the object. Let's remember the inner experience of our mental image of the color. When we do this, we distinguish between the outer color and our inner experience of it. Such inner experiences are definitely different in content from outer sense impressions. They are much closer in character to what we experience as pain or pleasure than ordinary sensory perceptions are.

Now let's think of such an inner experience arising in the soul without being caused by either an actual outer, physical, sense-perceptible object or a memory of one. People with supersensible cognition are able to have such experiences and to know that they are not imaginary but are expressions of beings of soul and spirit. If a soul-spiritual being calls forth the same impression as a red object in the physical, sense-perceptible world, it can be called red. In the case of the physical object, however, the outer impression is always present before the inner experience of color, while in true supersensible perception in present-day human beings the reverse must always be the case—the inner experience is there first, like a mere shadowy memory of color, followed by an image that becomes more and more vivid. This is how this process must take place, and the less attention we pay to this fact, the less we are able to distinguish between real spiritual perception and imaginary deceptions (illusions, hallucinations, and so on). The vividness of the image during soul-spiritual perception of this sort—whether it remains very shadowy, as if dimly visualized, or whether its effect is strong like that of an outer object—depends totally on the perceiver's inner development.

The general impression that a clairvoyant observer has of the human ether body can be described as follows: When people with supersensible cognition have developed such strength of will that they are able to disregard what their physical eyes are seeing, in spite of the fact that a physical human being is standing in front of them, they are then able to use supersensible consciousness to see into the space the physical person occupies. Naturally, it requires an intense heightening of their will for them to be able to disregard not only what they are thinking but also something that is standing right in front of them, and to such an extent that its physical impression is extinguished. However, it is possible to bring this heightening about—it happens as a result of the exercises for achieving supersensible cognition. When people first perceive in this way, they get a general impression of the ether body. The inner sensation that arises in their souls is approximately the same as the one they get from seeing the color of a peach blossom. This becomes increasingly vivid and enables them to say that the ether body has the color of peach blossoms. After that, they also perceive the individual organs and currents within the ether body.

However, the ether body could be described further by presenting soul experiences that correspond to sensations of warmth, sound, and so on, because the ether body is more than just a color phenomenon. The astral body and the other elements of our human makeup could also be described in this same sense. Having considered this, we will realize how spiritual scientific descriptions are meant to be understood (See chapter 2).

*The Astral World*

[2]     As long as we are only observing the physical world, the Earth as our dwelling-place appears like a separate cosmic body. However, if supersensible cognition rises to the level of other worlds, this separation ceases. This is why it was possible to state that imagination simultaneously perceives both the Earth and the Moon stage as it has continued to develop into the present time. In addition to the Earth's supersensible aspect, other cosmic bodies that are physically separate from the Earth are embedded in the world that we enter in this way. Those who perceive supersensible worlds do not observe only the Earth's supersensible aspect but to begin with they also perceive the supersensible aspect of other cosmic bodies. (People who are tempted to ask why clairvoyants don't

tell us what things look like on Mars, and so on, should keep in mind that clairvoyants are primarily concerned with observing the supersensible aspects of cosmic bodies, while they themselves, in asking this question, have physical, sense-perceptible conditions in mind.) That's why this book has been able to present certain relationships between the Earth phase of evolution and the simultaneous evolution of Saturn, Jupiter, Mars, and so on.

When the human astral body is carried off into sleep, it belongs not only to earthly conditions but also to worlds in which still other cosmic domains (the worlds of the stars) take part. Indeed, these worlds work into the human astral body even during the waking state, which is why the name *astral body* seems justified.[1]

## Human Life after Death

This book has described the time after the death of the human being when the astral body still remains united with the ether body. During this time, a memory of the entire life that has just ended is present but gradually fades (see chapter 3). The length of this period of time is different for different people and depends on how strongly an individual's astral body clings to the ether body—that is, on how much power the astral body has over the ether body. Supersensible cognition can get an impression of this by observing individuals whose state of body and soul dictates that they actually ought to be asleep, but who are keeping themselves awake through

[3]

---

1. From the Greek *astron* and the Latin *astrum*, meaning "star."

sheer inner effort. It becomes evident that the length of time individuals can keep themselves awake without being overcome by sleep varies from person to person. After death, our recollection of our past life—that is, the time of the astral body's connection to the ether body—lasts approximately as long as we would formerly have been able to remain awake in a case of extreme need.

. . . . . . . .

[4]     When the ether body is released from a human being who has died, something that can be described as an extract or essence of it still persists throughout this individual's later evolution. This extract contains the fruits of the life that has just ended and is the vehicle of everything that unfolds, like a seed for the next life, during the human being's spiritual development between death and a new birth (see chapter 3).

. . . . . . . .

[5]     The length of time that elapses between death and a new birth (see chapter 3) is determined by the fact that an I usually returns to the physical, sense-perceptible world only after enough change has taken place there for it to be able to experience something new. While the I is in the domains of the spirit, its earthly dwelling is changing. In a certain respect, this change is linked to all the great changes going on in the cosmos, such as changes in the Earth's relationship to the Sun. However, these are all changes in which certain repetitions appear in connection with new conditions. For example, they are expressed

outwardly in the fact that the point on the celestial sphere where the Sun rises at the beginning of spring makes a complete circle in the course of approximately 26,000 years. During this period of time, therefore, the vernal equinox moves from one celestial region to another. In the course of one twelfth of this 26,000 year period, or approximately 2,100 years, circumstances on Earth have changed enough so that human souls will be able to experience something that is different from their preceding incarnations. But since people's experiences differ depending on whether they incarnate as women or as men, as a rule two incarnations—one male, one female—take place during a period of this length.

These things also depend, however, on the character of the forces we take with us from earthly existence into death, so everything indicated here should only be taken as the general rule. The details can vary in many different ways. How long a human I spends in the spiritual world between death and a new birth depends on the above-mentioned cosmic conditions in only one respect. In another respect, it depends on the evolutionary conditions a particular individual undergoes during this time. After a certain time has elapsed, evolution leads the I to a state of spirit that can no longer be satisfied by inner spiritual experiences. It then begins to long for a changed state of consciousness that finds satisfaction in being reflected by physical experience. The individual's reentry into earthly life results from the interaction of this inner thirst for embodiment and the possibility the cosmos offers of finding a suitable bodily organism. Because these two things have to work together, incarnation may take place in one instance when this "thirst" has not yet peaked but an approximately suitable embodiment can be realized. In another instance, it takes place when the thirst has already exceeded its normal intensity because there was no possibility of embodiment at the appropriate time. A person's general attitude toward life, which is due to the makeup of his or her bodily nature, is related to these circumstances.

### The Course of a Human Life

[6]    The life of a human being, as expressed in the successions of conditions between birth and death, can be fully understood only when we consider the changes that take place in the supersensible aspects of a person's makeup, and not merely the physical, sense-perceptible body. We can look at these changes as follows: Physical birth represents an individual's breaking away from the sheltering physical body of the mother. After birth, the forces that the embryonic human being formerly shared with the mother's body are present only as independent forces within the newborn being. Later on in life, supersensible events similar to the events of physical birth take place and can be perceived by means of supersensible perception. Until a child begins to lose his or her baby teeth in the sixth or seventh year of life, the ether body is surrounded by an etheric covering, which falls away at this time, when the "birth" of the ether body takes place. However, the human being remains surrounded by an astral covering that falls away at puberty, sometime

between the twelfth and sixteenth years, when the "birth" of the astral body takes place. Still later, the actual I is born. (These supersensible facts yield some fruitful viewpoints on education, which are presented in my booklet *The Education of the Child from the Viewpoint of Spiritual Science.*[2] This booklet also provides further explanations of things that can be mentioned only briefly here.)

After the birth of the I, we find our way into the circumstances of life and the world around us, and we become active within them in accordance with the aspects of our makeup that work through the I—the sentient soul, the mind soul, and the consciousness soul. After that comes a time when the ether body reverses its development; it undergoes the reverse of its developmental processes from the seventh year onward. Previously, the astral body's development had initially consisted in developing the potentials latent in it at birth; later, after the birth of the I, it enriched itself through experiences of the outer world. After a certain point, however, it begins to nourish itself spiritually by feeding off its own ether body; it gnaws on the ether body. As life continues, the ether body also begins to feed off the physical body. The decline of the physical body in old age is related to this.

---

2. *Die Erziehung des Kindes vom Gesichtspunkte der Geisteswissenschaft* first appeared as an article in *Lucifer-Gnosis* (no. 33, 1907), the magazine founded and edited by Rudolf Steiner (in GA 34); contained in *The Education of the Child: and Early Lectures on Education*, Anthroposophic Press, Hudson, NY, 1996.

Thus, the course of a human life can be divided into three parts—one period when the physical and ether bodies are unfolding, a second when the astral body and the I are developing, and a third when the ether and physical bodies are reversing their development. However, the astral body is involved in all the processes that take place between birth and death. Because, spiritually, it is actually born sometime between the twelfth and sixteenth years of life and because it has to feed off the forces of the ether and physical bodies during the last period of life, what it is able to accomplish through its own forces develops more slowly than it would if it were not taking place within the physical and etheric bodies. As a result, after the physical and etheric bodies are cast off at death, the development during the purification period takes only about one-third as long as life between birth and death (compare chapter 3).

### The Higher Domains of the Spiritual World

[7]    Through imagination, inspiration, and intuition, supersensible cognition gradually ascends into the domains of the spiritual world where it has access to the beings involved in human and cosmic evolution. This also enables it to trace the process of human development between death and a new birth in a way that makes this process understandable. However, there are still higher domains of existence that can be mentioned only briefly here. When supersensible cognition has raised itself to the level of intuition, it lives in a world of spiritual beings who are also undergoing evolutions of their own. The

concerns of present-day humanity reach right into the world of intuition, so to speak. In fact, we also experience the effects of still higher worlds in the course of our development between death and a new birth, but we do not experience them directly; the beings of the spiritual world bring them to us. So by observing these beings, we can discover everything that happens to the human being. However, what actually concerns these beings, what they themselves need in order to guide human evolution, can only be observed by means of a mode of cognition that transcends intuition. This points to worlds whose lowest spiritual concerns can be viewed as including Earth's highest spiritual concerns. For example, rational conclusions are among the highest concerns within the earthly domain, while the effects of the mineral kingdom are among the lowest. In these higher realms, rational conclusions are the approximate equivalent of mineral effects on Earth. Beyond the domain of intuition lies the domain where the cosmic plan is fashioned out of spiritual causes.

## The Aspects of Our Human Makeup

When it was said in chapter 2 that the I works on the lower aspects of our makeup—the physical body, the ether body, and the astral body—and transforms them in reverse order into the spirit self, the life spirit, and the spirit body, this refers to how the I works on the nature of the human individual through the highest human faculties, which have only begun to evolve during the various stages of the Earth phase of evolution. However, this transformation is preceded by one that takes place on a

*[8]*

lower level, giving rise to the sentient soul, the mind soul, and the consciousness soul. When the sentient soul is forming in the course of a person's inner development, changes are taking place in the astral body. Similarly, the development of the mind soul is expressed in transformations in the ether body, while that of the consciousness soul is expressed in changes in the physical body. Details of these processes were included in this book's description of the Earth phase of evolution.

In a certain respect, therefore, we can say that even the sentient soul is based on a transformation of the astral body, the mind soul on a transformation of the ether body, and the consciousness soul on a transformation of the physical body. But we can also say that these three soul aspects are parts of the astral body, because the consciousness soul, for example, can exist only because it is an astral entity within a physical body that is adapted to it. It leads an astral life in a physical body that has been modified to become its dwelling place.

### The Dream State

[9]    In this book, the dream state has already been described from a certain point of view in chapter 3, "Sleep and Death." On the one hand, because the progress of evolution is such that earlier states play into later ones, we should think of the dream state as a remnant of the ancient pictorial consciousness that human beings possessed during both the Moon phase of evolution and a large part of the Earth phase. During our dreams, a remnant of what was formerly our normal state of consciousness appears

in us. On the other hand, this state is also different from ancient pictorial consciousness. Ever since the I first developed, it has been playing into the processes in the astral body that take place during sleep while we are dreaming, so what manifests in our dreams is a pictorial consciousness altered by the presence of the I. Since the I is not conscious of acting on the astral body, however, nothing belonging to the domain of dreaming should be considered part of what can truly lead to knowledge of the higher worlds in the sense of spiritual science. The same is true of so-called visions, premonitions, or "second sight." These come about when the I eliminates itself as a factor; as a result, remnants of ancient states of consciousness arise. Such states of consciousness are of no direct use to spiritual science, and what can be observed during them cannot be considered results of spiritual science in any true sense.

*Acquiring Supersensible Knowledge*

The path to acquiring knowledge of supersensible    *[10]*
worlds that has been described in greater detail elsewhere in this book can also be called the *direct path of knowledge*. In addition to this path, there is also another that can be described as the *path of feeling*. However, it would be quite wrong to believe that the first path has nothing to do with educating our feelings. On the contrary, it leads to the greatest possible deepening of our feeling life. The path of feeling, however, turns directly and exclusively to feeling as its starting point in its efforts to rise to spiritual cognition. It is based on the fact that if the soul surrenders

completely to a feeling for a certain period of time, this feeling is transformed into cognition, into a pictorial perception. For example, if the soul completely fills itself for weeks or months or even longer with the feeling of humility, the content of this feeling is transformed into a perception. It is indeed possible to discover a path to supersensible domains by making one's way through such feelings one step at a time. However, it is not easy for present-day human beings to actually carry this out under life's ordinary circumstances. Solitude and withdrawal from modern life are almost indispensable, because the impressions of daily life disrupt what the soul accomplishes by concentrating on specific feelings, especially in the early stages of inner development. In contrast, the path to knowledge that this book describes can be followed under any circumstances of contemporary life.

### Observing Specific Beings and Events in the Spiritual World

*[11]*     One can ask whether meditation and other methods of acquiring supersensible knowledge permit only a general observation of the human being between death and rebirth and other spiritual processes, or whether they also make it possible to observe very specific processes and beings— for example, a particular person who has died. The response to this must be that those who have acquired the faculty for observing the spiritual world through the methods described here can also reach the point of being able to observe detailed events in that world. They make themselves capable of establishing a connection to human

beings who are living in the spiritual world between death and a new birth. However, we need to keep in mind that, in the sense of spiritual science, this should happen only after we have gone through a genuine training in supersensible cognition. Only then are we capable of distinguishing between deception and reality with regard to specific events and beings. Anyone attempting to observe details without the right training may fall victim to many deceptions. Even the most elementary things, such as understanding how to interpret impressions of specific realities in the supersensible world, are not possible without advanced spiritual training. The training that leads to supersensible observation of the things described in this book also leads to the ability to trace the life of an individual human being after death. It also leads to being able to observe and understand all the individual beings of the world of soul and spirit who work from this hidden world into the outer manifest world.

It is only possible for us to observe details with certainty, however, if we base this observation on our knowledge of the great general cosmic and human realities of the spiritual world, which concern all human beings. If we desire the one without the other, we will go astray. We are granted access to the particular domains of supersensible existence that we long for above all else only after we have struggled with the serious and difficult paths leading to issues of general knowledge in our efforts to find the key to the meaning of life. This is a necessary part of what we must undergo to observe the spiritual world. Only if we have taken these paths out of a pure and unegotistical urge for knowledge are we mature enough to observe the details that would formerly have served only to satisfy an egotistical need, even though we might have convinced ourselves that we were only striving for insight into the spiritual out of love—love for someone who has died, for example. Insight into details is granted only to those whose serious interest in general spiritual scientific knowledge has given them the possibility of accepting even the details as objective scientific truth without any egotistical desire.

---

*Included here are introductions written by Rudolf Steiner for the various German editions of* Die Geheimwissenschaft im Umris.

## Introduction to the First Edition

When a book such as this one is handed over to the public, it should be possible for its author to imagine all possible contemporary criticisms of its contents with no loss of composure. For example, if people whose thoughts on a certain subject have always been in line with the results of scientific research begin to read how this subject is presented here, they might come to this conclusion:

> It's astounding that assertions like this are even possible in this day and age. The author throws around the simplest scientific concepts in a way that demonstrates an altogether incomprehensible unfamiliarity with even the most basic scientific knowledge. For example, he uses concepts like "heat" in ways that show no trace of having been influenced at all by any modern thinking in the field of physics. Anyone knowing even the basics of this science would be able to tell him that what he says here doesn't even deserve to be labeled "amateurish," but can only be described as absolute ignorance.

This criticism is certainly possible, and many more such statements could be made. On the other hand, it would also be possible to conclude that the book's readers will put it aside after a few pages—either with a smile or in indignation, depending on their temperaments—and say, "Fallacious thinking certainly does produce strange aberrations nowadays. We'd better just add these explanations to the collection of strange things we've encountered."

But what would the author of this book say if he actually experienced criticism like this? From *his* point of view, wouldn't he simply have to see this critical reader as incapable of sound judgment or lacking the goodwill to come to a discerning conclusion? Certainly not in every case. The author of this book is capable of imagining that his critic is a very intelligent person, perhaps even a competent scientist who is very conscientious in how he or she arrives at conclusions. The author is able to think his way into the soul of such a person and into the reasons that lead him or her to such criticism. However, in order to clarify his actual position, the author must do something that he generally finds inappropriate but that does seem urgently necessary in the case of this book—namely, discussing personal matters—although nothing that does not relate to the decision to write this book will be included. What is said in a book like this would certainly have no right to exist if it were strictly personal in character. It *must* contain accounts that *anyone* could arrive at, and it must relate them in a way that is free of personal coloring to the greatest possible extent. Thus it is not "personal" in this sense, but only in the sense of explaining how the author finds the above-mentioned criticisms understandable and yet was still able to write the book.

It would be possible to avoid bringing in such a personal element by demonstrating explicitly and in detail how the statements in this book actually concur with all the progress modern science has made. In that case, however, the present book would have required many volumes of introduction. Since it was impossible to produce those volumes, the author found it necessary to describe the personal circumstances justifying his belief that a convincing agreement between his own thinking and modern science is possible. He would certainly never have published what is said in this book about heat processes, for example, if he were not able to state that thirty years ago he had been fortunate enough to make a thorough study of the various branches of physics. Of particular interest to him, and the focus of his studies at that point, was the so-called "theory of thermodynamics." The author was involved in ongoing studies of the historical development of explanations associated with names like Mayer, Helmholtz, Joule, and Clausius.[1] His studies thus laid an ample foundation for him to understand all

---

1. Julius Robert von Mayer (1814–1878), physician and physicist who discovered the law of the conservation of energy. Hermann von Helmholtz (1821–1894), pioneering physician, anatomist, physiologist and physicist; James Prescott Joule (1818–1889), English physicist who calculated the quantity of heat produced through mechanical work; Rudolf Emanuel Clausius (1822–1888), physicist; founder of the theory of thermodynamics.

later developments of thermodynamic theory in the field of physics; he encounters no obstacles in investigating what science has achieved in this field.

Having to confess to any inability in this area would have been sufficient reason for the author to leave unsaid and unwritten what he presents in this book. He has really made it a matter of principle to speak or write about things in the field of spiritual science only when he would also be able to formulate to his own satisfaction what current science knows about these same things. This is not intended as a universal requirement, because others may legitimately feel compelled to communicate and publish anything their feelings, their powers of judgment, and their healthy sense of the truth lead them to, even if they do not know what can be said about these same things from the viewpoint of contemporary science. However, the author does intend to abide by this principle himself. For example, the few sentences in this book about the human glandular and nervous systems would not have been written if he had not also been in a position to attempt to speak about them as someone with a modern scientific education.

Thus, although readers may come to the conclusion that anyone who speaks about heat in this way knows nothing of the basics of modern physics, the author of this book believes that what he has done is fully justified because he really has made an effort to be aware of modern research; in fact, if he were not aware of it, he would stop speaking in this way. He knows that his motive in expressing this principle might very easily be mistaken for lack of modesty. With regard to this book, however, such things must be expressed so that the author's true motives are not mistaken for something still worse than lack of modesty.

It would also be possible for people to criticize this book from a philosophical standpoint. A philosopher might wonder whether its author had slept through all the work that has been done recently in the field of epistemology, and whether he had never heard of the existence of Kant, who would say that it is simply philosophically inadmissible to advance such views.[2] Again, it would be possible to go on and on in this vein. For the philosopher, the conclusion might be that uncritical, naive, and amateurish stuff like this is intolerable, and that it would be a waste of time to go into it further.

For reasons indicated above, and in spite of all misunderstandings that might arise as a result, the author would again like to present something personal. He began to study Kant at the age of sixteen and now truly believes himself capable of a completely objective assessment of this book's contents from the Kantian perspective. Here, too, he would have had reason to leave this book unwritten if he had not known what might move a philosopher applying modern standards of criticism to find it naive. The author really is capable of knowing that he is going beyond

---

2. Immanuel Kant (1724–1804), German philosopher, professor of logic and metaphysics; his best known works are *Critik der practischen Vernunft* (1788, *Critique of Practical Reason*) and *Critik der Urtheilskraft* (1790, *Critique of Judgment*).

the limits of possible knowledge in the Kantian sense, and that Herbart might discover in this book a "naive realism" that is not yet able to "elaborate concepts," and so forth.[3] He is even capable of knowing that the modern pragmatism of James and Schiller would find that this book oversteps the limits of "true mental images" that "we can make our own, assert, put into effect, and verify."

In spite of knowing all this, and even because of knowing it, he can still feel justified in writing the expositions presented here. The author of this book has dealt with philosophical trends of thought in several of his books: *The Science of Knowing*; *Truth and Science*; *Intuitive Thinking as a Spiritual Path: A Philosophy of Freedom*; *Goethe's Worldview*; *Views of the World and of Life in the Nineteenth Century*; and *The Riddles of Philosophy*.

Many other types of possible criticism could still be cited. Readers of one of the author's earlier works, such as *Views of the World and of Life in the Nineteenth Century* or the little booklet *Haeckel and His Opponents*,[4] might say: It's absolutely incomprehensible how one and the same person could write these books and then publish

---

3. Johann Friedrich Herbart (1776–1841), German philosopher and influential educator; he developed a metaphysical theory of "pluralistic realism" as related to pedagogical psychology, which rejected concepts of faculties and innate ideas; he followed along the lines of the educator Johann Pestalozzi and Jean-Jacques Rousseau.

4. *Haeckel und seine Gegner*, 1900. Reprinted in the essay collection *Methodische Grundlagen der Anthroposophie 1884–1901*, Rudolf Steiner Verlag, Dornach, Switzerland, 1989 (GA 30), pp. 152–200.

*Theosophy* and this present volume.[5] How can anyone first take Haeckel's side so strongly and then give a slap in the face to all the healthy "monism" resulting from Haeckel's research? I could understand it if the author of this *Esoteric Science* had fought Haeckel tooth and nail, but that he defended Haeckel and even dedicated *Views of the World and of Life in the Nineteenth Century* to him is absolutely outrageous. Haeckel would certainly have declined this dedication emphatically if he had known that its author would one day write stuff like this *Esoteric Science* with its crass dualism.

The author, however, takes the point of view that it is quite possible to understand Haeckel very well without believing that this means we have to think that everything not derived from Haeckel's own concepts and hypotheses is nonsense. Furthermore, he is of the opinion that it is only possible to understand Haeckel by exploring what he achieved on behalf of science, rather than by fighting him tooth and nail. And what the author—who defended the great natural philosopher against his opponents in a booklet entitled *Haeckel and His Opponents*—believes least of all is that Haeckel's opponents are right. That the author goes beyond Haeckel's hypotheses and places a spiritual view of the world alongside Haeckel's merely natural view truly does not mean that he necessarily shares the opinions of Haeckel's opponents. Anyone who makes an effort to look at this in the right way will

---

5. *Theosophy: An Introduction to the Spiritual Processes in Human Life and in the Cosmos*, Anthroposophic Press, Hudson, NY, 1994.

realize that the author's current writings do in fact agree with his earlier ones.

The author also understands completely that some critics might quite generally regard the descriptions in this book as the outpourings of a crazed fancy or of a dreamy game of thoughts. Anything that needs to be said in response is contained in the book itself, which shows to what a great extent rational thinking can and must become the touchstone for what is presented. Only those who apply the test of reason to this book as objectively as they would apply it to scientific facts will be able to decide what reason has to say in such a test.

Now that so much has been said about people who reject this book from the outset, a word to those who have reason to agree with it: for them, the essentials are contained in the first chapter, "The Character of Esoteric Science." However, there is still a minor matter that needs mentioning here. Although the book deals with research that cannot be carried out by intellects that are bound to the sense-perceptible world, it presents nothing that cannot be understood by any person choosing to apply the gifts of unbiased reasoning and a healthy sense of truth. The author states quite frankly that he wants, above all, to have readers who are not willing to accept what is presented here on blind faith but who will make an effort to test these accounts against the knowledge in their own souls and their own life experience. (What is meant here is not only spiritual scientific testing by means of supersensible methods of research, but primarily testing—and it certainly is possible—by means of healthy, unbiased thinking and common sense.—R. STEINER.) Above all, he hopes for *cautious* readers who accept only what is logically justifiable. The author knows that his book would be worth nothing if it depended only on blind faith and that it is viable only to the extent that it can be verified by unbiased reason. It is so easy for blind faith to confuse foolish superstition with the truth. Many who prefer to be satisfied with a mere belief in the supersensible will feel that this book expects too much of their thinking. But in the case of what this book communicates, the fact that something is being communicated is not the only important thing. It is also important that the communication is as it is because it conforms to a conscientious view of the domain of life in question. This is the domain where the highest things come into contact with unscrupulous charlatanism. It is where knowledge and superstition so easily meet in real life, and where, above all, they can so easily be confused with each other.

Anyone acquainted with supersensible research will notice in reading this book that it attempts to clearly respect the boundaries between the contents of domains of supersensible knowledge that can and should be communicated at present and those that will need to be presented at a later time or at least in another form.

*December 1909*

### Introduction to the Fourth Edition

Whoever undertakes to present results of spiritual science such as those recorded in this book must consider that most people nowadays see results of this sort as an impossibility. After all, the supposedly rigorous thinking of our times presumes that the things talked about here "can never be determined by human intelligence." Anyone who knows and respects the reasons that lead many serious people to make this claim will want to try again and again to point out the misunderstandings underlying this belief that our human understanding is denied entry into supersensible worlds.

Two things beg to be considered. First, if human souls reflect deeply, in the long run they will never be able to shut themselves off from the fact that their most important questions about life's purpose and meaning would have to remain unanswered if there were no access to supersensible worlds. We can deceive ourselves about this fact in theory, but the depths of our soul-life refuse to cooperate with this self-deception. Of course those who choose not to listen to these depths of soul will reject reports of supersensible worlds. Yet there are people—and not just a few of them—who cannot possibly remain deaf to the demands of these soul-depths and must constantly knock at the gates which, in the opinion of others, keep "the inconceivable" under lock and key.

Secondly, explanations resulting from "rigorous think-ing" are not to be underestimated, and those who become involved with them will certainly appreciate their serious-ness when they need to be taken seriously. The author of this book does not want to be seen as someone who light-heartedly dismisses the tremendous amount of thought that has been applied to determining the limits of the human intellect. This effort cannot be dismissed with a few platitudes about "academic wisdom," and so on, because in many instances it has its source in genuine acumen and a true struggle for knowledge.

But in fact, we ought to admit that reasons have been presented to show why the knowledge we now consider scientific cannot penetrate into the spiritual worlds, and that *in a certain sense these reasons are irrefutable*. Since the writer of this book readily admits this, it may well seem strange that he still attempts to give an account of supersensible worlds. It seems almost impossible that someone could accept, at least in a certain sense, the rea-sons why supersensible worlds cannot be known and yet continue to talk about these worlds.

And yet, this attitude is possible. And it is equally pos-sible to understand that it may seem contradictory. After all, not everyone is preoccupied with the experiences peo-ple have when they approach the supersensible realm with their human intellect. To those who are, however, it becomes evident that although intellectual proof may indeed be irrefutable, this is not necessarily decisive with regard to reality. Here, in place of theoretical arguments, an attempt will be made to bring about understanding by means of a comparison, while readily admitting that comparisons in themselves do not constitute proof. In spite of this, however, they can often make it possible to understand something that needs to be expressed.

As it functions in everyday life and in ordinary science, human cognition really is structured in a way that does not permit it to penetrate supersensible worlds. This can be proved irrefutably, but for a certain type of soul-life this proof is of no more value than proving that the unaided human eye cannot penetrate the cells of a living thing or the makeup of distant heavenly bodies. The claim that ordinary cognition cannot penetrate supersensible worlds is just as correct and provable as the claim that ordinary sight cannot penetrate cells. And yet the proof that ordinary sight is forced to stop short of seeing cells says nothing conclusive against cellular research, so why should the proof that ordinary cognition is forced to stop short of seeing supersensible worlds say anything conclusive against the possibility of spiritual research?

We can appreciate how this comparison makes some people feel. We can even empathize with their doubt that someone who uses such comparisons to counter the serious thought and effort expended in determining the limits of the intellect could have even the slightest idea of the full seriousness of that effort. However, not only is the person writing this imbued with that seriousness, he also experiences that effort as one of humanity's noblest achievements. While it would not be necessary to begin by proving that unaided human sight cannot penetrate the structure of cells, using precise thinking to become aware of the nature of thinking itself is indeed a necessary spiritual activity. It is all too understandable that those who devote themselves to this activity do not notice that reality can rebut them. And although this introduction is certainly not the place to go into the various "rebuttals" of earlier editions of this book by people who lack all understanding of what it is attempting to do or who level untrue personal attacks at its author, it must be emphasized that only those who choose to close their eyes to this book's entire manner of presentation will imagine that it underrates the efforts of serious scientific thought.

Human cognition, like sight, can be strengthened and enhanced. However, methods of strengthening cognition are completely spiritual in character; they are purely inner functions of the soul. They consist of what is described in this book as meditation and concentration or contemplation. Our ordinary soul-life is bound up with bodily instruments, but a soul-life that has been strengthened frees itself from them. To certain modern schools of thought, this claim necessarily seems totally senseless and based only on self-deception. From their point of view, it can easily be demonstrated that all soul-life is bound to the nervous system. Those subscribing to the viewpoint of this book certainly understand such proofs. They understand those who say it is superficial to claim that any soul-life is possible independent of the body and who are totally convinced that the experiences of a strengthened soul must still have some connection to the activity of the nerves, a connection that "spiritual scientific amateurs" simply fail to perceive.

What is described in this book is in such sharp contrast to certain entirely understandable habitual ways of thinking that in many instances there is no prospect of coming to an understanding at present. At this point we might begin to wish that it were no longer considered compatible with spiritual life in this day and age to immediately denounce a line of research as fantastic and visionary because it deviates substantially from one's own. On the other hand, however, it is already a fact that a number of people do have a certain understanding of the type of supersensible research presented in this book. These people realize that the meaning of life is not revealed by speaking in general terms about the soul, the self, and so on, but only by really going into the results of supersensible research. The need for this edition, the fourth within a relatively short time, is deeply felt by the author, not out of lack of modesty but with joy and satisfaction.

In being so immodest as to emphasize this, the author is only too aware of how little even the new edition corresponds to what an outline of a supersensible worldview ought to be. In preparing this new edition, he reworked the entire book, adding to it at important points for the sake of completeness and clarity. And yet he could feel in many passages how unbending the means of expression available to him are in comparison to what supersensible research yields. This is why it was scarcely possible to do more than point out a way of arriving at the concepts this book supplies about the Saturn, Sun, and Moon evolutions. In this edition, an important perspective on this subject has been given a new treatment. But experiencing these things is so very different from any experiences in the sensory domain that it is necessarily a constant struggle to find even somewhat adequate expressions for them. However, if you are willing to really go into the description attempted here, you may notice that although many things are impossible to say in dry words, the *style* of the description succeeds in approaching them. How this is done is different in the case of the Saturn evolution, for example, than for the Sun evolution, and so forth.

A great deal of supplementary and complementary material that seemed important to the author has been added to the second part of the book, which deals with the knowledge of higher worlds. The author has attempted to clearly describe the type of inner soul processes that free cognition from its limitations in the sense-perceptible world and adapt it to experiencing the supersensible world. He has also attempted to show that although this world is experienced entirely through inner ways and means, this experience is not merely of subjective significance to the individual who achieves it. This account was intended to make it clear that the soul's uniqueness and personal qualities are stripped away *within* the soul itself, so that the experience that is achieved happens in the same way for each person who effects personal inner development out of subjective experiences in the right way. Only when we think of knowledge of higher worlds as having this character are we able to distinguish it from all experiences of mere subjective mysticism, and so on. It can certainly be said that such mysticism is the more or less subjective concern of the individual mystic. However, as it is meant here, spiritual scientific training of the soul aspires to objective experiences. Recognizing the truth of such experiences is a purely inward process, and yet the universal validity of these experiences is apparent for this very reason. Again, this is a point on which it is very difficult to come to an understanding with many of our current habitual ways of thinking.

In conclusion, the author would like to express the hope that well-intentioned readers will also accept this account for what it contains. Nowadays attempts are often made to apply ancient names to spiritual currents; only then do they seem valuable in the eyes of many people. However, we might well ask what the account in this book would stand to gain from being labeled "Rosicrucian" or the like. The important point is that it attempts to see into spiritual worlds by using means that are both possible and suitable for souls at this present stage of evolution, and that it considers the riddles of human destiny and of human existence beyond the limits of birth and death by these means. The point is not that this attempt bears some ancient name or other, but that it is aiming at the truth.

On the other hand, people with antagonistic intentions have also applied certain names to the worldview presented in this book. Aside from the fact that the ones intended to hit the author hardest and discredit him the most are absurd and objectively untrue, such terms demonstrate their unworthiness because they belittle a wholly independent striving for truth by failing to judge it on its own merits and because these antagonists attempt to impose upon others their conclusion that this striving is dependent on one or the other school of thought, a dependence that they either invented themselves or assumed for no reason and carried further. Necessary as it may be to write these words in view of the numerous attacks on the author, he is reluctant to take the matter any further at this point.

*June 1913*

*Preface to the Seventh through Fifteenth Editions*

For this new edition of my *Outline of Esoteric Science* I have almost entirely reworked the first chapter, "The Character of Esoteric Science." I believe there will now be less cause for the misunderstandings I saw arise as a result of the earlier version. On all sides, I heard that while other sciences provide proof, this would-be science simply says, "Esoteric science states this or that." It is natural for this prejudice to arise, since the proof that supersensible cognition offers cannot force itself upon us through its very presentation as is the case when relationships of sense-perceptible reality are described. That we are dealing with a mere prejudice is a fact that I attempted to make clearer in the revisions of this first chapter than I seem to have succeeded in doing in previous editions.

I have made some additions to the contents of the rest of the book for the sake of clarity. I have attempted to change the wording of the content in numerous places throughout the book, wherever my repeated experience of the subject seemed to call for it.

*Berlin, May 1920*

## FURTHER READING

Essential Anthroposophic Works by Rudolf Steiner

*Anthroposophical Leading Thoughts*. London: Rudolf Steiner Press, 1973.

*Anthroposophy (A Fragment): A New Foundation for the Study of Human Nature*. Hudson, NY: Anthroposophic Press, 1996.

*Anthroposophy and the Inner Life*. Bristol, UK: Rudolf Steiner Press, 1994.

*At the Gates of Spiritual Science*. London: Rudolf Steiner Press, 1986.

*Christianity as Mystical Fact*. Hudson, NY: Anthroposophic Press, 1997.

*The Christmas Conference for the Foundation of the General Anthroposophical Society 1923–1924*. Hudson, NY: Anthroposophic Press, 1990.

*Cosmic Memory*. Blauvelt, NY: Garber Communications, 1990.

*The Effects of Esoteric Development*. Hudson, NY: Anthroposophic Press, 1997.

*The Evolution of Consciousness as Revealed through Initiation-Knowledge*. Sussex, UK: Rudolf Steiner Press, 1991.

*The Fall of the Spirits of Darkness*. London: Rudolf Steiner Press, 1995.

*The Foundations of Human Experience*. Hudson, NY: Anthroposophic Press, 1996 (previous translation titled *Study of Man*).

*The Foundation Stone & the Life, Nature and Cultivation of Anthroposophy*. London: Rudolf Steiner Press, 1996.

*The Four Mystery Plays*. London: Rudolf Steiner Press, 1983.

*Goethe's World View*. Spring Valley, NY: Mercury Press, 1985.

*The Gospel of St. John*. Hudson, NY: Anthroposophic Press, 1988.

*How to Know Higher Worlds.* Hudson, NY: Anthroposophic Press, 1994.

*Human and Cosmic Thought.* London: Rudolf Steiner Press, 1991.

*Individualism in Philosophy.* Spring Valley, NY: Mercury Press, 1989.

*Mysticism at the Dawn of the Modern Age.* Blauvelt, NY: Rudolf Steiner Publications, 1960.

*Polarities in the Evolution of Mankind.* London: Rudolf Steiner Press, 1987.

*A Road to Self-Knowledge* and *The Threshold of the Spiritual World.* London: Rudolf Steiner Press, 1975. (New edition is forthcoming in 1998 from Anthroposophic Press.)

*Rudolf Steiner, An Autobiography.* Blauvelt, NY: Garber Communications, 1977.

*Spiritual Beings in the Heavenly Bodies and in the Kingdoms of Nature.* Hudson, NY: Anthroposophic Press, 1992.

*The Spiritual Guidance of the Individual and Humanity.* Hudson, NY: Anthroposophic Press, 1992.

*The Spiritual Hierarchies and the Physical World: Reality and Illusion.* Hudson, NY: Anthroposophic Press, 1996.

*The Temple Legend: Freemasonry and Related Occult Movements.* London: Rudolf Steiner Press, 1997.

*Theosophy.* Hudson, NY: Anthroposophic Press, 1994.

*Truth and Knowledge.* Blauvelt, NY: Rudolf Steiner Publications, 1981. Also *Truth and Science.* Spring Valley, NY: Mercury Press, 1993.

## Anthologies of Rudolf Steiner

Barton, Matthew (ed). *Evil: Selected Lectures by Rudolf Steiner.* London: Rudolf Steiner Press, 1997.

McDermott, Robert (ed). *The Essential Steine*r. San Francisco: HarperSanFrancisco, 1984.

Meuss, Anna (ed). *Angels: Selected Lectures by Rudolf Steiner.* London: Rudolf Steiner Press, 1996.

Querido, René (ed). *A Western Approach to Reincarnation and Karma: Selected Lectures and Writings by Rudolf Steiner.* Hudson, NY: Anthroposophic Press, 1996.

Seddon, Richard (ed). *Understanding the Human Being: Selected Writings of Rudolf Steiner.* Bristol, England: Rudolf Steiner Press, 1993.

Other Authors on Rudolf Steiner and Anthroposophy

Barnes, Henry. *A Life for the Spirit: Rudolf Steiner in the Crosscurrents of Our Time.* Hudson, NY: Anthroposophic Press, 1997.

Davy, John; Adams, George, and others. *A Man Before Others, Rudolf Steiner Remembered.* Bristol, England: Rudolf Steiner Press, 1993.

Easton, Stewart *Man and World in the Light of Anthroposophy.* Hudson, NY: Anthroposophic Press, 1989.

—*Rudolf Steiner, Herald of a New Epoch.* Hudson, NY: Anthroposophic Press, 1995.

Lissau, Rudi. *Rudolf Steiner: Life, Work, Inner Path and Social Initiatives.* Stroud, England: Hawthorn Press, 1987.

Prokofieff, Sergei, *Rudolf Steiner and the Founding of the New Mysteries.* London: Temple Lodge Publishing, 1994.

Samweber, Anna. *Memories of Rudolf Steiner.* London: Rudolf Steiner Press, 1991.

Schmidt, Paul E. *Rudolf Steiner and Initiation.* Spring Valley, NY: Anthroposophic Press, 1981.

Shepherd, A.P. *A Scientist of the Invisible.* Rochester, Vermont: Inner Traditions International, 1983.

Turgeniev, Assya and others. *Reminiscences of Rudolf Steiner.* Ghent, NY: Adonis Press, 1987.

Wachsmuth, Guenther. *The Life and Work of Rudolf Steiner.* Blauvelt, NY: Garber Communications, 1989.

During the last two decades of the nineteenth century the Austrian-born Rudolf Steiner (1861–1925) became a respected and well-published scientific, literary, and philosophical scholar, particularly known for his work on Goethe's scientific writings. After the turn of the century he began to develop his earlier philosophical principles into an approach to methodical research of psychological and spiritual phenomena.

His multifaceted genius has led to innovative and holistic approaches in medicine, science, education (Waldorf schools), special education, philosophy, religion, economics, agriculture (Biodynamic method), architecture, drama, new arts of eurythmy and speech, and other fields. In 1924 he founded the General Anthroposophical Society, which today has branches throughout the world.